Changing times, Changing trains

Richard Brown

Published by New Generation Publishing in 2024

Copyright © Richard Brown 2024

First Edition

Paperback ISBN: 978-1-83563-362-5
Hardback ISBN: 978-1-83563-363-2
eBook ISBN: 978-1-83563-364-9

www.newgeneration-publishing.com

New Generation Publishing

Contents

Acknowledgments

I am hugely grateful to three old friends and colleagues who read draft chapters and made many helpful comments and suggestions: Nick Brown, Nick Mercer and Julian Bene. They provided much encouragement, too, to persevere and finish the book. Likewise I am grateful to all of my various colleagues over the years, from whom I learnt so much. They are too numerous to mention individually, although I mention many of them at various points in the story.

I am also very grateful to my two daughters, Sarah and Nicola, and my son-in-law Tim, for proof reading many chapters. Finally, I must thank my wife, Gweno, for her encouragement and patient support as well as regular advice on IT matters, together with much editing and proof reading.

INTRODUCTION

I started to write this book out of frustration and concern for the future of our railways in Britain. Frustration that having effectively nationalised control of Britain's railways the UK Government appeared to have little idea of how it wanted the industry to be structured or move forward. This was despite having commissioned a wide ranging review of the industry's structure in 2018 - the Williams Review - which was only published three years later and is yet to be implemented in any form. And concern that the potential restructuring of the industry which seems likely under a new Government risks creating as many problems as it solves and fails to learn from some of the hard won successes that have been achieved over the years.

At the same time there is growing concern that the industry is losing corporate memory and collective understanding of how the railway works as an integrated system. Corporate memory is going out of the door as experienced people retire or leave the industry for more satisfying careers elsewhere. And understanding of how the industry works as an entity is confined to fewer and fewer people with many leaders now having had experience of only one leg of the industry and often working within quite narrow silos. It is much harder for today's managers to gain wide experience and knowledge of how the industry works as a whole.

I write as someone who has spent 43 years working in railways, mainly in Britain, and in at least six fundamentally different organisational structures. I worked for British Rail for 18 years before privatisation, for National Express Group plc for six years, for Eurostar working closely with other European Railways for 11 years followed by spells as a non-Executive Director on the Boards of the Department for Transport, HS2 Ltd and Network Rail Ltd. I have been lucky enough to have worked with or for a wider variety of rail related organisations than most other people. I've learned a great deal about how to organise and run railways in this time, and how not to. I've therefore written this book to share some of my learnings and experiences in the hope of capturing some corporate memory. If it helps the current generation of leaders and policy makers direct and organise the industry in a better way, or just prompts thoughts on how to do things differently, then it will have been worth it.

I've written it largely as a memoir in roughly chronological order starting in Part 1 with my time with British Rail and then National Express Group. Part 2 covers my time as CEO and then Chairman of Eurostar including some of the key events that shaped the business, and my experiences of various non-Executive Directorships. Parts 1 and 2 are written partly as a personal memoir of my own experiences and feelings at the time. But because most of this time was one of tumultuous change, they are as much about the changes in the industry as a whole, but from the point of view of an insider looking outwards rather than a business historian looking in. Part 3 then includes a number of reflections looking back over my career as a whole, for instance on the differing nature of private and public sector organisations and the merits of different organisational structures. In the final chapter I've attempted to draw together some of the key themes and learnings, pointing to ways to organise and run our railways better. Whilst I do not believe there is a perfect structure for organising a railway system, it is very clear we currently have one of the worst possible structures and ways of running a railway in Britain. It shouldn't have to be like this.

I've been lucky to have had a very rewarding and interesting career in what is an important but too often derided industry. I've worked with many impressive and interesting people and had a lot of fun and excitement along the way. I've tried to convey some of this, as well as sharing what I've learned. It seemed a pity not to try to capture the richness of all this in writing.

I joined the railway industry largely by chance, rather than from any long held ambition or family connection. My early jobs involved preparing business plans and strategies, firstly at Freightliner Ltd and then for the InterCity Business Sector of British Rail, as well as roles in marketing and sales. I have therefore always tended to look at the railways through a financial and customer lens. I've always sought answers to questions such as what are the economics of a particular service? How could they be improved by attracting more customers or reducing their costs? What are customers' particular needs for this service and to what extent do we need to change to better meet them? And, more recently, what organisational structures and arrangements give managers the best chance of doing these things effectively?

Given the current state of Britain's rail industry these questions seem to me to be particularly relevant today. The economics of the industry are again very challenging, with large amounts of Government funding being required post Covid against a backdrop of severe pressure on Government finances more widely. There is an urgent need for the industry to become much more cost effective. At the same time centralised and detailed control of the industry in England by the Department for Transport, and by the Office of Rail and Road as Regulator, has meant that it has become increasingly remote from its customers. Really understanding and responding to the different needs of different markets is very difficult with such centralised control. So I make no apology for focussing on these issues in this memoir.

When I joined the industry it was probably close to the nadir of its fortunes. Even though it was nearly 30 years since

Nationalisation in 1948 there was a lingering expectation that the railways should pay their way and intense debate about what the cost should be for those services which didn't. The then Labour Government saw the passenger railway as mainly being used by the better off, whilst the Conservative opposition had an almost contemptuous perception of an inefficient nationalised industry. The railways were seen as a "problem" across the political spectrum. Under the leadership of Sir Robert Reid, first as CEO then as Chairman, the industry made good progress in the early years of my career in addressing these challenges, reducing its call on taxpayers and becoming much more customer and market orientated.

But perceptions lagged reality and the newly elected Conservative Government in 1992 was determined to privatise the industry, ushering a new era of fraught relations with Government and politics following the switch to a Labour Government in 1997. Labour had passionately opposed privatisation when in opposition but was not prepared to go as far as renationalising it when in Government. Instead it chose to snipe at the newly privatised companies and their performance, only tinkering with its structure with the creation and subsequent abolition of the short lived Strategic Rail Authority. A further watershed was reached with the Hatfield rail crash and subsequent weeks-long meltdown in services as Railtrack scrambled to understand where else it was at risk. Coupled with a radical increase in the financial settlement for Railtrack's successor, Network Rail, instigated by the then independent Rail Regulator, Tom Winsor, it was at last accepted across the political spectrum that the railways provided an essential service and needed to be properly funded.

There followed a number of years of relative stability in industry-political relations, with Governments, perhaps grudgingly, accepting the status quo and working with it.

The financial performance of the franchise sector steadily improved as each new round of franchise contracts offered better results, so the Treasury was content that the call on public funds was contained. But the seeds of suspicion and dissatisfaction with the performance of the privatised train companies had been sown, giving rise to regular public criticism and calls for either nationalisation or more penal contractual arrangements. Secretaries of State for Transport, of both political hues, too often responded by further tightening franchise contracts or seeking tighter regulation and control and often inadvertently added to the outcry rather than dampening it down.

So now there is widespread acceptance that the current structure of the industry has become dysfunctional and needs major reform. In a sense the industry has come full circle since I first joined it and is seen as a "problem" again by both main political parties, although the Conservative Government showed little appetite to tackle reform. The Labour Government has published its blueprint for rail reform, which seeks to build on and go further than the Williams Review, with an intention to renationalise the industry. The blueprint contains a number of laudable objectives but includes little in the way of substantive ideas on how these could be achieved or how the inevitable tradeoffs might be managed. The conclusion must be that somehow the industry needs to find a way to chart a route to reform itself, albeit it will still need Government to play its part and stand back from its day to day involvement. The imperative need for the industry to reduce its call on the public purse and get back to being focussed on its customers is urgent.

If this memoir helps people's thinking on what is needed, in even a small way, it will have been worthwhile. It is in no way a blueprint for reform of the industry's structure and organisation. That is a task way beyond the capabilities of any one individual. But it might at least point to what could usefully be some of the components of a reformed structure and of some better ways of doing things, learning from what has worked before or in other types of railway organisational structures.

And for anyone who doubts why this is important it needs to be remembered that rail is the most energy and carbon efficient mode of surface transport, other than walking and cycling, with great potential to get more efficient still. It can and must play a major role in helping achieve net zero in Britain. It is also essential to the economies and quality of life of most of our cities, particularly with falling car ownership amongst younger people, and for many rural communities. And there is massive scope for it to carry more freight, taking pressure off the road network, helping solve the shortage of lorry drivers and reducing the huge environmental footprint of road freight transport. But reform of the industry is essential if it is to contribute fully to addressing the challenge of climate change and helping our cities and regions to continue to grow in a sustainable way.

PART 1

CHAPTER 1 A career in railways - in the public sector and British Rail

In some respects I was an "accidental" recruit to the railway industry when I joined in 1977. I had no previous knowledge or interest in the industry, and unlike many, no previous family connection. I had applied on the "milk round" of graduate recruitment and as well as being offered a job by British Rail I also had offers from Shell and Mobil Oil. I took the railway job on the basis that it seemed to offer greater interest and the chance of a sustained career, despite it being the least well paid. The recruiters at both Shell and Mobil were surprised and not a little offended, since British Rail was not a well-regarded organisation, as I was to discover. I was also influenced by my view that the railways were a much more environmentally friendly industry than oil, and perhaps offered a more sustainable future. My own father was not particularly impressed either, questioning why I would want to join a declining nationalised industry. When you are young you do not necessarily see or concern yourself with such considerations.

I vividly recall the selection process that I went through before being offered the management traineeship. I found the whole process very impersonal and somewhat off putting, save for two individuals who effectively "sold" me on the job. One was the chair of the selection panel, Peter Corbishley, BR's Chief Planning Officer, who at the end of my interview said that of course if I were offered a job I might have further questions before accepting and giving me his phone number. I now understand this was a pretty clear signal that he had already made his mind up. But on receiving the job offer I did indeed call him and he readily answered my questions, which felt both impressive and encouraging. The other individual was a young freight salesman, Kim Jordan, who had recently completed management training himself who was there to answer questions more informally. He was clearly enjoying his job, which sounded both interesting and stimulating, and I could readily see myself in his shoes in due course. He clearly had something about him. The lesson I took with me throughout my subsequent career is that recruiting the right person should be a two-way affair, with the organisation "selling" itself as much as the job candidate selling themselves. The right candidate will always have a choice of jobs, often more than one, and while they may have applied for your job, they are not obliged to take it!

In later years I have been struck by how many other eventual senior leaders that I have met, not just of the rail industry but also of the wider transport and logistics sector during my time as a Vice President and then President of the Chartered Institute of Logistics and Transport, who started out by chance rather than with any pre-planned intentions. Many started their careers in the industry after doing a holiday or casual job with no longer term career intentions, or following a chance switch from another sector. There must be some useful lessons from this for those now seeking to recruit young people into our industry, given it has a much lower profile than many other potential careers.

The rail industry I joined

The British Rail that I joined felt very old fashioned and rather backwards looking. Its political and public stock was undoubtedly at a low ebb, with the outgoing Labour Government of Jim Callaghan not particularly supportive of railways. The Conservatives, soon to enter Government, were actively contemptuous of what they saw as an inefficient and outdated industry, with all the defects of a nationalised company. It was lumped together in their minds with the other nationalised industries particularly coal and steel, and therefore needing drastic reform and rationalisation. Margaret Thatcher on meeting the Board of British Rail over a lunch early in her 1979 premiership is reputed to have told them that none of them could have been any good or they wouldn't have been there.

The last steam trains had only been withdrawn a few years previously and the hangover from steam operation still had a big impact on staff attitudes and work practices. More importantly the industry was still in the process of adjusting from one where freight was the dominant market, with all the characteristics of a male dominated heavy industry culture, to one where passengers were the principal raison d'etre which required a very different service orientated culture to be successful. The culture was all about moving trains rather than facilitating passengers' journeys. It was also influenced by the post war involvement of the military when it was part of the British Transport Commission. Most employees enjoyed life-long careers in the industry meaning that it was slow to change and reluctant to embrace the new reality of a passenger dominated business.

British Rail's organisation into five Regions - Southern, Western, London Midland, Eastern and Scotland - was very siloed, with functional structures replicated at both regional and HQ level. The Regions were in turn divided into a number of Divisions covering specific geographic areas and also replicating the functional structure, with most functions then each overseeing several Areas, but whose boundaries were not necessarily co-terminous with each other. The main functions were three engineering departments, Civil Engineering, Mechanical and Electrical, and Signalling and Telecommunications, alongside Passenger, Freight, Parcels and Operations. Operations ran the trains and provided the glue which bound all the rest together, and the lubricant which allowed the whole to work. Regional and Divisional Managers were expected to be general managers who coordinated and integrated the various functions. The Regions still carried some of the cultural inheritance of the four pre-war railway companies, with people identifying with their region as much if not more than British Rail corporately, and with a consequent sense of independence. There was continuing tension between Board HQ departments and the Regions and ambiguity as to who was really in charge and in the lead.

The career paths of senior people were an important part of the structure and a key ingredient in making it work. You did not become a Regional General Manager unless you had previously been a Divisional Manager, and you usually had to have been an Area Manager at some point before becoming a Divisional Manager. Most of these various managers started their careers as Traffic Management Trainees (who were mainly graduate recruits, but with an appreciable number of staff entrants too), and would have done several ground level supervisory or junior management roles before moving up the hierarchy. Operations was the dominant career stream, providing most of the key personnel in Passenger, Freight and Parcels departments too. Managers were also encouraged or expected to undertake roles at Board HQ at some point, much as Officers in the Armed Forces are expected to do a job or two at the Ministry of Defence before moving onto more senior roles.

Senior Managers therefore had wide experience and knowledge of how the industry worked, at various levels, which enabled them to integrate activities in an otherwise very siloed structure. The majority of these senior managers had done real, ground level operating jobs as part of their early careers so understood how the railway operated as a system. In some respects the industry worked despite its structure and because of the knowledge and experience of its key managers. This career development structure produced many very good managers, contrary to the external perception of the industry. After privatisation it is striking how many of the more successful Train Company MDs had come out of this structure. Many of the more thoughtful managers coming into the industry after privatisation also told me that they were struck by the unexpected quality of the managers they came across. The industry produced many credible leaders who could comfortably engage with front line staff, whose respect had to be earned and solidly grounded. Barry Woledge, our HR Director at InterCity, went so far as to say he thought BR managers were of higher quality than those of British Airways, where he had previously been deputy HR Director.

Comparable hierarchies existed for the three engineering functions, so a Civil Engineer would progress from a Section Engineer to an Area Civil Engineer and then comparable posts in a Division or Region, with specialist roles in between. Top of the hierarchy was the Chief Civil Engineer at Board HQ. This too produced widely experienced and capable engineers who understood how the industry worked. Again it is striking how many key roles in the privatised industry, Railtrack excluded, were filled by engineers who had been developed by this structure.

Engineers at each level had a clear sense of responsibility for and a degree of pride in their "patch", which helped maintain standards, but which also could produce a degree of defensiveness and resistance to instruction or initiatives from levels above.

This structure and the career paths through it produced something of a collegiate even tribal culture; as you progressed you knew more and more of your colleagues. This was undoubtedly a strength as most people had a shared passion for the industry and what its purpose was, even if they did not always agree about how to achieve it. But there were also two fundamental defects in this structure. First of all it led to a very inwards looking and conformist culture, lacking in diversity of people or thinking. It took time to progress up the hierarchy, making for lifetime careers, as was the case in many other large industries of the time. But it meant that few people had experience of other sectors or perspectives. This was a particular weakness as the UK's economy was itself changing radically, with coal, heavy industry and manufacturing all declining, and consumerism growing.

To progress upwards you had to perform, but also conform with the expectations of your superiors. If you didn't fully conform you needed to perform exceptionally well and be lucky to have a boss who could tolerate lack of conformity. The culture was also very bad at assimilating outsiders in the rare cases of more senior appointments being made of people from other industry sectors. Too often these individuals left after a short time, frustrated at their inability to make an impact or "rejected" by the organisation because they didn't fit in. I came to liken the process of successfully integrating individuals at senior level to a heart transplant, where the surgeon needs to carefully select the donor organ to be compatible with the recipient and then manage the post- operative recovery very closely to avoid organ rejection. The process does not happen of its own accord but needs active and careful management.

The resultant culture and lack of diversity of both experience and background inevitably slowed the rate of innovation in the industry. It too often led to the rejection or overlooking of ideas and innovations from elsewhere and produced something of a "not invented here" mentality. It also produced a defensiveness when subject to outside scrutiny or criticism. In many ways British Rail people conformed to the public sector stereotype of looking inwards and upwards for inspiration and direction, rather than outwards to customers and the wider market. The mismatch between internal and external perceptions of the capability of railway people, and regular criticism of the industry in the media and by politicians led many managers, certainly myself included, to believe they were not as good as they really were, possibly further adding to the defensiveness. This of course did not help the industry's reputation or help build understanding of the industry's challenges.

More importantly the industry structure was essentially production led and bore no relation to the industry's evolving markets, making it very difficult to match revenues to costs. Revenues were essentially accounted for at point of origin, whilst costs were collected in the areas they fell. The underlying financial performance of different routes and services was therefore poorly understood. More crucially no one below the Chief Executive had meaningful accountability or responsibility for managing the profitability of an individual service or route. Regional General Managers would have substantial revenues for which they were responsible, but responsibility and management of a significant proportion of the costs of carrying these revenues lay elsewhere. The problem was even greater at Divisional level, where most revenue was earned on services travelling beyond the division's boundary. It was symptomatic of this lack of financial awareness that no part of my management training covered financial issues. My training manager was completely nonplussed when I asked to go on a finance course and never sent me on one. I had to learn about financial management and transport economics via two of the exam modules I took for membership of the Chartered Institute of Transport.

The production led organisation also meant that there was limited specialisation of passenger, freight and parcels management by market sector, and so poor understanding of the evolving needs and expectations of different market segments. The exception was freight and parcels management at Board HQ, where there were managers overseeing specific market segments, such as coal, iron and steel and petroleum. Day to day management was still undertaken by generalist managers at Divisional and Regional level however.

This industry structure therefore directly influenced the wider perception of the railways as lacking innovation and being more interested in running trains than serving passengers and freight customers. And for the Government, the industry's poor financial control and analysis undermined confidence in it, and led to continuous concern over its financial performance and viability.

These shortcomings were increasingly seen and understood by BR's management and with the appointment of Bob Reid, later Sir Robert, as Chief Executive, the industry embarked on a process of fundamental reorganisation evolving between 1982 and 1992, switching to a market and profit centre led structure, of which much more below.

Life as a trainee

I enjoyed my time as a management trainee, which gave me a broad oversight of the industry but also gave me an appetite to want to change and improve it because of frustration with its shortcomings. I was actually a Planning and Marketing Trainee not a Traffic Management Trainee. This was a much smaller training scheme - there were just two of us in my year - and the idea of working in a more commercial and analytical area, and in London, was one of the things that had attracted me to choose this scheme. I hadn't wanted to get posted to some remote marshalling yard or depot and wasn't particularly interested in the minutiae of running trains. However, I quite quickly developed a deep respect for the operations function as the glue that bound the various silos together and allowed the railway to work as a system and have always enjoyed working alongside them.

My time was spent on a series of secondments to four different functions, passenger, freight, parcels and operations. I was mainly given projects to undertake as a means to learn about each. Most were paper exercises with little if any useful output, but two I remember as being particularly interesting and revealing about scope for the industry to improve. The passenger function at Board HQ asked me to look at the utilisation of the the large number of sets of passenger coaches then being used solely for excursions and summer holiday trains. They apparently had no hard numbers on this as the records were kept at the London Midland Region's operations HQ in Crewe and were thought to be too voluminous to be able to analyse properly. I spent four weeks living in a railway hostel in Crewe going through the records line by line to produce a comprehensive analysis of how often each set was being used. The conclusions were striking as most sets were being barely used on more than ten days each year, but still needed appropriate maintenance and secure storage so couldn't have been remotely profitable. I like to think I made an early contribution to reducing BR's costs, although I never found out what these costs actually were!

The other interesting project was for the Red Star Parcels Manager, who wanted an analysis of how the pricing of this express parcels product compared to competitors. I pretended to be a parcels customer and managed to get a pretty detailed rundown on how a number of competitor road based express parcels companies priced their services - it felt quite a thrill getting hold of information that apparently BR did not have and certainly helped develop my commercial skills. My clear conclusion was that Red Star were pricing their service in a very different way to their competition and in general were under-priced. I made several recommendations on how its price structure could better match the market. To my knowledge none of my recommendations was adopted, and my report was merely politely received.

To call what I received "a management training programme" would be a misnomer. It would be better described as "an industry familiarisation programme". I hardly attended any actual training or courses, but learnt by observing and doing. I took every opportunity I could create to get out and around the network to see as much as I could. It allowed me to become reasonably familiar with the different departments or functions, I suppose with the idea that it would help me choose where I wanted to work and help them get a feel for where I might be most suitable. I suspect this experience was in practice very similar to many other corporate management training schemes. Nevertheless, I felt more than ready to start doing a proper railway job when I finished "training".

Into the real world: Freightliner Ltd, a market orientated subsidiary

After finishing my management training my career took an unusual direction when I was sent to an operating subsidiary, Freightliner Ltd, as my first appointment. This had originally been set up in 1968 as a specialist operating division within British Rail, one of the many positive initiatives originating from the Beeching era. It was subsequently transferred to the newly created and publicly owned National Freight Corporation where it became a limited company. It had come back to full British Rail ownership in 1978, the year before I joined, an example of the all too frequent vacillations of Government policy towards the railways.

Freightliner specialised in inland container transport and was originally set up to try to retain general merchandise traffic on rail. It used containers to eliminate the costly and slow process of loading and unloading railway wagons, and to access traffics from customers who did not have or want to retain their own sidings and railheads. But it was also ideally placed to cater for the rapidly growing market for maritime containers, providing transport inland from key ports such as Southampton, Tilbury and Felixstowe. Freightliner owned and operated nearly all of its terminals, had its own specialist wagon fleet and a large container lorry fleet to provide a "last mile" service from the terminal to the final customer. It bought in the rail haulage of its container trains from British Rail's freight department.

I was not initially happy to be sent to Freightliner as I had been told that I had done well in my training and would be given a choice of two or three first jobs to go to. But as it turned out it was a very good place to start my career and I was lucky that for the bulk of my time there its Managing Director was Cyril Bleasdale, a free thinking and entrepreneurial leader who was very good at recognising potential and bringing on younger managers. I did four different jobs in planning, marketing and sales in five years, quickly gaining a good knowledge of the road freight market - the principal competitor - and of the deep-sea container shipping sector. My first job was an analyst in a small team producing a comprehensive review of Freightliner costs, revenues and business strategy giving me a good understanding of how the organisation and its business model worked. Each job involved a new stretch and put me outside my comfort zone, the ideal way to rapidly gain experience and confidence. My last job there had the rather grand title of National Account Sales Manager, Deep Sea, one of four National Account Managers each responsible for sales to a specific market sector. Deep Sea by then was Freightliner's largest sector, with £40 million of sales from some 40 deep-sea shipping lines needing to move their containers inland to and from their customers. It made up around 40% of the company's revenue but more importantly it accounted for all of the company's profit. The other three market sectors, Domestic, European and Irish were collectively loss making.

Whilst Freightliner had been set up by British Rail and a number of its managers had come from BR, it had a distinct culture, more commercial and more bottom line orientated than BR. This was partly down to the years it had been part of the National Freight Corporation, also then a nationalised company. It was unsubsidised and had to stand on its own feet financially and without any of the public service obligations that constrained BR's flexibility. Freightliner retained its own separate accounts and balance sheet after returning to BR ownership, and had to finance its own investment, which incentivised it to remain bottom line orientated. A good example of this was the monthly results statements, which showed me not only volume and revenue earned but also profit contribution from each route and customer. I and my team took as much pride in seeing the profit contribution grow, as in sales and volume growth. We also took care to ensure that in providing price quotations we included a margin over costs, as well as trying to be innovative in how a particular flow of business was carried to keep costs down.

Being a relatively small company, at least compared to British Rail, and having only two main tiers of management, Head Office and the twenty plus operating depots, ensured greater scope for impact by those managers who wanted to innovate. It helped that it also had a very focussed market, inland container transport, in which one could get much closer to customers and understand their needs and trends in the market. I had a team of three Account Executives two of whom were relatively recent management trainees like myself, and it seemed natural to us to push boundaries and try out new things, although I realise with hindsight we were unusually innovative. As an example, one of them, David Spaven, based a young sales agent, David Smith, in the traffic office of one of our customers at the Port of Ipswich, so that he got a printout first thing every morning of each container movement on offer so that he could pitch first for those most attractive to us. I don't think he ever got formal authority to create the post, or to locate it on a customer's premises, he just did it. It very quickly transformed our market share at the port and cemented a very strong relationship with the customer shipping line.

I myself negotiated what we would now call a joint venture with the then largest road haulier operating at Felixstowe, to serve Evergreen Line whom Freightliner had always had difficulty in establishing a productive relationship with. The deal gave us first refusal to move its containers by rail on a sub-contract basis whenever we had the capacity, and allowed the haulier to leverage our capacity to move large volumes of containers by rail to grow their own market share at Felixstowe. I cleared the idea with the Marketing and Sales Director, and ran the agreement that I wrote past the Company Secretary, but was otherwise left to get on with it. Unfortunately, I left Freightliner soon after completing the deal so never got to see how it actually performed but the concept seemed powerful to both myself and my younger opposite number at the haulier, John Williams. Interestingly his career subsequently blossomed to become owner and Executive Chairman of Maritime Transport, now one of the UK's largest logistics companies which makes extensive use of both rail and road for trunk movements.

With hindsight the generally "light touch" oversight and direction from senior management, even after Cyril Bleasdale moved on, was a great opportunity for us. What drove us was youthful enthusiasm and the desire to make our mark, and the monthly management accounts and reports which tracked our progress and pointed us in broadly the right direction, by showing us our profit contribution as well as sales revenue and volumes. We were not formally given bottom line accountability, but didn't wait to be given authority and generally sought forgiveness rather than permission, no doubt helped by the fact we were the company's main profit earner. The lack of senior management direction resulted in a somewhat more passive approach in other market sectors, which were struggling to cover their costs.

Overall, I think the assumption of senior management was that Freightliner was a volume hungry business and that provided the company maintained or grew the volume of containers carried and filled each train, profits would somehow follow. The idea that it might be a good thing to really understand one's costs, customer by customer and traffic flow by traffic flow, and seek to grow the profitable business and shrink or price off the unprofitable parts didn't seem to register. This was confirmed soon after the arrival of the new MD, Bryan Driver, who told the sales teams to go out and increase volumes across the board. We then grew our sector by some 20% over the next twelve months, when the market was growing by around 5% a year. But we were then told we could not be charging enough, and to increase our prices, even though all of the business we won was profitable and we had increased our overall profit contribution significantly!

The lesson for me was how important a well-constructed set of management accounts and reports are in ensuring management teams are aligned with the needs and strategy of the organisation as a whole and take the right decisions; and how motivating these could be to people who want to see the month by month impact of their efforts. We had that, but could probably have contributed much more to the company's performance had we also been given appropriate targets to beat and a coherent strategy to follow. Growing our profitable part of the business made perfect sense, but growing the unprofitable parts risked reducing these profits as costs would be increasing faster than revenues. Such reports and accounts are particularly important for sales teams in choosing what business to pitch for and at what price, and also for those managers who are making decisions about what services to run and which markets to address. The task at Freightliner was relatively straightforward, since it knew the costs of handling a container at each of its depots, what it paid British Rail to run each train together with the costs of its specialist container wagons, and how much it cost to provide a container or road delivery where the customer wanted these. The task for passenger rail services is rather harder, with a more complex cost structure and much higher level of shared costs to allocate appropriately, but is equally important. British Rail got to be very good at this in the last years before privatisation, of which more below.

The one area where Freightliner's cost accounts were very poor in giving the right signals to managers was in the prices paid to British Rail for rail haulage. Freightliner had a Rail haulage contract with BR in which it paid the direct costs of operating each train, with a percentage add-on to cover the costs of rail infrastructure. Early in my time at Freightliner the then Head of BR Freight, Henry Sanderson, announced his intention to significantly increase this percentage, on the grounds that it did not adequately cover the costs of infrastructure. I was covertly given the task of trying to quantify these avoidable costs across those parts of the rail network used by Freightliner's trains, so that Freightliner could challenge the proposed increase. Using knowledge of BR's infrastructure accounting systems gained during one of my management training assignments I established that the quantified avoidable costs of Freightliner's services were in fact lower than the percentage we were already paying. This allowed the company to successfully resist the increase, much to the displeasure of BR's Chief Freight Manager. Had the increase been applied it would have tipped a significant part of Freightliner's business into clear losses, triggered a number of service withdrawals and in turn meant Freightliner paying BR a lower absolute contribution to infrastructure costs. This was possibly not what BR's Chief Freight Manager intended, particularly as it was questionable whether all the costs concerned were truly avoidable. The lesson to be learned is that charges for rail infrastructure costs need to be very carefully designed and quantified, to avoid giving the wrong price signals to users. Again, this is a very complex area, that BR got very good at prior to privatisation but has since then been completely negated under the regulated infrastructure charging regime.

I learned later that part of the problem was a lack of understanding of the difference between cost accounting and management accounting. The former looks backwards, the latter forwards. Management accounting needs to not only reflect costs accurately but also be informed on what drives these costs to vary going forward and over what timescales they can be varied.

It is striking that Freightliner has continued to operate as a stand-alone company throughout the post privatisation era, taking still greater control over its costs by taking over ownership and operation of the locomotives it uses. Prima facie this is clear evidence that the organisational model is robust. Indeed, other companies with similar structure, such as GB Railfreight and several open access passenger operators, have also grown up since privatisation. The key ingredients are discrete and readily identifiable markets, and direct control over a sufficiently high proportion of their costs to be able to meet and adapt to changing customer needs with agility.

With hindsight I was hugely fortunate to have spent the first few years of my railway career at Freightliner, absorbing and learning from its commercial culture, trusted with significant freedom of action as a young manager and sharpening my instincts and confidence to engage fully with customers to really understand what they were looking for. It also taught me a lot about working with colleagues across the organisation, primarily with Freightliner's Terminal and Port Managers who were key in responding to each customer's particular requirements. I developed a particularly productive and enjoyable relationship with Freightliner's then National Operations Manager, John Bates. He was a master at operationalising my requests for new or amended services and maintaining collaborative relations across the organisation, from which I learned a great deal.

CHAPTER 2   Moving on: BR's emerging Sector and Profit Centre organisation

After five years at Freightliner I moved back to mainstream British Rail, first and briefly as Personal Assistant to one of BR's two Joint Managing Directors, Jim O'Brien, and then as Business Planning Manager for BR's recently established InterCity passenger sector. The Personal Assistant role was one that I did not enjoy and felt as if I was little more than a highly paid bag carrier. I was given no real responsibility and quickly became bored so moved on having barely completed half of what was the normal term in the role. I guess I had taken it somewhat reluctantly in the first place as when first approached about the role I had gone to Bryan Driver, the MD of Freightliner, to ask his advice. I had expected him to urge me to stay at Freightliner as I was still relatively new in my job and, I felt, starting to make a big contribution. Instead he urged me to go, which came over at best as very lukewarm recognition of my performance and contribution. So I decided to bale out forthwith!

Moving to InterCity, initially as Business Planning Manager, started nine of the most exciting and rewarding years in my career. It was where I really cut my teeth managerially and became instilled with InterCity's customer focus and values. I started with a team of two as Business Planning Manager and ended as a Profit Centre Director with responsibility for some 3,500 staff and a piece of vertically integrated railway. InterCity had a strong team of managers and leaders from whom I learnt a great deal and with whom it was a privilege to work. I worked successively for each of InterCity's three Managing Directors - Cyril Bleasdale, Dr John Prideaux and Chris Green - and experienced and learned from each of their very different leadership styles.

Bob Reid had by this time taken over from Sir Peter Parker as Chairman and had embarked on a continuous process of structural reform to BR's traditional regional and functional structure. The first step had been to create five Business Sectors, of which InterCity was one, working in a matrix structure alongside the existing Regions and Functions. This evolved over a number of years into a structure in which the Sectors were the lead organisations, with a number of mainly geographic Profit Centres in each and a complete end to the Regions and HQ Functions. It was an exciting time indeed to be a younger manager involved in setting up and leading parts of the new structure. The huge turnaround in financial performance that InterCity achieved as a business is itself a remarkable story which Chapter 3 tells in more detail. Being part of that story was a wonderful privilege and a very formative experience.

Bob Reid was a classic example of the railways' career development, having joined the industry as a Traffic Apprentice, as traffic management trainees were then called, and worked his way up via Divisional and Regional management, eventually becoming Chief Executive under Sir Peter Parker's chairmanship. As a result of all the jobs he had done on the way up there was very little he didn't know about how the industry worked. His key insight was that the inability to match costs to revenues at route or any other level, meant that it was only at the national level that this was truly possible. As Chief Executive he was the only person therefore who had true bottom line accountability. It meant that it was very difficult to determine which services were remunerative and which were not, with spending decisions taken with inadequate regard to the ability of the services concerned to support the costs. It made the task of improving the industry's financial performance exceptionally difficult.

This was a very serious shortcoming at a time when the Government was concerned about the net cost of the industry, seeing it as an excessive burden on the public finances. So Bob Reid's reforms were a necessary and appropriate response. Their prime thrust was to re-orientate the organisation to business units, the Sectors and Sub-Sectors, each of which had their own bottom line accountability and targets to improve performance, so reducing losses and subsidies and to improve delivery for customers. Both the theory and practice were that having a number of managers, not just one, driving bottom line performance produced much faster improvement in the financial performance of the organisation as a whole, as well as better spending and service decisions. Each Sector was given a financial target agreed with Government, with the overall objective to drive down the amount of taxpayer financial support to the industry. InterCity was given the target by Government of breaking even by 1988. The year before I joined in 1984 it was significantly loss-making, with losses amounting to some 20% of sales revenue. The clear expectation was that when profitable it would be a candidate for being privatised, along with Freight, the only other part of the railway that was profitable. As Business Planning Manager I was involved in a wide range of studies and reviews seeking ways to help achieve the target which, as at Freightliner, helped me build a detailed understanding of InterCity's economics and business model.

Initially Sectorisation, as the reorganisation came to be known, was largely an HQ level initiative with new Directors appointed to lead InterCity and Other Provincial Services, with small teams to support them. The General Manager of the Southern Region doubled up as Director of the new London and South East Sector, and Freight and Parcels were largely unchanged in structure but relabelled as Sectors. InterCity and Provincial Services appointed Managers in each Region to provide local oversight, but these managers initially reported to the Region with only a dotted line of responsibility to the new Sectors.

Sectorisation produced a wholly different dynamic in the industry, and unleashed a great deal of energy focused on business improvement. Each sub-sector was responsible for a group of train services from end to end, with costs and revenues attributed to their operation on an increasingly accurate and specific basis. For the first time it was possible to have a clear picture of the profitability of each service. Items of cost that were not supporting any particular service were challenged and driven out, and service decisions on frequency, stopping patterns and pricing could be taken knowing what it cost to operate the service. The process accelerated when, as a further step, the Regional Passenger Manager organisations were abolished and staff were allocated to one of three passenger sub-sectors within each Region. This gave more resources to sub-sector teams to challenge and manage costs and to market their services in a more focused way. Investment decisions became business led rather than production led.

At Sector level rolling stock strategies focused on cost-effectiveness nationally with a whole series of initiatives to improve utilisation and reduce costs. The infamous Pacer trains and the family of Sprinter trains were conceived and introduced as part of this. The clarity of clear profitability analysis of each train service had shown just how unremunerative a number of rural services had become. With Treasury pressure to reduce their losses, or close them down altogether, these lower cost and more productive train sets were a logical response. It is ironic that much as the Pacer trains were subsequently derided, their introduction had almost certainly saved a number of rural branch lines from complete closure.

The new structure produced an equally sharp focus on track and infrastructure costs. Each section of route was allocated to a prime user sponsor, who picked up the whole costs of that section, unless they could demonstrate that they did not need additional lines or junctions to run their services. For instance, on the main lines out of London, InterCity would usually be the prime user and pick up the costs of maintaining and renewing the fast lines, and Network SouthEast picked up the costs of the slow lines. Each junction and set of points would be attributed to an "owner" who picked up their costs, and equally each signalling workstation and shift was attributed to a sector for cost allocation purposes. This produced a strong drive to remove unneeded facilities whenever the opportunity arose. As part of the resignalling of York and Newcastle station areas prior to electrification of the East Coast Main Line in the 1980s, the number of points was roundly halved, for example, as a result of the process of challenge and attribution of each to an owner. This drove substantial savings in subsequent maintenance and renewal costs and improved reliability, with fewer pieces of equipment to fail.

The same process of removal of unneeded facilities was applied to all aspects of infrastructure, including sidings, depots and station facilities. Christopher Garnett, Chief Executive of GNER, in a speech several years after privatisation observed that it was remarkable how closely matched every part of the East Coast Main Line's infrastructure and facilities were to the service and demand levels that existed at the point of privatisation. This explained how extensive was the work and investment needed to cope with the growth in services and passenger numbers that took place after privatisation. He was one of the few post-privatisation Train Company Chief Executives who came from outside of the rail industry and was therefore more perceptive and objective in his appraisal of what he inherited. It showed how well British Rail had optimised its facilities for current demand, under relentless Government pressure to reduce costs.

Organising for Quality

The final step in Bob Reid's wholesale reform of the rail industry's organisational structure was the abolition of Regions and HQ Functions altogether, and vesting in the five sectors full responsibility for all aspects of their business, from day-to-day operations to ownership and upkeep of their own infrastructure, stations and depots. This was a vertically integrated structure, which was known as Organising for Quality as it was taken forward alongside a wide-ranging total quality management programme. Each Business Sector included a number of Profit Centres, with their own management teams covering operations, train maintenance, infrastructure, marketing, personnel and finance. The majority of Profit Centres were vertically integrated, responsible for most of the track on which their services ran, allowing them to run their section of railway as an integrated system. There was a complex system of trading between each Profit Centre, providing services from one to another and giving access to each other's track, stations and depots where needed.

There were a number of key virtues of the structure. Firstly, it ensured that the true economics of each Profit Centre's services were fully exposed, and actively managed by a fully-fledged management team focussed on improving performance. In effect there were now 25 or so CEOs driving performance not just one. Secondly, it aligned all members of the workforce behind a clearly identified set of train services. People could see better how they fitted into the whole, and how their particular job or department contributed to a successful railway service. I know that many employees, particularly those in more behind the scenes departments, such as civil engineers and maintenance staff, found this refreshing and motivating. Thirdly, the parcel of services managed by each Profit Centre had different market characteristics, with different mixes of commuters, business and leisure passengers, and shorter and longer distance services within the passenger sectors. Each could therefore work to meet the needs of its particular markets, encouraging a variety of strategies to do this rather than a single, centrally driven strategy.

A good number of the managers in Profit Centres in the Organising for Quality structure recall it as being the best structure they had ever worked within. Managers could see what their customers and markets needed and were prepared to pay, had control of all the levers they needed to improve things, and had the management information systems to be able to track the results.

However, the long term success of the structure could never be tested. Within weeks of the new organisation going live in April 1992, a Conservative Government was re-elected in May with a manifesto plan to break the railways up, split track from train operations, franchise passenger train services and sell off much of the railway via a large number of newly created service companies, such as Train Leasing Companies and Infrastructure Maintenance Companies. The Organising for Quality organisation continued for a further two years and produced some further improvements in financial and train service performance. But most energy was inevitably diverted to another major reorganisation to prepare for privatisation. It is at least debatable how durable the structure might have been, given the inherent tensions caused by different objectives and strategies between the Sectors and widespread inter-dependencies between Profit Centres. There was also very little investment during these two years, and therefore the ability of the structure to conceive and deliver cost effective investment schemes particularly in shared infrastructure was never tested.

There was however unanimity amongst the Directors of the Profit Centres that the structure had great potential, and was felt to be a much better basis for Privatising the railway than that adopted by the Government. This was the clear message at an infamous meeting of all of the Directors with the then Secretary of State for Transport, John MacGregor, who listened politely and then completely ignored an impassioned series of contributions from all in the room. These were that vertically integrated, market focused Profit Centres were a much better way forward than the planned splitting of track from train and, and breaking the industry up into numerous small and separate pieces.

A final lesson from Bob Reid's business led railway was that effective change is best achieved through evolution than from a single "revolutionary" change in structure. The reforms he initiated took the best part of ten years to reach their culmination in the Organising for Quality structure in 1992, with a number of intermediate steps, each of which was felt at the time to be a substantial change in itself. Reaching the point where there is a sufficient critical mass of people who see the need for change and agree on what that should look like, takes time and a great deal of engagement. At each stage there were the doubters who needed to be persuaded, and the opponents that needed to be managed, and all of this in a heavily unionised environment with due regard to the need to consult with employee representatives and seek their agreement for the changes involved. I doubt whether Bob Reid and his key lieutenants had a detailed blueprint in mind when they started out, but the principles were always clear: that a better organisational structure for the railways is one that is focused on the different markets served, overtly highlights the financial performance of different services and gives bottom line responsibility for managing them to a whole raft of focused managers, rather than a single central individual. Most importantly it is one that brings together the management of track and train and aligns the many different groups of staff behind an identified group of train services. Each Profit Centre's performance was clear to all so that the jobs and careers of its managers were on the line.

All change! - towards a privatised railway

The privatisation of Britain's railways in the 1990s was one of the most radical reorganisations of an industry ever attempted - a truly "revolutionary" restructuring. The Government had decided to learn from the earlier privatisations of other industries, such as gas and telecommunications, which left the original industry structure largely intact and therefore still monopolistic. Instead it broke the rail industry up into many smaller pieces. The task was more complicated than for other privatisations as significant parts of the industry required large subsidy to continue to operate so a straight sale or flotation was impossible. Government also wanted to see competition on the rails between different services, with the belief this would reduce costs and improve service quality. A hybrid solution was adopted which tore up all the existing industry structures and split track from train operations. It created a large number of support service companies which were sold one by one and split the passenger sectors into 25 Train Operating Companies (TOCs) which were let as time limited franchises. The structure was designed to facilitate so called open access operators as new entrants to the industry, with the expectation that these would in time supplant the franchises and offer passengers a choice of train services on each main route.

In many ways it is remarkable that the Government managed to complete such a radical programme within its five-year term of office. It required the creation of some 50 separate companies from scratch and development of a track record of performance to allow their subsequent marketing and sale or franchising. John Major's Government unquestionably drove the process hard, wanting to demonstrate its credentials as a reforming Conservative administration, staying true to the spirit of its Thatcherite predecessor. Its approach was clearly ideologically driven. It also probably had half an eye on the

1997 election, which it would lose by a landslide to a resurgent Labour Party under Tony Blair, wanting to ensure a fait accompli for the next Government.

But the lion's share of the actual work was done by the railway management who had become well practiced in managing reorganisations during the years of evolution toward full sectorisation in 1992. The reorganisations had also required the development of a sophisticated system of trading and internal contracting between Profit Centres, which readily leant itself to morphing into arms-length contracts between the new privatised entities. With hindsight it is a real tribute to the industry's managers that they completed the task in such a short space of time, even though many had strong reservations about the wisdom of the new structure. There were probably a range of motivations. For many it was the chance to "run their own show" in a smaller company freed of the inevitable constraints of a monolithic nationalised corporation. For some it was the chance to demonstrate that they were as good as their private sector counterparts, with whom they had been unfavourably compared for so many years, by successfully moving into the private sector. Almost certainly the most important factor was their loyalty to the industry and their colleagues, and the determination to make it work come what may.

The sheer scale of the upheaval is well illustrated by my own pre-privatisation organisation, the Midland Cross Country (MXC) profit centre of the InterCity Sector. This gave birth to seven new organisations or parts thereof: two complete TOCs, Midland Main Line and Cross Country Trains, with track infrastructure split five ways, divided between two Railtrack zones, Midland and Northeast, one whole Infrastructure Maintenance Company and part of another, and a Track Renewals Company. It was certainly a leadership challenge to successfully manage this dismemberment, whilst keeping the train service running throughout, and at the same time making some modest improvements in both financial and operational performance.

The first milestone in the privatisation process was the creation in April 1994 of Railtrack plc, to own and operate the railways track and signalling infrastructure. The original intention was that this would remain in public ownership, being a natural monopoly. As half of the old British Rail, it was still a very large organisation. However, its first, acerbic Chairman, Sir Bob Horton, assiduously lobbied across Government to make the case for its privatisation via a large flotation. He had previously briefly been Chairman and Chief Executive of oil giant BP plc, leaving under something of a cloud, and was keen to once again be a Footsie 100 Chairman. The Government was also tempted by the financial rewards of a sale, and saw private sector ownership as driving greater cost discipline.

Railtrack was almost certainly doomed to eventually fail from the outset. Its first Chief Executive, John Edmonds, was a hugely experienced rail manager, but who had a barely disguised contempt for engineers as people he thought spent money unnecessarily. Railtrack contracted out all of its maintenance and renewal activities to the new Infrastructure Maintenance Companies and Track Renewal Companies. The large bulk of British Rail's civil and signalling engineers therefore transitioned to these companies, taking with them their knowledge of how rail assets perform and how they need to be maintained. As importantly, because British Rail had no central database or register of the condition of its assets, knowledge of asset condition was also effectively outsourced. Railtrack was therefore never properly structured to perform as the asset management company it needed to be. To illustrate the point, one of Railtrack's first Zone Directors, equivalent in the hierarchy to British Rail's earlier Regional General Managers, was instructed by the Chief Executive that he must have no one with the title "Engineer" in his organisation!

Because of the huge land and property estate that Railtrack inherited, its Board and Chairman saw it more as a property company than a railway company, with little regard to fostering the skills necessary to maintain and operate a complex railway network. As long as John Edmonds was Chief Executive this was not as risky as it might seem, as there was little that he did not know about railway operations ensuring generally sound decisions. The various Zone Directors - Railtrack's equivalent of BR's Regions - were all ex BR too, so were knowledgeable about how the railway worked. However, his successor, Gerald Corbett, had no such experience having previously been Finance Director of Burger King. To paraphrase the former US Defence Secretary, Donald Rumsfeld, in a number of areas he didn't even know what he didn't know, or how fatal Railtrack's lack of corporate memory and asset knowledge would prove. I well remember him doing a short presentation to TOC MDs shortly after his appointment, asserting that there was little wrong with Railtrack's performance as its share price was steadily going up, as shown on the one slide he used! This was despite an increasingly poor operating and punctuality performance and widespread dissatisfaction amongst his customers, the train operating companies. A major asset failure and accident like the Hatfield crash was almost certainly inevitable given the way Railtrack was set up and run and its lack of asset knowledge.

The lesson for today's railway is the critical importance of understanding the skill sets and knowledge needed to run an effective rail system, and ensuring these skills are properly developed and managerial experience and future leaders are nurtured and continuously grown.

Preparing for Privatisation

The four years spent preparing for Privatisation were in many ways the most stimulating and challenging of my career. After the ten-year programme of organisational evolution culminating in the final big push to create the pure profit centre structure in 1992, it initially felt devastating to be expected to rip up the new structure and put in place the completely different set of organisations mandated by privatisation. We had spent much time and effort in winning over hearts and minds in support of the new Profit Centres, particularly amongst the often sceptical production functions. One of the hardest things I have ever had to do, after the general election in May 1992, was to break the news to our people that it was all change again. We would have to split up the structures we had just put in place, with people who had only recently come together going off again in a number of different directions. I tried to put a positive face to the announcement by committing us to handing over each part of the railway we had only just taken on in a better state than we had inherited it, and to giving full and open support to each of the new organisations that we would be handing over to. As it happened the professional pride that this appealed to undoubtedly helped us keep the railway running smoothly for our passengers, in what could otherwise have been a profoundly demoralising and disruptive period of change.

It also helped that the new Profit Centre structure, which in the event was in place for two whole years, was hugely energising and empowering. For the first time it brought together in a single chain of command all of the key functions necessary to run the railway. With all of the key people in one organisation it was possible to really drill down and understand what might be causing trains to run late and decide how best to improve things. It was up to us as to how best to allocate resources between departments and teams to try to improve train service performance. And it was up to us how to make the many trade-offs involved in railway operations, for instance stopping train services earlier in the late evening to give more time to the engineers for overnight track maintenance to reduce costs or speed up the delivery of some improvement. We had both profit and cash targets, and the ability to reinvest savings within the year encouraged the development of strong financial control and forecasting. Our Head of Finance, Geoff Evans, led this process magnificently, putting in place strong controls and processes and educating all of us in how to manage our finances. In many ways he was a prime example of the strength of British Rail's personnel development, having started as a junior clerk, becoming a qualified accountant and developing into an accomplished Finance Director.

It was also the case that both the Midland Main Line (MML) and Cross Country routes had been cinderellas under the old BR organisation, with MML split between the Eastern and London Midland Regions and neither Region giving it much attention or priority. Cross Country ranged across all five Regions, stretching from Inverness to Penzance and Poole, and was seen as something of a nuisance and distraction by them. Both routes therefore had significant unrealised potential for improvement through a clearly focused and dedicated management team. Local staff also welcomed the fact that they were now part of a clearly recognisable entity with senior management attention focused on their railway. Infrastructure staff in particular could now identify themselves with a distinct railway and see the impact of their endeavours on passengers. A small indicator of the engagement this fostered was our annual Christmas staff party. I insisted that all staff were invited, not just salaried staff from headquarters. The numbers attending each year grew, so that at the final "Farewell to MXC" party in March 1994 there were significant numbers of traincrew, station and maintenance staff attending. This was a huge change from established tradition where each grade group tended to socialise with themselves.

The years 1992 to 1994 were difficult ones for the UK economy putting pressure on passenger numbers, and leading to tight financial targets being set, and virtually no investment ahead of privatisation. In its second year of operation MXC had to absorb a £6.1 million centrally imposed reduction in its original cost budget of £178.5 million, as the economy and the industry's finances deteriorated. But we then bettered this by reducing costs by a further £3.5 million. Profit of £5.8 million was £4.5 million better than target, allowing an additional £4.2 million investment in a range of projects, including station, depot and infrastructure improvements. And this was achieved in a year when much attention was on designing and preparing the switch to the new organisations required for privatisation at year end. It really did feel as if the profit centre structure was working and opening up the opportunity for much better performance, and I think all of us were proud of what we achieved against the odds in those two short years.

As a leadership team these two years were an especially challenging time as we were in effect trying to do two jobs simultaneously: running MXC as a new organisation, with tough targets to meet and a desire to harness the benefits of the new structure and show that it worked; and planning the breakup and complete creation of seven new organisations or parts thereof. It was initially a time of great uncertainty as no one, least of all the Government, really knew what the privatised structures would look like and everyone was apprehensive as to whether they would still have a job, and if so where. To start with I was pretty disillusioned with what seemed like a kick in the teeth from Government. It had completely changed its whole approach to privatisation from what we had previously been led to expect, which was that InterCity as a business would be privatised. I started a process of external coaching with a view to leaving the industry and finding a new job. It was not easy keeping one's personal feelings to oneself, whilst trying to remain an effective leader, providing support to colleagues and flagging the way forward. I was then incensed when told that all profit centre directors would have to reapply for their jobs in the new structure. Ironically this made me determined to secure a job as an MD of one of the new TOCs and not let others move in ahead of me, and culminated in my being appointed as designate MD of the Midland Main Line Train Operating Company, which included the largest single part of what had been the Midland Cross Country profit centre. But before telling the story of Midland Main Line it is important to tell InterCity's story first.

CHAPTER 3 InterCity: A passenger railway without subsidy

I joined the InterCity sector of British Rail as Business Planning Manager in 1985, three years after it was first set up. Up until then passenger railway networks the world over were usually organised in one of two ways, on a geographic basis or on a functional basis, or some mix of the two. InterCity was therefore a radical change since it was organised on a market basis, embracing a group of longer distance train services serving separately identifiable markets. London and the South East predominately serving the London commuter market, and Regional (initially called Other Provincial Services), comprising the remainder of mainly regional city commuter and rural markets, were the other two passenger sectors.

It was generally thought that InterCity services were profitable, or at least should be, and the Government had set British Rail the target to break even from 1st April 1988. The BR Board had set the additional target that InterCity should make a 2% return on its asset base, valued at current not historic costs, from the 1989/90 financial year. This was so that InterCity would   become sufficiently profitable to be able to finance the replacement of its assets over time. The informal understanding was also that this would pave the way for InterCity to be privatised as an entity, and this was certainly the understanding of most of us in the business.

But in the year I joined InterCity recorded a loss of £125million on a current cost accounting basis, from passenger income of £639 million, a negative margin of 20%. Much of my time over the next nine years, and that of everyone in InterCity, was therefore spent in seeking ways to achieve and improve profitability, both service by service and overall. It is remarkable that InterCity did in fact move into profit in 1988/89, delivering a turnaround in financial performance that was both bigger and faster than other big turnaround stories of the 1980s, such as British Airways, British Steel, British Leyland and ICI [1]. Many initiatives contributed to this, some of which would be familiar to today's railway managers, but some of which would not be practical given the fragmented structure of the industry and therefore less familiar. Given the increasingly challenged financial position of Britain's railways today it is likely there are some useful lessons which could be applied as the industry moves back to a more integrated structure under Great British Railways.

In my ten years with InterCity I was lucky enough to be closely involved in most aspects of the turnaround and am therefore well placed to tell a number of aspects of the story. I joined as Business Planning Manager, then moved to InterCity Manager in Birmingham, responsible for both the West Coast Main Line and Midland Main Line sub-sectors, and ended as Director of the Midland Cross Country Profit Centre.

An important part of the story was the creation over time of a cadre of managers at both the centre and in each of the eight sub-sectors with the skills and knowledge of InterCity's markets, customers and economics to be able to deliver the turnaround. All those involved deserve a share of the credit as it was a genuine team effort. The vast majority of this cadre came from within the industry, which was a testament to the range of talent that British Rail had attracted and developed through its various management

---

[1] A lecture given to the Royal Society of Arts entitled "InterCity - Passenger Railway without subsidy" given by InterCity's MD, Dr John Prideaux, in May 1989 provides an excellent account of InterCity's journey to profitability.

training schemes. It was only in later years that a small number of people were brought in from outside the industry at senior levels, Barry Woledge as HR Director coming from British Airways and Geoff Ashton as Finance Director from Trust House Forte Hotels, being the most notable.

It took time to build up the new teams and for them to acquire the knowledge and understanding of the new business and its dynamics to be fully effective. A key first step was to get a clear understanding of the real financial performance of each route and service within it. This was an evolving task over a number of years as the art of drilling down to establish what each activity really cost and how shared costs should best be attributed to different services was progressively refined. How revenues were allocated to each service also evolved as in the early days a significant proportion of fares revenue came from so called "blank tickets", where the passenger's origin and destination stations were not recorded, so the revenue was merely allocated pro rata to directly recorded revenue. As a result, different routes' profitability shifted over time, as costing and recording systems improved, sometimes with dismaying results for the managers concerned. For instance, both the East Coast and West Coast sub-sectors were both shown to be less profitable than initially thought, as their true infrastructure costs became clearer.

But with each service's revenues matched increasingly closely to all of the costs incurred in operating them, this focus on profitability began to drive decisions and strategy. An early decision was to redeploy a number of the Western Region's High Speed 125 Train (HST) sets to the Midland Main Line and Cross Country sub-sectors. This both reduced costs by displacing a large number of older locomotive hauled train sets and their locos, and increased revenue because of the sharp improvement in service quality for passengers. Train mileage and service frequency on Western was of course reduced, but many of the services involved were underperforming so costs were reduced faster than revenues. It is hard to see how a comparable redeployment of rolling stock assets could be achieved on today's passenger railway, with train sets on fixed term leases and services mandated by franchise or concession agreements also for varying fixed terms. But in a rational world ensuring that your best assets are deployed to maximise their earning capability is surely one important component of optimising financial performance. Currently asset deployment can be optimised within a franchise or concession, but not across the network as a whole.

Focusing on service quality for passengers

An early focus was also on improving product quality, recognising that the travel experience on competing airline and coach services was steadily improving. As was car travel, with the road building programme reducing journey times and new car specifications continuously being raised, with air conditioning, in-car entertainment and the like increasingly becoming the norm. InterCity under its first Director, Cyril Bleasdale, reintroduced Pullman services on all key business travel routes and built first class waiting lounges at a number of main stations in direct imitation of airport lounges. It also embarked on a programme of refurbishing coach interiors to ensure comfort, decor and facilities kept up with passenger expectations.

In parallel with these moves to improve the "hardware" of the service, much was done to try to improve the softer aspects of InterCity's service quality. A good example is its initiative to introduce Senior Conductors (now usually called Train Managers) to replace train guards. Most guards had started life working on freight trains, had not been selected for their customer service skills and, more importantly, had never been given any customer service training. The result was at best an uneven approach to on-board customer care, with the better guards feeling frustrated with their lack of recognition or training. InterCity therefore negotiated a new employment grade for Senior Conductors and put those selected through a week-long residential training course in customer service. In parallel it provided smart new uniforms, looking more like a business suit than a guard's traditional workwear, and a new set of authorities to help Senior Conductors address service problems in real time such as upgrading people into first class accommodation or authorising free refreshments.

I attended a number of the training sessions at the end of the week to give a wrap-up talk about InterCity and what we were trying to achieve. I well remember the very first of these courses when a number of the Senior Conductors present were almost in tears with gratitude to InterCity and pride at being part of the new business. As well as this being the first customer service training they had ever received for what was an absolutely key front-line customer service role, they explained that this was the first time they had ever met and talked with a senior manager and had the business and their important role in it described. It was also the first time they had felt properly recognised and valued for their contribution to the business. It was a very emotional moment and a wonderful object lesson in how to initiate constructive change in a group of staff. It is not just a question of doing the right training but of addressing all aspects of a job and giving people the tools and authorities to do it properly. Up front and visible leadership of the initiative played a role too.

At InterCity Birmingham we hired a BBC Radio presenter to train our station announcers in how to make more passenger friendly public address announcements. Alongside other sub-sectors we introduced Customer Action Teams (CATs) made up of volunteer office-based staff who would go out to a heavily delayed train to assist the Senior Conductor and on-board staff in helping address passenger concerns. This was before the era of ubiquitous mobile phones, when phones were very expensive and the size and weight of a small brick. Teams were equipped with one of these phones to allow passengers to call ahead to waiting friends and relatives, not a problem on today's railway but a useful assistance to passengers then.

InterCity's strategy

Re-reading the InterCity Strategy Review of November 1987, which I project managed and wrote as Business Planning Manager, I was struck by the attention we paid to the competition to InterCity train travel. We commissioned specific studies on potential trends in both coach and airline competition and reviewed what InterCity needed to do to remain competitive. By no means all of the competitive developments that were then foreseen actually occurred, but what was important was that it was an outward looking, market focused strategy, unlike much of what British Rail had produced before. And it was also unlike the current approach of the Department for Transport (DfT) as ringmaster and "controlling mind" of the industry which seems to treat rail in isolation from competing modes of travel. Perhaps because the DfT is responsible for all forms of transport it is not able publicly to acknowledge the linkages, for instance between petrol prices and rail travel demand, as it believes it needs to be agnostic between modes. It is ironic that privatisation sought to introduce competition between rail services, but has resulted in competition between rail and other modes of travel being overlooked. A key theme of the turnaround strategy was that it was not static but dynamic, seeking to regularly invest to ensure services kept pace with, and ideally ahead of the competition.

The way the strategy was produced was itself interesting. I was seconded from my day job as Business Planning Manager for a number of months, and created a small seconded team to help produce it. John Prideaux set up a steering group of people from outside of BR to challenge our thinking and ensure we were always outward looking in our approach. The group included a rising star transport economist from the London School of Economics, Prof. Stephen Glaister (who much later became Chair of the Rail Regulator), and an industrialist who had recently been a Special Adviser in the Prime Minister's office at No 10. John also opened the door for me to set up a number of joint working groups with a variety of other departments to look at ways to reduce costs.

The main thrust of InterCity's turnaround strategy was of necessity on driving down costs, and no stone was left unturned in seeking opportunities to achieve this. This included asking difficult questions as to whether particular routes should be closed, or services transferred out of the sector into one of the subsidised rail sectors. An early task I was given was to investigate the potential savings from closing St Pancras station and the Midland Main Line south of Leicester, as well as the Berks and Hants Line from Reading to the West Country via Westbury. For the former, whilst InterCity appeared to benefit from withdrawing from the route, the negative impact on other sectors outweighed any benefit so fortunately there was no withdrawal. It is ironic indeed that in subsequent roles I became directly responsible for the Midland Main Line, and was an enthusiastic user of St Pancras whilst at Eurostar! How the UK rail scene has changed! The Western Region opposed the closure of the Berks and Hants line, even though it would have saved InterCity money with minimal impact on other sectors, and in due course managed down its infrastructure costs so it eventually became viable.

It is important that even though InterCity was being managed as a distinct business with clear and very challenging financial objectives, it was still part of a wider corporate entity and therefore had to take account of its potential impact on other parts of the railway in its decision making. It is not clear that this applied to the franchised railway after privatisation, where a successful franchise bid could easily impact on others for instance in taking a larger share of revenue on a passenger flow served by two or more services (major service reductions or closures have long been a thing of the past since privatisation) but this did not appear to be reflected in the DfT's decision making. And because InterCity was part of a wider corporate railway a number of its cost reduction initiatives were developed in close collaboration with others.

Win-win collaboration

A very good example of a successful collaboration was between InterCity and BR's Civil Engineers. Track renewal costs were a substantial item of cost for InterCity and a joint discussion was held, with InterCity challenging the engineers to find ways to reduce their unit costs for track renewals. The engineers' response was to ask for more time each weekend to undertake their renewal work since their costs were greatly impacted by the length of time they had to do the work. Typically, they were taking two, or more usually three weekends to complete a renewal job, with the consequent need to transport staff and plant to site and set up and close down their worksite multiple times. Longer possession times for renewal work would reduce their unit costs significantly, particularly if they were given long enough to do the job in a single weekend.

At the same time, we challenged them to find ways to increase the speed that they initially handed back newly re-laid track for passenger service, knowing that faster journey times were a key issue to improve our competitiveness with the still growing motorway network. Typically hand backs were at 20mph for the following week to give time for the newly laid track ballast to settle. The outcome of all these discussions was a completely new approach to track renewal, with the work ably led by the Deputy Director of

Civil Engineering, Tim Green. The engineers were given much longer track possessions at weekends, 30 to 40 hours rather than the traditional 15 hours, allowing them to do a complete job in one weekend, and so disrupting many fewer weekends for passengers. This was coupled with InterCity investing in a number of innovative new items of on-track plant, christened Dynamic Track Stabilisers. These were designed to simulate the passage of trains on the newly re-laid track and consolidate the ballast in one night, so allowing the new track to be handed back for passenger service on a Monday morning at speeds much closer to the normal line speed of 125mph.

Slowing trains from line speed to negotiate the temporary 20mph speed restrictions, and then accelerating back to full speed, added up to 5 minutes to journey times for each renewal site, with allowances included in timetables to accommodate this. In total these allowances added up to a full 20 minutes between London and Edinburgh for instance, so this was a strategically important improvement. The new approach therefore allowed InterCity to reduce journey times significantly, with consequent benefits for passenger revenue alongside substantial reductions in civil engineering track renewal costs. InterCity's own costs were also reduced, because of the saving in braking and energy costs from slowing down and then accelerating back to line speed. A remarkable win-win outcome for everyone! Track renewal techniques have of course moved on substantially since the 1980s when this work was done, but I have no doubt that a similar open- books collaboration between the train operators and infrastructure engineers would find ways to reduce current track maintenance and renewal costs, whilst minimising the disruption to passenger services.

The goal of seeking cost reductions at the same time as improving the service for passengers was applied even more successfully to coach maintenance. The work here was part of British Rail's Manufacturing and Maintenance Strategy initiative and involved decoupling the maintenance of coach interiors from that of their running gear, particularly bogies and wheel sets. Traditionally passenger coaches had been sent back to main works every two years on an eight-year cycle of minor and major overhauls. Both ride quality and coach interiors tended to deteriorate towards the second half of this two-year cycle as depots could leave any significant items of work to be done to the next works overhaul. The works overhauls were also costly and involved significant downtime away from revenue earning service. This was therefore not a good approach, with high costs, high asset downtime and steadily falling quality over the two-year cycle! I well remember many journeys in my early career travelling in a coach which was "hunting". This was an uncomfortable and sometimes slightly alarming oscillation in the vehicle caused by worn bogie components which needed replacing. The problem largely disappeared with the new approach to coach maintenance.

The new strategy turned this on its head by investing in maintenance depots' equipment and staffing to do much more work at each depot, particularly during vehicles' natural overnight downtime. Depots were staffed and equipped to maintain coach interiors on a continuous basis, but with a major refurbishment in main works every eight years or so, not just replacing interiors as new but also adding in new features such as plug-in sockets or better seats. Depots were also equipped with wheel lathes and lifting gear, allowing them to maintain wheel sets and bogies to more consistent standards and improve ride quality. Coupled with more regular replacement of key bogie components, this allowed the full bogie exchange to be extended to two years, nearly doubling the previous periodicity. The result was significantly better quality for passengers, at the same time as substantially lower costs and better asset utilisation.

Reshaping InterCity's train services

With today's railway largely the result of detailed train service specifications set by the DfT, it is hard to appreciate that InterCity had widespread freedom to decide what level of service it provided on each route. It could cut or withdraw services altogether provided it could persuade the BR Board this was appropriate and was able to handle any political or passenger push back. Radical changes to the portfolio of sleeper services provide a case study of the power of this approach. When InterCity started as a separate business it had a considerable range of sleeper services, many of them comprising sleeper coaches attached to the rear of overnight seated trains. It became quickly evident that none of them were profitable, but in the absence of any single manager having bottom line responsibility before InterCity, few changes had been made under the Regional Management structure. Sleeper services are inherently challenging economically, with only one loaded vehicle journey every twenty-four hours, higher cost vehicles with much lower passenger occupancy, and higher staffing costs both on board and at servicing depots because of bed making, laundry etc. They can only be made economic with consistently high loadings over the week and seasons, and high fare levels. Given these obvious facts the lack of change is a striking indication of the general sluggishness of the old regional management structure.

An early change was to concentrate all Anglo Scottish sleeper services to depart from Euston and run on the West Coast route to Scotland. This was primarily to free up night time capacity on the East Coast route to facilitate electrification works, but also enabled some modest savings in London terminal costs. Next to go were sleeper services attached to the rear of seated trains, for instance between London and Liverpool and Manchester. Load factors on these were generally very poor, a reflection of the substantial reduction in day train journey times over the years which made it largely unnecessary to travel overnight.

There were also a number of instances where one or more sleeper coaches were detached from a longer distance service, to provide through sleeper services, two examples being to Stranraer, to connect with ferries to Northern Ireland, and to Barrow-in-Furness. On learning of our proposal to withdraw these services BR's then Chairman, Sir Robert Reid, instructed me to make sure, as the responsible manager, that I properly informed the services' customers what we proposed and why. For the Stranraer sleeper this involved meeting a delegation of Northern Ireland Unionist MPs who had expressed concerns about the withdrawal. I remember going to the meeting in a Committee Room of the House of Commons with considerable trepidation, since the Ulster Unionists had quite an aggressive reputation. I needn't have worried. When I took them through the statistics on the Northern Ireland to British mainland travel market, it was clear they had had no idea how few people were travelling by sleeper or indeed rail, as the airlines had long since taken virtually the whole market. They themselves routinely flew to and from the Province so when they understood how very small the residual rail market was, they readily endorsed what we were doing as sensible and necessary! It was a good example of how the perceptions of politicians and the media can sometimes be widely adrift from the real situation, and how effective communication can preempt unnecessary opposition.

Another example was the Barrow sleeper withdrawal, where the main customers had been managers from Vickers Shipbuilding, who again readily accepted what we were doing once the situation had been explained to them. The icing on the cake was that for a few years we inserted an additional stop in one of the west coast sleepers at Oxenholme, which was much more convenient for passengers from the Lake District than Barrow was. When I consulted with the North West Rail Users Consultative Committee they actively welcomed the withdrawal of the Barrow sleeper as a result. RUCCs were not usually known for welcoming service withdrawals!

The endgame on the sleeper strategy was to concentrate the service on just two long, 16 coach trains out of Euston each night, one for Glasgow with a section for Fort William being detached at Carstairs Junction, and one for Edinburgh where sections were detached for Aberdeen and Inverness. This greatly reduced the haulage costs and freed up overnight capacity for track maintenance and freight services. At the same time a number of initiatives were implemented to improve service quality. The sleeper coaches were put through a comprehensive interior refurbishment, a lounge car was introduced into each train providing late evening drinks and snacks, train speeds were constrained to 80 mph to improve the comfort of ride whilst passengers slept, and drivers were specially trained on braking technique on these very long but sensitive trains. Finally, boarding and alighting times were extended at both ends so passengers could enjoy a longer night's sleep if they wished, and access was made available to InterCity's first class lounges prior to boarding. It is interesting that this pattern of two sleepers each way, each night, continues to this day in the franchised railway more than 30 years later.

It is also hard now to appreciate the extent to which InterCity's, relatively limited, investment programme was largely driven by business need rather than any wider political agenda. The one exception to this was of course East Coast Electrification, which was given the go ahead by the Government largely in recognition of Bob Reid's success in getting the industry's finances under control. There was a business case, albeit not an overwhelming one, and it certainly stretched InterCity's finances for a few years since much of the investment involved had to be charged to revenue account and not capitalised. But most investments were those decided upon by InterCity itself, and driven purely by commercial need either to enable cost savings, to retain or grow passenger revenue or replace assets approaching the end of their lives. This is increasingly a far cry from the current approach in the industry, where investments are controlled and decided upon by the Department for Transport, and only ever with Treasury approval. Inevitably political, not rail industry priorities tend to dominate, with a real risk for the industry that many investments do less than they could to improve its finances.

Whilst many investment schemes were of course managed day to day by British Rail's various engineering and technical functions, the sector was required to be the sponsor for them and ensure they delivered the promised benefits. John Prideaux's sponsorship of the East Coast Electrification project was for me a textbook example of how effective investment project sponsorship should work. As Sector Director he saw it as his personal role to sponsor and oversee this strategically crucial project. At every stage of the project he was looking not only to ensure it was being delivered on time and within budget, but more importantly he was always seeking out additional benefits to build on the original business case. For instance, he required InterCity's sub-sectors to bid for allocations of the still relatively new InterCity 125 HST train sets released from the East Coast as electric trains took over. This ensured the 125s were then used on the most profitable services, bettering the assumptions in the original business case.

He also charged the Project Director, Don Heath, and myself as Business Planning Manager, with undertaking a review of potential line speed improvements on the East Coast Main Line on the back of the major investments in electrification and resignalling, with a target to get from London to Edinburgh in 4 hours. This we achieved as a result of dozens of small line speed improvements that we identified, boosting the revenue gains that electrification on its own would have brought. And he personally led reviews of track layouts in the areas being resignalled, producing substantial reductions in the number of points, with resultant savings in subsequent maintenance costs and improved punctuality because of fewer points failures. The lesson for me was that investment project sponsorship needs to be by a senior business leader with accountability for the benefits and costs, and the authority to vary specifications where appropriate. The Project Director needs to be accountable to the sponsor, not the other way round, as is often the case currently at Network Rail.

Focusing on asset utilisation

There was a strong focus on maximising the utilisation of rolling stock assets, an approach of course adopted by all the new business sectors. Under the old regional structure, where many InterCity services operated over two different regions, there was rarely a single manager or management unit with clear authority looking at the performance of a route as a whole, allowing often inefficient practices to persist. Even where there was clear management responsibility, as on the Western Region which of course oversaw the entirety of Great Western InterCity services, the focus was on optimising the use of their allocated fleet of HST units, rather than questioning whether some of them might be more gainfully used elsewhere. Having InterCity as a market and profit focused national business made it so much easier to question and change often long-standing practices and achieve large efficiencies.

Persuading regional production managers of the need for changes on occasions took considerable time. On the West Coast Mainline, for which I was InterCity Manager from 1988 to 1991, InterCity had ordered a number of Driving Van Trailers (DVT) in order to operate the route with fixed formation train sets, with a locomotive permanently coupled at one end and the DVT allowing the set to be driven from the other end on the return journey: so called "push pull" operation. This allowed the saving of a significant number of locomotives, which no longer needed to be detached then moved to a holding siding ready to be attached to a subsequent train, plus the staff necessary to undertake all the attaching and detaching. It also increased platform capacity, by enabling faster reoccupation of platforms by an arriving train after each departure, and in due course allowed track layouts at terminal stations to be simplified by no longer having to provide holding sidings for locomotives awaiting their next working.

But it first needed the discipline of coaches being kept together as whole sets. This was not the practice on the London Midland Region, who operated the large bulk of West Coast InterCity services. The Region's Operators were in the habit of detaching coaches with defects, such as inoperable air conditioning, at stations en route, when the defects first came to their attention. This was partly the result of a poor relationship between the Operations and Mechanical Engineering functions on the region, with the operators wanting to highlight what they saw as poor maintenance. But the result was a vicious circle of problems, as the detached coaches often took many days to be collected and returned to their allocated depots to be fixed, so that coach availability fell putting pressure on depots to let "borderline" coaches go out each day to ensure the right number of coaches were provided train by train. But this of course increased the number of coaches that developed defects during the day.

The solution was to have a strict discipline of keeping sets of coaches together throughout the day, if necessary locking off individual defective coaches from passenger use, so that depots could fix problems straight away on the sets' return to depots overnight. Over time the result was both better coach availability and reduced levels of defects experienced by passengers. But It took nearly two years and a number of strong words to break the London Midland Region's habit of random coach detachments, ahead of the introduction of DVTs and proper unit train operation.

As with all the new business sectors, the focus on cost reduction was all pervading and by no means confined to maximising resource utilisation - "sweating the assets" as Chris Green, when Director of Network Southeast, put it - or to better maintenance and technical practices. Every item of cost was scrutinised, so that whenever a post became vacant because the incumbent had moved to a different job or left the railway, sub-sector managers immediately challenged why the post could not be withdrawn permanently or at least be part of a rejigging of responsibilities to save staff elsewhere. This was the easiest, and in the absence of across the board redundancy programmes, the quickest way of reducing staffing levels and costs and improving productivity. Railway managers, not just sector managers, became adept at challenging and managing costs down in this way. Whilst each saving was small, the relentless and continuous challenging of every item of cost produced steady and cumulatively significant increases in cost-effectiveness with little organisational disruption. It was in some ways akin to the zero-base budgeting approach used in some companies today.

This was in significant contrast to today's railway, where too often a manager's response to a new vacancy is to look to recruit to fill it, without much thought. This is also a widespread behaviour in the public sector, where there is a reluctance to offer up savings in staff or costs, in order to protect budgets and organisational standing. Given the steadily widening direct influence of Government in the industry through the Department for Transport, and growing proportion of the industry that is not subject to market or competitive pressures, for instance via franchise competitions, it is perhaps not surprising. I was certainly struck by the general lack of this management discipline when I first joined Eurostar and when a member of the Network Rail Board.

The key component in this approach is having a small cadre of managers with proper bottom line accountability for a service or group of services, who see and have to approve the full range of costs involved - trains, infrastructure etc - and who are in a position to make sound judgements as to what costs can be supported in delivering the service to passengers, and which costs can be dispensed with. There are always additional things that can be done that might improve services. In the absence of regular challenge in this way, costs have a habit of creeping up without regard to their contribution or cumulative impact on the service they support. The lack of this challenge capability is a major weakness of the current industry structure, with Network Rail's costs, which amount to broadly half of all industry costs, effectively determined by the Rail Regulator with hardly any reference to their contribution to the variety of services they support. And franchisee's costs are also largely fixed once a franchise is awarded, by franchise agreements and contracts. This produces a lack of agility in continuously adjusting a service's cost base, certainly in any downwards direction, to respond to changing commercial pressures, eventually requiring larger and much more disruptive adjustments to costs.

The final group of costs that InterCity sought to challenge and reduce, but with less success, was overheads and centrally allocated costs. The InterCity Strategy Review that I project managed revealed that these amounted to an astounding 27% of InterCity's total costs. Over half of these were so called administrative and general expenses, mostly at national level, which were simply allocated to sectors without any trail of cost causation. Part of the problem was British Rail's still immature system of cost analysis; for instance, employers pension contributions were included as overheads but should logically have been attributed to each local cost centre employing staff. But most were from the budgets of Headquarters Directors, who jealously defended their need to decide what should be spent. However, by definition there was little linkage to the service enjoyed by passengers and so InterCity's ability to optimise and match costs to revenue, service by service, was significantly blunted. A disproportionate share of InterCity's turnaround effort had therefore to be focused on direct operating and infrastructure costs.

Overall then InterCity's turnaround was based on a very wide ranging and largely successful attack on unit costs and a programme to sweat its assets and rolling stock utilisation. In contrast it is striking with hindsight how modest was the projected revenue growth assumed in the strategy. Of the £54 million profit improvement that the 1987 Strategy Review projected by 1989/90, roundly only a quarter, £14 million, came from revenue growth. At the time, the art of passenger revenue forecasting was still very simplistic, and forecasts had to be credible in the eyes of the Department of Transport and Treasury. British Rail and InterCity had a forecasting model called the Leeds Model, based on analysis of past revenue trends by the University of Leeds Transport Studies Unit. This showed an historic correlation with national GDP, with each percentage increase in GDP apparently driving a 1.5% increase in InterCity rail usage but with an underlying negative time trend of minus 2.5% each year, attributed to road building and decline in population in cities, which were traditionally strong markets for rail. There was superficial logic to this model, which essentially said that as incomes grew people's propensity to travel grew faster, and there is no doubt that the motorway construction programme which continued into the late 1980s had a significant negative impact on rail travel demand. But its logic also implied that InterCity's own efforts to improve services and attract new customers counted for little.

InterCity actually achieved profitability in 1988/89, despite the 1987 Strategy Review that I wrote forecasting this was not achievable. A large part of this was down to higher revenue growth, with national GDP growing faster than the 1987 forecast. However, some of the outperformance was attributable to all of InterCity's programmes to improve service quality and attract new passengers, but which could not credibly then be included in its forecasts. Certainly, in later years reductions in journey time, frequency improvements, coach refurbishments and other quality improvements had a material effect, and began to undermine the Leeds Model.

It is a common attitude in many public sector and Government services that demand is seen as something that is exogenously driven but needs to be met (or sometimes not, in the case of some health services!), whereas the private sector sees customer demand as something to be stimulated and if possible grown by product innovation, marketing or whatever. The Leeds Model, and the public sector attitudes it reflected, were a significant dampener on InterCity's freedom of manoeuvre, and it was only the advent of franchises for whom revenue growth was the key to maintaining their financial viability, that consigned the Model to history.

For me the key to InterCity's successful turnaround, in service quality for passengers as well financially, lay in its sub-sector or route-based teams, backed by a small but highly experienced Headquarters organisation which set overall strategy and led on nationwide initiatives. The sub-sector teams got to know each of their individual services intimately, and as well as challenging costs as described above, were able to agilely adjust service frequencies, stopping patterns, fares and marketing programmes to respond to market trends and opportunities and improve profitability. A good example of this agility was InterCity Birmingham's response to the unexpected growth in passenger demand in 1988 and 1989, when the opportunity was taken to increase the frequency of trains from Manchester and Liverpool to London from the previous two trains every three hours to a regular hourly service. This made the services significantly more attractive to passengers who had hitherto used British Airways' Manchester Heathrow shuttle service, and with skillful train planning was achieved with no increase in the number of train sets needed.

On the Midland Main Line the team bid for and secured the first HST set displaced from the East Coast Main Line as a result of the line's electrification. This one additional train set enabled an increase in frequency from Sheffield, Derby and Nottingham to London to hourly and to half hourly from Leicester to London, a dramatic and transformational improvement in the Line's fortunes. At the time it felt as if much of British Rail had forgotten how to grow the business after years of cut backs and retrenchment, and that we were learning from scratch how to manage growth.

The sub-sector organisations not just of InterCity but those of all the new sectors were, with hindsight, wonderful learning and development environments for a relatively new generation of railway managers, very many of whom went on to run the new passenger franchises after privatisation. It is an interesting speculation as to how successful the franchises might have been without their experience and drive. It is also an object lesson in what it takes to develop a new generation of managers, and how powerful a successful development programme can be even if it was not entirely planned that way.

CHAPTER 4 Transitioning to the private sector - Midland Main Line Train Operating Company.

April 1st is always a memorable date, and was even more so in 1994 as it marked our first important step toward privatisation. This was the date that Midland Main Line (MML) became a separate organisational unit, alongside 24 other "Train Operating Units" destined to become Train Operating Companies (TOCs) and in due course let as separate franchises. Importantly, InterCity ceased to exist as a national organisation at the same time, so whilst MML was still part of British Rail it began to operate rather more autonomously with little strategic direction from above. Nevertheless, it still had tough targets to meet and was subject to close central oversight and controls. Managerially we were largely "on our own" which was both exciting and initially somewhat daunting, but was an excellent preparation for the private sector ownership that followed.

It also marked the start of an incredibly intense period for us as a management team. In effect we were now doing three distinct jobs, each of which was hugely demanding and time consuming. Firstly, we were required to work with BR HQ and a raft of lawyers and advisers to set MML up as a formal company and prepare it to be let as a franchise. Each step of this process was largely new to us, involving a steep learning curve. Secondly, we were of course required to manage MML as an embryonic train company and meet safety, train performance and financial objectives. Doing this as well as possible was doubly important, not just in terms of our professional pride as railway managers but also to demonstrate a strong track record which would mark us out to potential future private sector owners. Finally, we had decided to mount our own management bid to run the franchise, which involved getting the necessary financial backing in place and putting together a competitive bid to the Franchising Authority. Again, this process was entirely new to us, with its own distinct learning curve. Moreover, British Rail required that this last task was all done in our own time, in evenings and weekends. It was a frenetic but very exciting period. One colleague described it as being like driving a sports car whose roof had suddenly blown off, with the wind now racing through your hair!

The pressure on us was further increased because of our wish to move MML much higher up the "queue" to be franchised. At the outset MML had been penciled-in as one of the last Train Companies to be privatised because of the perceived legal difficulties of granting satisfactory access to use St Pancras station, our London terminus. St Pancras had recently been transferred to the ownership of London and Continental Railways, the private sector consortium which had won the concession to build the Channel Tunnel Rail Link. The expectation was that MML services would be hugely disrupted during rebuilding of St Pancras to accommodate Eurostar international services, and there was doubt as to how the privatisation powers in the 1994 Railways Act would apply in this special case. BR's Finance Director, Derek Fowler, even expressed the view that privatising MML was unlikely to be possible at all because of the special difficulties of access to a separately privatised station. But when we researched the programme of bus company privatisation, which was the closest parallel to the process we faced on the railways, it was very clear that management bids were only successful for the first few sales, before a clear market of bidders became established. We therefore concluded we needed to be much nearer the top of the queue if our management bid was to have any chance of success.

By this time, we had largely got over our initial anger and dismay over the way privatisation was being done. Alongside everyone else we had long since accepted that we had no influence over how the privatised industry would be organised. The broad structure was at least now clear and we just wanted to get on with it, and, I suppose, to prove to ourselves and the wider world that we could survive and thrive in the private sector. Two things also added to my own determination. My new boss, one of two MDs charged with preparing the Train Companies for franchising, helpfully told me at our first meeting that nothing would give him greater pleasure than to see me screw up, as he would have liked my job as MD of Midland Main Line! I was as a result determined not to give him the opportunity and have always been grateful for his openness, whether intended ironically or seriously! And secondly, the way that British Rail treated the Train Companies at times, for instance requiring us to formally sign documents denying we were guilty of any financial or any other impropriety, felt unjust and offensive. At one point I felt that the last BR Chairman, John Welsby, was being deliberately difficult so as to increase our desire to be privatised and out from under British Rail. With hindsight I don't think he was that Machiavellian, but was just trying to keep a lid on things as the industry was broken up.

Preparing Midland Main Line for privatisation

Our management team was ready formed from the start as we had all worked together at Midland Cross Country so we were able to hit the ground running in many respects. The main adjustment was from running an integrated piece of railway to running a narrower business which was more of a pure customer service organisation. The first step toward privatisation was to get MML incorporated as a distinct company, albeit still under British Rail ownership. This required putting in place clear contracts with all of those other new rail organisations that we would need to provide services to us, or from us. The most important was with the new Railtrack company to ensure access to their infrastructure. Fortunately, Peter Strachan, the Director of the Railtrack zone which managed the bulk of the track we ran over, had also worked at InterCity and understood our particular needs. We were therefore able to establish a good relationship which made the task of negotiating the myriad access contracts much easier. It was also more closely tuned to what we saw as our particular needs, with only a very loose template from the centre on what it should look like, unlike current access contracts which are now tightly specified by the Rail Regulator. The local relationship was in sharp contrast to Railtrack HQ with whom we never established any sort of relationship. Symptomatic of their attitude to their customers was the way we learned what our track access charges would be: via an article placed in the Financial Times! Having been used to understanding and managing every detail of the costs of track and signalling, to be paying a single, very large, fixed lump sum for access and to learn about this through the media was galling to say the least. Unfortunately, this proved to be not untypical of Railtrack's attitude to its "customers".

Another important contract was with London and Continental Railways to ensure adequate and continuing access to St Pancras during and after the rebuilding to accommodate Eurostar services. Nick Brown, our Operations Director who was in due course my successor as Managing Director, played a blinder in negotiating this, working out our minimum operational needs to allow us to reduce the number of platforms we used from 7 to just 4, and agreeing a detailed set of contingencies and remedies to allow continued operations during the actual rebuilding period. This removed a significant barrier to our being one of the earlier franchises to be let and cleared the way for us to move up the "queue".

As well as negotiating a whole swathe of contracts, we had to demonstrate clear financial control over our new business and had to undergo a rigorous process of safety validation, to satisfy the BR Safety Directorate that we had the controls, procedures and capability to run a safe railway. This involved producing a detailed written Safety Case and undergoing a thorough cross examination by a special validation panel. Both tasks were necessary before we could be "incorporated" as a limited company with our own balance sheet and accounts. Each of those tasks was of course helpful in getting us into the mindset of running our own business, and no longer looking "upwards" for direction or support as is so often the mindset of the public sector.

An early challenge - the 1994 Railtrack signallers strikes

An early need to be self-sufficient and self-directing was triggered by the Railtrack signallers' strikes of August and September 1994. The strikes were over the union's pay claim, and were badly mishandled by Railtrack who were still Government owned at this stage and therefore needing to agree the terms of any settlement with Government. Nationally most of the rail network was shut down on each strike day, but the Midland Zone of Railtrack told us from the outset that they would be able to operate four out of our five signalling centres, with staff from several East Midlands centres prepared to work and managers operating the others. This would allow us to operate most of our daily trains if we chose to.

Our initial reaction was one of caution, being concerned about the risk of provoking the union by being seen to be strike breaking by running trains, and potentially triggering picketing of our stations. But on reflection we decided we had a duty to try to run a service; after all what was the railway for but to serve its customers? With a little trepidation we therefore ran a service from day one of the strikes, with only Sheffield and Chesterfield excluded. I will always remember the atmosphere on our stations when I toured them that day: there was a palpable sense of pride amongst our staff, who were of course not on strike themselves, that we were keeping faith with our customers and running trains for them.

But it was immediately apparent that our problem was not being able to run trains, but not having many passengers. On that first day we only carried about 10% of our normal numbers of passengers. This was simply because the national media was dominated by stories of no trains running, so the large majority of our regular passengers were either unaware or disbelieving that we were actually running. As the strike days continued our sense of dread about the risk of damage or worse to our business grew. This was amplified after I and our Operations Director, Nick Brown, attended a national briefing for senior British Rail managers when it became clear that BR centrally had no contingency plans and there was no reassurance that the strikes would be settled any time soon. We therefore decided that we were on our own managerially and that we would have to rely on our own efforts to get passengers back.

This prompted a frenetic period of activity aimed at getting local publicity and word of mouth telling people we were operating virtually normally by this point. We had no budget for advertising, nor were we then allowed to advertise, and so had to rely on stunts and gimmicks to get ourselves talked about. It was a wonderful way of engaging staff in the new business and unleashing a wave of creativity, with a number of groups set up by our Marketing Director, Andrew Harvey, to brainstorm ideas on how we could build awareness. Most prominent was an initiative to erect large-scale banners at some of our stations telling passers-by that Midland Main Line was "keeping on running". This generated some media coverage as well as complaints from several Local Councillors, including from Camden Council, whose offices were directly opposite St Pancras station and who complained to BR's Chairman, John Welsby. He in turn rang me to "reprimand" us, but of course privately was very pleased.

Another idea was a "mystery" train providing free travel one Saturday, which was widely publicised but without saying which train this would be. A number of stations offered free car cleaning to first class passengers, and we gave out car stickers to all members of staff and any passengers who would accept them, again trumpeting that Midland Main Line was "keeping on running". This all got us talked about and passenger numbers grew steadily with each day's strike.

A small problem was that whilst we knew we were winning passengers back, BR's then sales information systems only gave us monthly totals, with a very crude estimate of weekly totals. We therefore instituted a daily manual count of passenger numbers on each train to track our progress, which became a valuable source of information on a permanent basis long after the strikes were over. By the last strike-day we had built numbers back up to 75% of normal, a considerable achievement given the continuing national media coverage of "no trains", and with negligible expenditure incurred and no advertising. We also started to grow revenue again ahead of the previous year within just four weeks after the end of the strikes. It was a wonderful demonstration of the power of out of the box thinking and action, and of the importance of word of mouth as an influence on passenger behaviour. As a management team it gave us a lot of confidence and courage to follow our instincts and try new things out. We had also taken the first steps in establishing Midland Main Line as a brand that worked for its customers, and as a company that people were proud to work for because of this. It was a classic example of applying the management dictum that one should "never waste a good crisis".

Preparations for franchising

With Midland Main Line established as a proper incorporated company, preparation for privatisation switched to preparing the necessary suite of information documents for potential bidders to be able to understand the business and base their bids on. In total this involved the preparation of 12 Long Form Reports setting out in huge detail what the business involved, including its assets, staffing, finances, contracts and operational performance. Each detail in these documents had to be signed off by us as management, as well as the Information Memorandum, equivalent to a Sales Prospectus had this been a conventional sale rather than a franchise. The amount of diligent reading and checking involved was huge!

All of this required us to engage with a whole new set of people, lawyers, merchant bank advisers and the like, with whom we had had little or no previous contact. We quickly learnt that it was much better to work collaboratively with them as we could learn a lot from them, and it made what would otherwise have been a very tedious process bearable, if not actively enjoyable. It also showed us that open, collaborative relationships could be far more productive and in a number of cases evolved into real partnerships which benefited both businesses involved. Perhaps the best example was with the lawyers we chose to advise and support us as a franchisee, Edwards Geldard, a Derby-based firm of commercial lawyers. They continued as our lawyers after privatisation, also then acting for our new owners National Express Group on rail issues, as well as for other privatised rail companies based in Derby. They were also of course regular users of MML, gave us much friendly feedback on our service and introduced us to a number of useful contacts in the East Midlands. It was from them that

I learned that whilst it was important to take legal advice, one didn't necessarily have to follow it. The lawyer's job is to point out the legal and contractual risks, but for the client then to decide whether they want to take that risk.

Alongside all this early activity my fellow designate Train Company MDs elected me as the first Chairman of the Association of Train Operating Companies. This was one of the many new organisations created for privatisation and whose role was to provide a range of common services to the Train Companies, particularly those deemed by Government to be so called "network benefits" such as Railcards, which they were determined to retain. As one of the youngest and least experienced MDs my election was a great surprise to me. We had by then moved MML up the queue to be privatised and started to establish ourselves as something of thought-leader, but I believe I was mainly elected because I was the least objectionable candidate and there were doubts about the leadership credentials of some other candidates.

There was of course no organisation to start with so a key task was to start to create an embryonic team to set up and run it. As the "representative" of the TOCs, I was also expected to work with Government and the newly established Office of Passenger Rail Franchising (OPRAF) in designing the numerous new structures and processes that would be needed to ensure rail services continued to operate as a seamless network. This was less a collaborative process and more a series of diktats from Government and OPRAF as to how things were to be done. Much of this was not welcome to the TOC MDs, so I became something of a go-between, developing useful diplomatic skills in the process. It is striking that most of the structures and arrangements that were put in place continue to this day, although some, such as the fares structure, ticketing and reservation systems, have long since passed their sell-by dates and are now urgently in need of reform. The whole episode was my first real exposure to the workings of Government, and was a classic example of how it can behave like a bulldozer, paying scant attention to and barely listening to wider views when the political drive is behind it.

Recognising that we had much to learn if we wanted to succeed and thrive post privatisation, we took every opportunity to engage with and listen to anyone who might usefully give us advice. One of the things I did was set up a sort of "shadow board" of the new company, with half a dozen or so prominent business people and customers from the region, who we gave a dinner to every few months, shared our latest challenges with and obtained useful advice from. At least one went on to be one of our nominated Non-Executive Directors of our Management Buyout company had it succeeded. It gave us confidence that we were working on the right lines.

Building our confidence was more important than many people have acknowledged. I think a lot more people than are prepared to admit, are "swans", appearing outwardly serene and confident but paddling away furiously beneath the surface. We had all spent our careers to date as British Rail managers. British Rail was not a well-regarded organisation, and was regularly lampooned and criticised in the media and by most politicians, and over time this criticism inevitably rubs off on all but the most thick-skinned people who work there. The accepted wisdom was that British Rail was not well run and that private sector management was better. To help prepare our team I encouraged each individual to update and if possible to upgrade their professional qualifications, where they had them, and to attend an advanced management programme relevant to their role, for example at Insead Business School in France.

I myself was lucky enough to attend the Advanced Management Programme at Harvard Business School in the

USA which exposed me to a wide range of overwhelmingly private sector managers from all over the world. I was the only British Rail manager ever to be sent there, which resulted from my pointing out to Sir Bob Reid, BR's Chairman ([2]), that I had never had any management training or education after my initial period as a trainee. As well as learning a lot about finance, it showed me that I was the equal of most of those present, further adding to my confidence. Interestingly I didn't feel I learnt much about strategy, marketing or HR, suggesting that my career experiences to date and self-learning had already taught me more than I realised.

Mounting a Management Buyout Bid

In parallel with all this we were working on our own Management Buyout Bid (MBO) for the franchise. We engaged Ernst and Young Corporate Finance as financial advisers at an early stage, who were very helpful in guiding us through what was an entirely new world to us. We obviously could not afford to pay them but the Government had allowed BR to pay a very small retainer to MBO advisers, as they wanted to encourage management bids. E and Y were prepared to then work on a no-win, no-fee basis beyond this. We also needed to get our own legal advisers, separate to those working for MML Ltd, to help us navigate the intricacies of the Franchise Agreement we would need to enter into.

Our thinking was greatly stimulated by a number of private meetings we had with Brian Scott, MD of the Great Western and his then deputy, Richard George, who had both been fellow Profit Centre Directors at InterCity. Despite our very

---

[2] Confusingly Sir Robert Reid, BR's Chairman who initiated the whole sectorisation programme, was succeeded in 1990 as Chairman by Sir Bob Reid, who had previously been the UK Chairman of Shell.

different backgrounds and experience Brian and I had often found ourselves in close agreement on many issues that had been discussed at InterCity Directors Group, and I had great respect for both his and Richard's perspectives. Nick Brown, Geoff Evans and myself often found ourselves buzzing with new ideas on possible options on the drive home after these meetings. It was also very therapeutic to be able to share ideas and problems totally openly with colleagues facing similar challenges.

A key task was to line up financing for our bid company, to ensure we had access to adequate working capital and financial backing to support the two financial bonds we would be required to provide. One was a performance bond, to cover the Government for their costs in reletting the franchise if we failed to "perform" satisfactorily, the other was to cover the value of the season ticket cash we held on account, in case we "ran off" with it! We met with a variety of banks and finance houses, learning all the time about this esoteric new world.

We decided at an early stage that our bid would be strengthened and look more credible if we had a so-called industrial partner as a shareholder, alongside ourselves and a venture capital company. There being no companies in the UK who had any experience of running railways the next obvious choice was one of the recently privatised bus companies, who were already expressing strong interest in moving into passenger rail and applying the skills they had learnt from bus privatisation. We met with four out of the five of them, but either didn't particularly like what we saw or they didn't like us. Ironically, we got on best with National Express, who of course were to win our franchise in due course, but who were not interested in bidding alongside a management team.

We approached a number of other potential industrial partners, including British Midland Airways who were probably in a more similar business to us than the bus companies, and eventually lined up Atkins, a large transport and engineering consultancy, as our partner. But barely two weeks before our bid was due to be submitted I met with their Chief Executive who clearly had not been briefed on any of our discussions and who demanded even more attractive terms than those we had negotiated - "sweet equity" he called it! These terms had obviously been shared and agreed with our other backers and so no change to them at this late stage was possible and the deal was off. E and Y then earned their notional fee handsomely in lining up Electra Fleming as an additional financial backer for us at short notice, sitting alongside 3i Capital, our venture capital backer. But it was nevertheless a very fraught time for us all.

In the event our bid was significantly behind the winner, National Express Group (NEG), and a new chapter in my rail career commenced. I think the fate of our bid was sealed when we met with 3i for a final time a day or two before it was due to be submitted and we took them through our final business plan and financial projections. They demanded that we reduce our forecasts for revenue growth as being too ambitious compared with past trends, which meant we had in turn to significantly reduce our profit forecasts and the "premium" that we were able to pay to the franchising authority (MML being a profitable train company, franchise bids were judged by how much the bidder was willing to pay to OPRAF each year, rather than the amount of subsidy sought). NEG's bid was therefore significantly ahead of ours, so there was no real contest. It was ironic that in due course we grew passenger revenue considerably faster than even NEG's forecasts, so 3i missed out big time! In effect 3i fell back on a traditional BR/public sector approach to revenue forecasting.

It was also disappointing as we had given particular attention to marketing and initiatives to grow revenue, seeking to break away from the rather pedestrian traditional railway approach. We hired a marketing specialist, Brian Barrett, on a two-year retained basis to advise and support us and developed a close partnership with Steer Davies and Gleave Ltd, then a leading rail consultancy, to help us identify and analyse market opportunities. Brian was subsequently hired by Virgin, no slouches at marketing, to be the first Chief Executive of Virgin Trains for both the West Coast Main Line and Cross Country routes.

With hindsight I believe it was a very good thing that our Management bid failed. The way the franchise model worked meant that you were on a perpetual treadmill, receiving lower franchise support payments or having to pay an ever-higher premium to Government via the Franchising Authority each year, meaning that they were very risky businesses vulnerable to recessions, strikes or major disruption such as the Hatfield crash caused subsequently. The franchised train companies were always very thinly capitalised with limited reserves to be able to withstand these inevitable financial downturns, so needed the backing of financially much stronger owning groups to support them through the bad times.

It was certainly in British Rail and the Government's interest to encourage management teams to bid as it kept them engaged and helped focus them on the future. But I think this support was at best skin deep and somewhat cynically they didn't expect many MBOs to succeed. For us it was nevertheless a valuable experience. It wised us up to some of the realities of owning and running a private sector business - we would have had to put our homes on the line to raise the necessary finance - and it made us reach out to some of our future competitors rather than waiting for them to come to us.

So it was that we all became employees of National Express Group (NEG). One of the hardest phone calls that I have made was to their Chief Executive on the day we heard that they had won the franchise, and when we were still coming to terms with what felt like bitter news that our bid had failed. I had previously been given advice by Sir Nigel Rudd, Chairman of Williams Holdings, a very successful 1980s engineering conglomerate based in Derby which had grown by a series of hostile takeovers, on how best to respond to being taken over oneself. This was to hide any personal feelings, engage positively with the new owners and present oneself as someone who would be important to the future of the business. Encouraged by my colleagues, I swallowed my personal disappointment and congratulated NEG on their win and said that we would be pleased to help them implement their bid plans if they wanted us. They told me much later that they were very impressed, and relieved, by my call. A few days later I met their Chief Executive for the first time face-to-face, was offered a substantial pay rise reflecting the difference between public and private sector management salaries, and told it was up to me who was on my management team. And so began an exciting period for the first few years after privatisation, when we had substantial freedom and autonomy to manage our business, and provided we delivered, were trusted to get on with it.

Early days with National Express Group

National Express was at that time already a broadly-based passenger transport company, with a large bus operation in the West Midlands and an Airports Division, on top of the original National Express coach business. It had a growing number of operating subsidiaries and its approach was to choose and appoint the MD of each operating company, agree a business plan and then leave management to implement the plan. They saw themselves as a passenger transport holding company and had no corporate policies and procedures to follow other than the requirement to report on financial performance and cash flow in detail each month, and on progress against the business plan. It was a hugely motivating structure to work in and after BR it felt very liberating. They also believed that passenger transport businesses were essentially local and regional businesses, with a strong local identity being important. They didn't believe in rebranding their businesses to incorporate their corporate identity. As a result, we felt we were continuing to run our own business not someone else's.

Perhaps the best example of just how motivating the new environment was is the project to refurbish our Intercity 125 train sets. This was a £3.5 million commitment in NEG's franchise bid. I had written a six-page paper setting out the business case for the necessary investment and our intended approach to delivering it and had prepared a full presentation to our new Board, expecting a detailed cross examination. After just two minutes NEG's Chief Executive, Ray McEnhill, who now chaired our Board, simply said "approved, next item please"! What a contrast with my previous experience with BR Investment Committees, when in one case it had taken two years to get approval to renew a key bridge in Birmingham. It sent such a clear message of "we trust you, we will not second guess you, and it is entirely up to you to deliver".

Delivering the refurbishment was an exciting project, from which we learnt a great deal. We immediately invited tenders to produce designs and specifications for the whole project, and received two particularly attractive proposals, one from Saatchi and Saatchi Design, and the other from a sole practitioner, Ray Stenning of Best Impressions, who had made his name designing bus liveries. We liked both sets of proposals and agonised over which to accept. My solution, based on one of the mantras I had learnt at Harvard of "it's not either or, but both and....", was to negotiate and agree with both to split the job, giving Ray Stenning the external livery to design and Saatchi and Saatchi the interior work. They were both disappointed to start with but then worked well together.

Choosing the final external livery was itself an eye-opening lesson in the importance of good customer research. Ray Stenning presented us with two alternative liveries, one a maroon red, close to the old Midland Railway red and so in tune with the MML's heritage, the other based on teal green. As a management team the large majority of us preferred the red, but Ray Stenning and Andrew Harvey, our Marketing Director, both insisted we should choose the green. We argued at length about it and eventually I decided the only way we could resolve the issue was to ask some of our passengers. Andrew then commissioned a quick piece of research with some 400 passengers and several hundred staff. The results were both fascinating and sobering. The large majority of women preferred the green, as did a majority of men under forty. The only group who preferred the red livery were men over forty. I looked around our board table and observed we were overwhelming men, mostly over forty! It so clearly demonstrated that boards and management teams are rarely the right people to take such decisions. We therefore went with the green livery, even though some of us were instinctively uncomfortable with it. It was of course a great success with passengers. Since then I have always tried to ensure key decisions were based on proper passenger research, not on personal taste.

An interesting post script came several months later when we had a model of the new train livery on display at one of our regular meet-the-management "surgeries" with MPs on the route at the House of Commons. We were still a little shy about the striking new livery and therefore nervous when one Tory MP took a particularity close interest. It hadn't been long since British Airways had launched their infamous "tail fin" livery, with Margaret Thatcher covering up a similar model with her handkerchief in disgust. The MP proceeded to tell us that one of his hobbies was colour therapy, and that if we had asked him to suggest two colours for a new train livery it would have been green, for calm, and orange for a touch of excitement. Exactly as we had eventually chosen! Quiet sighs of relief all round followed!

Another interesting lesson was choosing new seat cushions. It had quickly become clear that train manufacturers had no expertise or particular interest in seat design or ergonomics, and just provided whatever was available. We arranged for several different seat cushions to be on show in our offices and invited staff and visitors to rate their relative comfort. This showed that comfort of the seat base was overwhelmingly the most important feature for passengers, and a thick, soft seat back as we then had was of limited value. So we focused on choosing the best seat base cushion but at the same time were able to reduce the thickness of the seat back cushion by at least a full inch. This effectively meant that the seat pitch - the legroom between the seat and the one in front - was comfortable for taller people by three to four inches, a really significant improvement. I have not noticed that learning applied to a number of more recent train refurbishments nor new trains ordered by the Department for Transport.

Getting talked about and winning new passengers

Growing our passenger numbers and revenue proved to be rather easier than we expected, and we outperformed both our own MBO and National Express's forecasts from day one. More significantly, we demonstrably outperformed what either the Leeds Model or BR and the Department for Transport's Passenger Demand Forecasting Handbook would have forecast. I believe that a lot of this was simply down to getting noticed and talked about as a new and different operator. National Express had committed to provide free tea and coffee to all passengers throughout the franchise term, as a way of positioning us as "hosting" and not just "carrying" our passengers to their destination. We were initially horrified at this as it cost us £1 million a year in lost buffet sales, but it was so warmly received by passengers that it certainly got us talked about positively, and without doubt paid for itself very quickly.

We were also quite innovative with some new types of fare. Most notable was "4-Sight", a flat fare of £49 return for four people travelling together, priced to match the then cost of a tank of petrol. This was valid for up to four people travelling together, they didn't have to be the same family, in theory they could have only just met. It was undoubtedly abstractive but again it got us widely talked about, and was backed by our only TV advertising campaign at the time. Likewise, "London Day Out" was another very popular new fare, priced at a flat £19 return from any of the East Midlands Cities and Sheffield. You could travel first class for £29 return, with breakfast thrown in at weekends, which was especially popular on Rugby International days at Twickenham when we also sold a lot of Champagne over breakfast!

For the "from-London" market my successor as MD, Nick Brown, arranged packaged days out to both Chatsworth House via Chesterfield with a special coach link, and to Alton Towers via Derby. All of this coupled with our striking train refurbishment and close attention to the details of service, such as ensuring that trains departed from the same platform and were consistently the same way round with first class always at the front arriving in London, ensured we got truly "noticed" and talked about in a very positive way. Our earlier worries that we would lose out from the ending of InterCity's high-profile TV advertising campaigns and our inability to afford advertising on anything like that scale on our own, proved completely unfounded. With hindsight I am not sure InterCity's advertising had been particularly helpful to Midland Main Line. It had usually featured InterCity's best new trains and top-level service, which I think was a bit of a downer for potential passengers on less glamorous routes with older trains where the perceived travelling experience was not quite up to the advertising. It proved to me that being seen to be striving to deliver what passengers really want and being "on their side", can be more powerful than glossy and award-winning advertising.

I encountered anecdotal proof of the power of being noticed positively over a taverna meal on holiday in Greece, when I was randomly sitting next to a couple from Nottingham. On hearing that I worked on the railways the wife started to give her poor opinion of rail travel in general only to be interrupted by her husband saying "but, my dear, we are talking about Midland Main Line here" and proceeded to extol our virtues as he saw them. He clearly saw our service as being different and better, and it turned out he was the owner of one of Nottingham's largest car dealerships. It certainly made my holiday!

Not everything we tried worked out. One of my ideas, I had thought a good one, was to serve strawberries and cream on leisure trains during Wimbledon Tennis fortnight to further emphasise our "hosting" philosophy. Sales were abysmal and I'm afraid restaurant and buffet car food wastage soared during the fortnight as a result. At least we were trying new things out. More successful was an initiative to give out free mince pies to first class passengers on selected trains during the run up to Christmas. Behind it all was the recognition that just providing a reasonably good train service is not enough to be truly successful. It is also necessary to continuously look for new ways to add value for passengers and to keep the service "fresh" by doing new and different things and so getting talked about by our passengers.

We were fortunate that MML ran closely parallel to the M1 motorway throughout, providing a huge pool of potential passengers to win over from their cars. This opportunity had been pointed out to us by Brian Barrett and the then small rail consultancy he worked for, Steer Davies and Gleave, but having grown up with BR's passenger demand forecasting methodology we probably didn't fully appreciate its significance at the time. BR's, and the Department for Transport's rail demand forecasting models are not dynamic and only extrapolate from existing rail demand to take account of the effect of service changes such as journey time reductions or frequency increases. If you start with a relatively low number of passengers, the models take this as their base and are not able to reflect any transformational changes. They do not model the dynamics of competition between modes, or the impact of intangible but still important variables such as awareness and reputation. In effect we successfully repositioned MML as an attractive and viable alternative to the M1, consistently beating what the models said.

Some new trains at last

The rail franchising model required the franchisee to commit to a fixed payment to or from the Franchising Authority which rose in real terms each year in the case of a profitable franchise paying a premium to Government. So success meant beating one's original forecasts, either by reducing costs or by attracting more passengers. Once the franchise was underway most costs were effectively fixed, with the large fixed payments for track access accounting for roundly half of all costs and most other costs fixed for the duration of the franchise term through train leasing or other contracts. The scope for cutting costs on MML was also very limited, as we had already been running the route as a management team for four years, two as MXC and two as MML immediately prior to privatisation, and under pressure throughout to reduce costs. In practice then most of MML's financial success came from revenue growth ahead of forecast.

The best indicator of this success was National Express's decision to take up their option to extend the franchise term from the initial seven to ten years by acquiring a new fleet of trains and doubling the frequency of service from Derby, Nottingham and Leicester to London. They had to be sufficiently confident that MML would be able to deliver and beat its forecasts over a ten-year period to be able to justify this decision to investors.

The go ahead to acquire an additional fleet of trains in turn gave the route a substantial further boost. Our train leasing company, Porterbrook, had already taken the speculative decision to order a large number of new Class 170 trains from Adtranz in Derby in anticipation of franchise demand, so we were able to take the first train sets off Adtranz's production line and quickly put them into service. The resulting doubling of service frequency also allowed us to reduce journey times from Derby, Nottingham and Leicester to London by spreading the intermediate station stops south of Leicester across more trains, stopping any one train less frequently. The extra capacity also enabled us to go ahead with one of the very few new stations to be built on an intercity route after privatisation, at East Midlands Parkway, close to Junction 24 on the M1. Not only did this provide a faster option for travel to London for the considerable number of passengers who lived south of Derby and Nottingham city centres, but it was also a cost-effective way of providing additional car parking capacity for the two cities whose city centre stations were constrained on space for parking.

Our announcement of the acquisition of the new Class 170 trains gave me a salutary lesson on the cynicism of the political world and the way the media worked. Perhaps naively, we believed that the purchase of new trains built and financed in Derby (Porterbrook Leasing was based in Derby) and then serving Derby would be good news politically. We therefore invited the local MP, Margaret Becket, to lead our press announcement. Her constituency included Adtranz's Derby works and she had campaigned passionately for new trains to be built in Derby prior to privatisation. By this time she had been appointed Secretary of State for Trade and Industry in the new Labour Government and her office asked us to move our press conference from Derby to London so she could more easily attend. But just one hour before our press conference was scheduled, we learned that the Government had referred National Express's acquisition of the Midland Main Line franchise to the Monopolies and Mergers Commission (MMC) for an inquiry, an overtly political move, and that the MP/Secretary of State would not after all be attending the press conference. The MMC referral of course then dominated the news agenda and our new train order was ignored in the national media. I can only conclude that the move was a deliberate political ploy to prevent National Express or the newly privatised MML getting any credit for their investment and support for Derby. I spent the rest of the day on the defensive, fronting media interviews about the MMC referral. I particularly remember the ITN reporter that evening sympathising with me about the "spiking" of our trains' announcement and apologising that he could only ask me questions about the MMC referral. Such is the power of the Government to set the national news agenda.

CHAPTER 5 Life in the private sector - National Express days

Looking back, most of my time with National Express feels like the least satisfying part of my career. There are few things that I can point to that I feel proud about, few achievements that I recall I contributed to. This may seem surprising to many for whom promotion to a plc Board might seem to be the pinnacle of a managerial career. My five and half years with the company certainly started very well as I've already described in the previous chapter. It was exciting and hugely empowering to join a company that trusted us and left us free to manage our business and get on with the job of providing the best rail service we could. And having spent my whole career until then with British Rail in the public sector it was exciting to be working in the private sector and moreover to feel that one was making a real success of it. But my time as Commercial Director on the main Board was increasingly frustrating and unsatisfying and in the end being made redundant was the best thing that could have happened to me.

I did three successive jobs at National Express, starting as MD of Midland Main Line immediately after the route was privatised. After less than a year I was then asked to step up to the newly created role of Trains Division Chief Executive, to oversee National Express's five passenger rail franchises, three of which they had only just won: ScotRail, North London Railways and Central Trains. Then after a further two years I moved on to the main Board into another newly created role of Commercial Director. Each role meant that I was increasingly well paid, but ironically my job satisfaction moved in inverse proportion. This was partly because each role moved me further away from the "sharp end" of running a rail business with regular contact with customers and staff, and partly because both National Express and the wider rail industry were changing substantially at the same time, the former not for the better.

When I joined, National Express was run very much as a transport holding company, with arm's length subsidiaries in, by then, four different sectors, trains, buses, coaches and airports. It had an extremely small head office, composed solely of finance, legal, corporate communications, a small business development team and three Executive Directors. It was deliberately not resourced to get involved with the running of the operating subsidiaries, hence the high degree of freedom enjoyed by their management teams. When I moved into the role of Trains Division Chief Executive I was keen to ensure that the five train company MDs and their teams enjoyed a similar degree of freedom to what I had experienced at Midland Main Line and therefore adopted a very hands-off approach to their management.

National Express's Trains Division

This approach inevitably meant a rather narrow role for me as Divisional CEO and a very small divisional team of just four people. In line with National Express's established approach, a first task was to undertake due diligence on the management teams of the franchises we were taking over, followed by some often painful conversations where we concluded that some individuals were not up to the job that was needed. Producing a Business Plan to deliver the commitments and subsidy profile that had won the franchise bidding should then have been a fairly straightforward process. But in at least two cases it was quickly apparent that after the first few years the bids could not be delivered financially because of over optimistic assumptions about the scope to cut costs made by a bidding team who had already moved on to different roles within National Express. In the short term the Trains Division was performing very well financially and had contributed to a significant rise in National Express's share price, so the business's reaction was largely to put its head in the sand and assume that it would be able to negotiate its way out of any large problem when the time came.

The overhang of potential longer-term losses on our two largest franchises encouraged us to redouble our efforts to be seen as diligent and responsible stewards of our franchises by fully delivering on all of our non-financial commitments and engaging constructively with the Franchising Authority. Initially this was the Office of Passenger Rail Franchising (OPRAF), and subsequently the newly established Strategic Rail Authority (SRA). This was at a time when several other Franchise owning groups were seen to be performing badly and the new Labour Government felt the need to hold franchisees' "feet to the fire", in the absence of any move to renationalise the industry. Perhaps naively we believed there was an opportunity to differentiate National Express from other Franchise owning groups and be regarded as a "good performer" that could be trusted to deliver and in future retain and win new franchises. In practice it turned out that there was no long-term reward for good performance given the way new franchise competitions were run, with little or no regard to the previous track record of bidders.

It quite quickly became apparent that this very lean structure meant there were no "reserves" of talent when someone senior in any one of the companies moved on for whatever reason. I was several times scrabbling to find a replacement MD or working with one to find a replacement Finance, Marketing or Operations Director. At times I was spending a quarter of my time on watching out for and securing potential management talent, in effect being my own head hunter. In most cases I was having to go outside of National Express to the wider rail sector to find the necessary people, a situation that was the same for all the other franchise owning companies. The lack of any real talent management and development process across the rail franchises - "growing your own people" rather than hiring in - has undoubtedly been a significant weakness in the franchise model.

Trying to engage with the SRA proved to be increasingly frustrating. Its first Chairman was Sir Alastair Morton, a towering figure who had driven through the financing and completion of the Channel Tunnel project and came to the SRA with big ambitions. He called on the franchises to think big and come up with much more ambitious proposals to invest in and develop new services. He recognised, for instance, that most London termini stations were operating at capacity and saw the answer as constructing cross London links so trains no longer needed to be turned round in London - several Crossrails in fact! We responded by developing a radical plan to extend services in the West Midlands, linking New Street and Moor Street stations by a new tunnel, and a plan for a London orbital service linking the North, West and East London lines. The latter was in due course implemented by Transport for London as part of their Overground network. In reality we were tilting at windmills, as National Express did not have either the financial firepower or infrastructure project management capability to implement such schemes, and the industry structure would have been a huge impediment. It did not reflect well on the SRA or its chairman that they did not recognise this.

Following my term as the first elected Chair of ATOC, the Association of Train Operating Companies, I continued to spend time representing the franchised passenger sector throughout my time with National Express. This included speaking for the sector at two Rail Summits called by John Prescott, the Deputy Prime Minister and Secretary of State for Transport and the Environment in the incoming Labour Government. These summits were pure window dressing, a chance for the new Government to look good holding the rail industry to account for what was seen as falling levels of train punctuality and rising cancellations. I found myself defending the Train Operating Companies against both the Government and Railtrack, who had convinced themselves that declining train performance was mainly the TOCs' fault not theirs. It was actually very stimulating and quite satisfying to out-debate Railtrack whose Chief Executive used very busy slides prepared for him by McKinsey's the Consulting Firm. Neither he nor they really understood many of the issues. But it was also frustrating that the Government was not really interested in some real problems or indeed what we were trying to do to solve them, they just wanted to be seen to be holding the industry to account.

I was elected Chair of ATOC for a second time just before the dreadful train crash at Hatfield on the East Coast Mainline which led to a meltdown of the whole rail network for many weeks afterwards as Railtrack imposed widespread precautionary speed restrictions as they checked each section of track and replaced many sections. On most lines journey times were doubled or even trebled as a result and train service frequencies dramatically reduced. This time the Government set up a weekly Crisis Management Committee chaired by the Prime Minister himself, where I again represented the TOCs. It was a fairly unimpressive forum, despite being well chaired by Tony Blair, who asked many probing questions. But Railtrack were floundering in their response to the crisis and desperately trying to rebuild their knowledge of their key asset, the track, having outsourced responsibility for it to multiple maintenance contractors. The safety regulator, which at that time was the Health and Safety Executive, was relatively passive and unhelpful as Railtrack struggled to perform the risk assessments it demanded before removing speed restrictions, nor were the Department for Transport helpful.

It was clear that Railtrack were inadvertently exporting safety risk to the roads, by actively discouraging passengers and freight from using rail so necessitating them switching to road. I remember witnessing a major accident on the A1 one weekend in which at least three people were killed and more injured, and observing at the next Monday's Crisis Management Committee that I hoped none of those involved would otherwise have travelled by train but for Railtrack's draconian speed restrictions. I well remember Tony Blair saying that was a good point and asking the meeting who was responsible for road safety. There was a lengthy silence only broken when the Permanent Secretary of the Department for Transport somewhat sheepishly said "I suppose I am, Prime Minister". A classic example of one standard for railway travel and a completely different one for road transport.

Searching for opportunities to grow

After 1997 all of the UK rail franchises had been let, meaning that the short-term opportunities to grow what was seen by investors as a successful and profitable new division of National Express were very limited. So to continue to expand its rail interests National Express became a shareholder in the London and Continental Railways consortium which won the contract to construct the Channel Tunnel Rail Link (CTRL) and run the UK part of the Eurostar service. This led to my joining the Board of Intercapital and Regional Railways Ltd (ICRRL), a joint venture with French and Belgian Railways set up to oversee Eurostar's operations in the UK, as the National Express shareholder Director. In due course this fortuitously led to my moving to Eurostar as CEO, of which more later in Chapter 6.

The negotiations with the Department for Transport for a management agreement for ICRRL to oversee Eurostar (UK) Ltd were my first exposure to high level contract negotiations with Government. With hindsight they were a triumph of optimism over realism, and an example of how Government can sucker one into a deal that subsequently proves a bad one. National Express, with negotiations led by its then Finance Director, was very keen to do a deal, and based on its early experience with rail franchises was naively over-optimistic on what it could achieve. The Government was determined to remove Eurostar (UK) Ltd from LCR control after the latter's need to go cap in hand to Government for more money to build the Channel Tunnel Rail Link, and cleverly tried to present Virgin Trains as a potential counter bidder and competitor to ICRRL. Virgin were another shareholder in the original LCR Consortium, whom no one involved wanted to win the management contract for Eurostar, so National Express and its French and Belgian railway partners were prepared to over bid to keep them out. The result was a contract with the Department for Transport that eventually cost National Express many £ millions in losses over its term.

Alongside Eurostar, National Express also looked for other privatisation opportunities abroad. One of these was in the State of Victoria in Australia. The Liberal (ie conservative) Government there had decided to franchise their Train and Tram operations in Melbourne and rural Victoria on similar lines to the UK. They set up a small team to run a competition, with advice provided by Roger Salmon who had successfully led the UK's franchising programme as first Director of the Office of Rail Franchising (OPRAF). Victoria had five franchises on offer, smaller than those in the UK but with a broadly similar franchise model. The one big difference was that franchisees also had responsibility to maintain their infrastructure as a vertically integrated operation, but this did not concern us as we already had direct experience of managing track and signalling infrastructure as part of BR's Profit Centre organisation. At the time we were also lobbying in the UK for some franchises, particularly in Scotland, to take over management of their infrastructure from Railtrack to create a similar "vertically integrated" operation and we thought that experience and a track record in Australia would help our case.

I spent much of 1999 commuting between Britain and Australia to support our bid team there and build our credentials with the State Government who were much keener than the UK Government to "vet" bidders and ensure they were capable and reputable. Part of this was the need to overcome any perception of us being seen as an arrogant "Pom" company, which required development of a good degree of cultural sensitivity. We developed a very good relationship with the Government's Franchising team, but because their job was to let franchises on the best terms, this probably also contributed to us being "sucked in" too much to the process and distorted our judgement in our subsequent bids.

The Victorian franchises appeared attractive and National Express was keen to build on its developing reputation for sound stewardship of its rail franchises in the UK so we were again guilty of over-optimistic bidding, both on our ability to reduce costs and grow revenues. In the subsequent words of National Express's CEO we all got "bid fever". This was further encouraged by the CEO saying that if we won he wanted us to have at least two franchises to justify the expense and time in overseeing businesses so far away. We therefore tabled a highly competitive hybrid bid for three franchises which we duly won.

Australia was a much more car orientated culture than we were used to, and fares were already quite cheap, so the scope to attract more passengers was more limited than we assumed. We misjudged the willingness of the Victorian Rail Unions to negotiate changes to working practices, after they had appeared quite reasonable in our initial discussions. But with a change in Government to a Labour administration very soon after the franchises started, they became much less accommodating. As in the UK the new Labour government declined to renationalise the operation but instead enforced the franchise contracts vigorously making it very difficult to negotiate any mitigations linked to other betterments. After the first year or two the result was another loss-making business, which National Express had subsequently to withdraw from. The whole experience underlined the potential pitfalls of trying to set up operations in a different country, without adequately understanding the different environment for doing business. Australia's shared language and historic ties with the UK too easily masked real differences in its industrial relations culture and customer expectations.

Onto NEG's Main Board as Commercial Director

At the same time as bidding in Australia I was invited by Phil White, the CEO, to join the main Board of National Express Group (NEG) as Commercial Director. National Express by that time had five divisions: coaches, buses, airports, trains and US buses, mainly consisting of a large and growing Yellow School Bus operation. It was a very interesting but diverse set of businesses, from which I learned a lot, but there was little synergy between them. Coaches were the original part of the group and were a consistently profitable but relatively small part of the Group. We did not actually own any of the vehicles or employ their drivers, these were contracted in on a per mile operated basis from a variety of other bus and coach operators. The division was therefore primarily a marketing, sales and route planning operation, with a very high return on capital. The resulting strong cash generation was used to finance the acquisition of other businesses, first of all West Midlands Travel which operated a large and very profitable network of buses in the West Midlands and formed the core of the bus division. Both National Express coaches and West Midlands Travel had been the subject of earlier management buy outs which had not prospered. The original team that built up NEG had done similar things in other sectors and were adept at making necessary changes in management and agreeing successful new business plans but then leaving the new management largely free to deliver them. In many ways the business model was similar to today's venture capital sector.

Airports were the third leg to join the group, with firstly East Midlands, then Bournemouth and finally a small ex US Air Force airbase in New Jersey, Stewart Airport. Airports were and still are strategically very attractive businesses to own in the UK. To rephrase Mark Twain, "put your money in airports, son, they don't build them anymore", because of shortage of suitable sites on a crowded island, restrictive planning rules and intense neighbours' opposition. East Midlands Airport also became highly profitable, but required high levels of capital investment to develop its potential. NEG originally paid some £27million to acquire it from its previous Local Authority owners, invested over £100 million in its facilities and eventually sold it to Manchester Airports Group for £274 million.

The Trains Division, which I had set up and run, initially consisted of five UK franchises, Midland Main Line, Gatwick Express, ScotRail, Central Trains and Silverlink (the renamed North London Railways). Soon after I joined the Board we bought out Prism Rail plc who operated four more UK franchises, c2c, West Anglia Great Northern, Wales and West and Cardiff Valley Lines. These businesses all had a very different business model, requiring relatively little capital and therefore potentially high return on capital, but had very volatile and usually low profit margins. Consequently, they were risky businesses.

The US Bus Division was the most stand-alone, and was led by the owner of one of the originally acquired Yellow School Bus operations. It was steadily growing through acquisition of the many smaller "mom and pop" Yellow Bus operations, as the owners sought to sell out and retire, as well as a number of City Transit Bus contract operators.

There was very little in common between these different divisions, other than that they all provided passenger travel services. Each had its own local or regional markets, sector specific labour forces, particular procurement needs and usually strong management teams in place. There was therefore very little scope for a Group level Commercial Director to add any value in terms of group wide marketing, sales or procurement. The main role would have been in business development, but the Finance Director who joined the Board soon after me saw that as his role and had had experience of acquisitions and deal making in previous jobs. I therefore struggled from day one to carve out a useful role for myself. I was also now at arm's length from the Trains Division as Phil White the CEO had at the same time created the new role of Chief Operating Officer. Ray O'Toole, who took up the COO role, then arranged for the Train Company MDs to report to him directly and he took a much more hands-on approach to them than had previously been the practice at NEG. Trying to create space between an ambitious Finance Director and a hands-on and controlling COO was not a comfortable task!

Inevitably, few of the business development opportunities that we looked at came to anything. We looked at buying rail operations in New Zealand, Portugal and Greece, and at getting involved in several light rail/tram projects. An interesting, potentially major, missed opportunity was an approach from a trio of US entrepreneurs who wanted our backing to launch a dial-up taxi service in the States using mobile phones and GPS tracking: remarkably similar to what is now Uber! My colleagues were not keen on getting involved with taxis so we never took it further. The one clear success was the acquisition of Prism Rail plc and their four UK franchises.

The slate of Non-Executive Directors (NEDs) on the Board was also changing at the same time. All four of the original NEDs who had been with the Group since it was first started, and were fully aligned with how it worked, stood down over this period to be replaced by a very different line up. Not only were the new NEDs unfamiliar with the business but at least two were more or less openly critical of management and appeared to believe they could do things better. None of them had had any experience of running public transport services. The atmosphere at Board meetings became unproductive and a "them and us" attitude between Executives and Non-Executives developed. As Executives we were wary of being too open with the NEDs for fear of the openness being used against us, and frustrated about their lack of understanding of the realities of the business. The NEDs in turn were no doubt frustrated at the lack of engagement. It did not feel like a recipe for good governance! It was certainly an object lesson in how not to select and induct Non-Executive Directors into an established business. They had been selected primarily on how their profiles would look to investors rather than their desire and ability to contribute constructively to the business and were then not adequately briefed on how the business worked. They became critics rather than critical friends.

Learnings from National Express

I have reflected much since on the question of what value National Express Group added to the rail industry. It was essentially a deal orientated business, good at buying and selling businesses and spotting and exploiting opportunities. At its best, it was also good at judging and selecting management and then giving them the space to run and develop their business as if it were their own. This worked well for businesses that were strong in their sector, such as coaches, or relatively self-contained, such as airports. It also worked well in the early days of rail franchising when the focus was on delivering the franchise commitments and empowering management teams that had been constrained in the public sector under British Rail.

The great strength of the franchising system is that once a franchise is let, it becomes a contractual commitment, which the franchisee is then totally focused on delivering. This plays to the strength of the private sector which is much less susceptible to short term political or other distractions and therefore ensures much greater stability of direction for the development of the franchise over its term. But it does require the outcomes expected from the franchise by the Franchising Authority to be correctly specified with the right incentives and financial structures in place to support them.

National Express was of necessity a very lean organisation at the centre, too thinly resourced to do much more than just deliver its contractual commitments in the franchise agreements. This was partly a deliberate consequence of its management philosophy and partly the result of the expectation of investors that the bottom line should show continuous growth, so adding central overhead costs was always difficult to justify. There was no central HR function at all and no management training or graduate scheme to develop future leaders. The "make or buy" decision for management was too often to buy-in rather than develop and promote one's own people, so it did little to grow the wider management capability of the industry.

The leanness of the organisation also meant there was virtually no "slack", so when a critical vacancy occurred or a new problem or opportunity emerged, too often managers were moved to cover it creating a new gap and problem behind them. Midland Main Line undoubtedly suffered subsequently from a lack of management continuity with regular changes of MDs. Likewise, there was very little spare resource to develop its bidding capability for new franchises or contracts, and after its initial successes NEG's record for successful franchise bids was overall surprisingly poor. Over time other owning groups developed sophisticated bidding teams, which of course didn't come cheap but met with higher success rates.

The pressure on overhead or head office costs constrained the ability to develop new systems and ways of working, for instance new IT systems or ways of engaging with customers. National Express did try to develop an internet ticket sales platform, which we branded QJump. We sold this to Trainline which had been launched by the Virgin Group. As a private company they were much more able to devote the substantial resources of risk capital necessary to build and market such a platform effectively.

Overall it was certainly difficult as a publicly listed company to reconcile the expectations of investors and shareholders with the particular challenges of rail franchises. The share price is an important measure of financial success and the market determines this, based amongst other factors, on current profitability and how fast it judges this is likely to grow in future. It particularly values a steady upwards trajectory in earnings year by year which is difficult to reconcile with the much more volatile earnings that franchises can produce (including periodic losses!). Whilst a franchise might produce reasonable earnings over its full term, this is rarely steady year by year. It is noteworthy that there are now only two publicly listed franchise owning groups, whereas there were at least seven such owning groups at the start of UK franchising. The pattern of earnings is much more amenable to non-listed owners such as foreign owned railways who can take a more relaxed view of fluctuations in earnings in any one year.

I was never very impressed by the investor community or by investment analysts. The latter took a very mechanistic approach to valuing a company and paid little attention to more qualitative factors such as management capability or the relative attractiveness of different markets. There was a significant degree of herd behaviour and a tendency for investors to overreact to either good news or bad news. The first couple of years of rail franchise results helped boost the Group's share price to record levels, with investors mainly seeing the upside and few asking how sustainable the results were. The price fell back during the dot com boom and at one point the company was valued at less than Lastminute.com which at that point had never made a profit.

An interesting feature of National Express's management culture was that it tended to closely reflect the behaviours and values of the people at the top. This was perhaps not surprising given it was a relatively young company with insufficient time for any particular style or way of working to become embedded or institutionalised. The culture and atmosphere within the Group began to change with the new COO and Finance Director, and changed again substantially for the worse when a new Chairman and CEO were appointed several years after I left. Older, longer established organisations with a more embedded culture are often more resilient to a change in leadership, but harder to change as a result. I definitely felt the company I left in 2001 was not the same company I joined in 1996. I regret not having had a more positive impact. It was another object lesson in one of the more sobering aspects of being a leader: that an organisation over time often comes to reflect the strengths, weaknesses and values of its leader. A scary thought if you are a leader aware of your own weaknesses!

It became clear to the Board that there was not a substantive role for a Commercial Director so I was made redundant at the end of 2001. I was never a deal maker in the mould that National Express had developed and, on reflection, I was always much more suited to running a discrete business than buying and selling them or bidding for contracts. I would probably have resigned after another year or two's frustration in the role, so I was actually done a favour by being made redundant. And it freed me up to look for my next challenge which very soon led to my move to lead Eurostar.

PART 2

CHAPTER 6   Transforming Eurostar

I joined Eurostar as CEO in August 2002. I was the fifth person to lead Eurostar in the UK in its then still short eight-year life, and the first to lead both the UK company, Eurostar UK Ltd (EUKL), and Eurostar Group Ltd (EGL). The latter was the marketing and common services company jointly owned by all three Eurostar partner railways. I took over from two people, the MD of EUKL and the Chief Executive of EGL, and from the start set out to lead Eurostar as if it were a single integrated operation. To understand how this was more easily said than done I need to explain briefly how Eurostar was then organised, together with a little history.

Eurostar at that time is best described as an unincorporated partnership between three railways, EUKL in the UK, French National Railways (SNCF) in France and Belgian National Railways (SNCB) in Belgium. EUKL was originally set up by British Rail in the dying days before privatisation as European Passenger Services Ltd, to be the UK partner in the Eurostar project. Its ownership had been transferred to London and Continental Railways Ltd (LCR), the consortium which had won the contract to finance and build the Channel Tunnel Rail Link (CTRL) linking London to the tunnel to carry Eurostar. EUKL was a fully-fledged train operating company, owning a number of Eurostar's train sets, managing its own stations and train maintenance depot and employing train crew and other staff. But its operational responsibility for Eurostar only extended to the French "border", at the midpoint of the Channel Tunnel. LCR had eight shareholders, including my previous company, National Express, SNCF and Bechtel a large US consultancy who were to be the Project Managers for building the new railway. LCR had been given ownership of EUKL because it was originally expected to be cash positive and could therefore help it finance construction of the CTRL.

Each railway partner was responsible for operations in its own country, with a notional "handover" of responsibility at the midpoint of the Channel Tunnel and at the French-Belgian border. Each railway owned a number of Eurostar train sets and was responsible for their maintenance, at three different maintenance depots. Each contributed a number of train crew to the operation and each managed the stations in its own territory. The French and Belgian Eurostar staff were still employees of their parent railway, not of Eurostar. There was a revenue sharing protocol which governed how passenger revenues were shared between the partners, and cost sharing arrangements for train crew and maintenance. EGL's primary role was to lead marketing of the service and also to manage a small number of key contracts, the most important being that for on-train catering. Both EUKL and EGL were based in a shared office in London, at Waterloo Station, overlooking the Eurostar platforms there.

To add spice to this already complex structure a company called Intercapital and Regional Railways Ltd (ICRRL) had a contract to oversee management of EUKL, with a highly geared incentive arrangement to try to ensure it secured EUKL's financial turnaround. This rather bizarre contract had been put in place by the Department for Transport after LCR had had to go cap in hand to the then new Labour Government to seek additional funding to be able to complete construction of CTRL. In a somewhat petulant reaction the Government had deemed LCR unfit to manage EUKL, hence the need for a management contract bearing only a passing resemblance to a franchise. ICRRL had National Express, SNCF, SNCB and British Airways as its shareholders. I had been the National Express shareholder director on the Board of ICRRL, so was already partly familiar with Eurostar before I joined as CEO, and had led several of the initial cost cutting initiatives. One of ICRRL's initiatives was to set up EGL in order to provide a proper focus for the marketing of Eurostar.

British Airways was a shareholder in ICRRL because it had been thought that it might be possible to extend some Eurostar services to Heathrow, so allowing BA to cease flying between Heathrow and Paris. This was during Robert Ayling's tenure as BA Chief Executive, when a number of unconventional ideas were tried out. One such initiative was the London Eye, as part of London's Millennium celebrations, and the same team who ran that project worked on the Heathrow proposal. An early task after ICCRL won the management contract for Eurostar was a detailed feasibility study into a Heathrow extension which showed that there was no business case. British Airways thereafter became a sleeping shareholder.

Ironically, I had been the de facto Chair of EGL as David Azema, its first Chief Executive, was also officially Chairman, or Président et Directeur Général as is common on French Boards, but found it impractical to both report to the Board and chair it. It was also how I first got to know Guillaume Pepy, who was the SNCF representative on the ICCRL Board. It was Guillaume who picked up the phone to me after I was made redundant from National Express and in effect offered me the role of CEO, replacing David Azema who had resigned to go to a senior position at Vinci. My appointment was also of course approved by SNCB, whose Directors I also had got to know at ICRRL, and LCR, then led by Rob Holden. Rob and LCR were slightly more hesitant about my suitability as they apparently saw me principally as a cost cutter not a revenue builder. I took this as rather a compliment as I saw myself as being much better at winning new passengers than cutting costs!

All of the various parties recognised that this structure was pretty dysfunctional and another one of ICRRL's initiatives was to try to set Eurostar up as a proper joint venture between the three railways, ensuring unified management control of the whole operation. Project Jupiter to achieve this had been started by David Azema in 2001 and the idea was that I would lead EUKL and EGL in the interim and finalise the Project, then becoming the first CEO of the new joint venture company. I was told the project would be 75% complete when I joined, but in the event it proved to be far from completion and was abandoned early in 2004 when the UK Government in effect vetoed a number of key aspects.

For all my time as CEO I had to work with this dysfunctional structure. I had full managerial control over EUKL and EGL, but in both France and Belgium I had no such authority or control and had to operate by persuasion and influence only. It was immensely helpful that Guillaume Pepy who became de facto Chairman was also then deputy CEO of SNCF, so that most decisions we took at the Board affecting operations in France were followed through. Jacques Damas, my Deputy as Chief Operating Officer, was on secondment from SNCF and widely known and respected there, so was also able to get what we needed in France. The combination of a Brit and a Frenchman as number one and two in the organisation was a powerful one and important to our success. Whilst we had two SNCB Directors on the Board their influence within SNCB was less strong, so it was a constant battle to affect how things were done in Belgium.

Whilst I refer to the "Board" it was in fact always two Boards, with EUKL and EGL Board meetings held jointly, even though several non-Executives were technically only a member of one of them. Guillaume Pepy was Chairman of these meetings, even though Rob Holden was actually Chairman of EUKL as its sole shareholder. ICRRL had their own Board meeting ahead of each of these meetings, also attended by me, to determine their position on EUKL issues. On paper, of course, I was also accountable to this Board as it held the management contract to oversee EUKL. It required a great deal of sensitivity and patience to make this all work, and it is a great credit to all parties that there was almost always a strong sense of collaboration to do this. In practice LCR too continued to take a close interest in both EUKL and Eurostar's overall performance since they had to fund EUKL's continuing losses out of the funding they had raised to build the Channel Tunnel Rail Link. I therefore did periodic presentations to the LCR Board as well, reporting on progress. So there were four Boards with an interest in and influence over Eurostar's performance in the UK and to whom I was accountable!

When I arrived at Eurostar, EUKL alone was losing roundly £80 million a year, on passenger revenues of £190 million and there was understandably considerable concern about its financial performance. There were no profit and loss reports for either the French or Belgian parts of the business and it was my assumption that they too were losing money. I never saw any management accounts for either country's share of Eurostar, if indeed they existed at all, and there were of course no statutory accounts as there were no separate corporate entities in either country. The losses were primarily because passenger numbers were very substantially lower than the original traffic forecasts on which the Channel Tunnel and Eurostar projects were based. To make matters worse passenger volumes had actually been falling slightly for the previous few months before I joined, and media coverage of the service and its general reputation was steadily turning negative after an optimistic start at the service's launch. Turning this situation around was going to be a big challenge. The lack of cost information in France and Belgium meant that our prime focus was of necessity on growing revenue to achieve this. Chapter 7 describes how we set about growing revenue and passenger numbers.

Tackling Eurostar's management culture

From the start I set out to run Eurostar as if it was a single organisation. I saw it as part of my job to hide the complexity from our customers and concentrate on growing the business as a whole. Fixing the management culture proved to the first hurdle to overcome. Because I was taking over and combining two previous leadership roles, MD of EUKL and CEO of EGL, I found I had five direct reports on commercial issues alone: two Marketing Directors, a UK Sales Director and two Heads of Communication. I had already decided to appoint a new Commercial Director to lead all revenue generating activity, which inevitably dismayed all the five incumbents who were in any case largely working in their own silos with very little collaboration between them. They all chose to leave over the next few months.

What was much worse was the lack of collaboration or engagement between EUKL and not just EGL but also SNCF and SNCB as the two partner railways. A trivial but telling example was EUKL reporting out-bound train punctuality at the handover to SNCF at the midpoint of the tunnel. It was not as if any passengers ever finished their journeys there! For whatever reason they had not liaised with SNCF and SNCB to present punctuality at final destination, presumably seeing their responsibility ending at the border. EUKL had also initiated two disputes with SNCF over revenue shares which hardly endeared it to SNCF colleagues, or did anything to grow the size of the "cake" to be shared. I quickly insisted on the disputes being settled or withdrawn.

My efforts to get everyone to focus on Eurostar as whole, not just their national share, created quite a strong reaction from key EUKL directors. So much so that I received a phone call from one of the EUKL non-Executive Board Members early in 2003 asking to see me. She explained that I needed to be aware that five of the EUKL executive directors had approached the EUKL Chairman to complain about my approach as "being too close to the French"! This was a stark illustration that the UK side of Eurostar simply didn't recognise the reality of the business. Over 75% of a passenger journey between London and Paris was on French territory and therefore the responsibility of SNCF. EUKL itself accounted for less than half of Eurostar's business, whatever measure was chosen. Only by the three railways working collaboratively together could Eurostar ever truly succeed. I never found out formally who the five were as they never had the courtesy to speak to me directly about their complaint. Four of them chose to leave over the next few months.

There was also a wider malaise in the management culture partly driven by the many changes in leadership and direction in Eurostar's short life. There was no formal decision-making structure at a management board level and a consequent lack of many of the normal governance processes and scant respect for lines of authority. For example, I found that the legal team was suing a small airline called Buzz for breach of trademark by using Eurostar colours in its livery. The suit had been continued even after Buzz had been taken over by Ryanair, a much larger and more aggressive airline. I could find no evidence of the legal action ever having been approved or even reported to any Board, and the executive concerned was dumbfounded when I told her to drop the case, as if she felt I didn't have the authority to do that!

An even more extreme case of lack of respect for authority, or indeed for customers, occurred after I received an email from an old British Rail acquaintance who ran a tour operator called Great Rail Journeys, asking to meet me. When asked for a brief, the then Head of Leisure Sales' response was to tell me not to bother myself with them as they were too small a customer! Unsurprisingly this set my antennae twitching and when I met with Howard Trinder,

Great Rail Journeys' MD, he had a number of complaints about our service but also a number of helpful suggestions and he clearly wanted to grow his business with us which had a lot of potential. Having been thus wrong footed the sales team picked up all of my feedback and over time Great Rail Journeys grew into one of our largest customers. It is now a very large company with regular advertising in national newspapers and television.

Another example was a plan to cut Eurostar's "lead-in" fare - the lowest permanently available return fare - from £69 to £59 return, and to switch extensively to single-leg pricing, so that each leg of a return journey could be priced differently depending on the demand on each train used. I learnt about the plan only weeks before it was planned to start. There appeared to have been no prior discussion with me or any other member of the management team, nor with the Board. This radical plan was the brainchild of the UK Sales Director, and when he had taken me through it in detail, describing the market and competitive background, I saw that it made good sense. But to his considerable disquiet I insisted that we presented it to the Board for approval, as it clearly affected all partners through the revenue share mechanism and was an important strategic decision. The Board approved it, fortunately, as by the date of the Board all of the new pricing had been loaded into the ticketing system. Had we not obtained proper Board approval I suspect we would have encountered pushback subsequently from Eurostar's Continental partners who would have taken umbrage over the UK taking an unilateral initiative without consultation.

EGL too had managed to embark on one or two spectacularly ill-conceived projects. The worst example was the launch of a customer loyalty card to try to match airlines. To differentiate this from the usual plastic cards someone had the "bright" idea of making this from brushed metal. Within hours of its launch, and initial distribution to frequent passengers, reports started coming in of the card setting off airport security scanners, and of several passengers having cut their fingers on its relatively sharp edges. It was quickly withdrawn and the cards destroyed but it did little to instill regular passengers' confidence in us. The process of critical vetting and risk analysis of project proposals had clearly been inadequate.

Another equally ill-conceived project was a plan to compete with low cost airlines by offering cheap fares on a regular service to Disneyland Paris, seeking to mirror the likes of Ryanair offering cheap fares to low cost, but out of the way airports. The project would have actually increased our costs, as the trains would still have had to run on to Paris for maintenance. And it would merely have abstracted revenue from the main service direct to Paris, as well as worsening that service by switching frequencies from there to Disneyland. The plan had completely misunderstood how the low-cost airline model worked.

There was also a lack of alignment amongst the different directors and heads of department about what sort of business Eurostar really was and what its strategy was. The IT Director for instance clearly saw Eurostar primarily as a marketing and distribution business, with a passenger carrying business on the side, and was planning to spend several millions on a new IT distribution and ticketing system that would serve all UK train operators not just Eurostar. This was despite there being no approved business case and no certainty of either technical success or likely demand from other companies. Equally mad, Eurostar had two competing websites, one run by EUKL and one by EGL.

At the time Eurostar had no Strategy Director, or anyone close to one, so I personally wrote a strategy document and led a number of seminars with senior and middle managers to take people through the key parts of it. My purpose was to build alignment with a single corporate strategy and try to ensure everyone was working in the same direction.

Looking back now, perhaps I should not have been surprised about the lack of normal management controls and processes. When British Rail set up what was then European Passenger Services it appointed a number of highly capable directors to set up and lead the business. Only one of the original team was still around, Malcolm Southgate, who was now a non-executive and deputy chairman of the EUKL Board. The others had all left at the same time as the first MD Richard Edgeley, who had been dismissed by LCR as soon as they had taken over ownership of EUKL. Adam Mills the CEO of LCR had then doubled up as MD of EUKL for a number of months whilst they searched for a new MD. This was just at the time LCR were struggling with raising finance and finalising designs for the Channel Tunnel Rail Link, so presumably he could give only passing attention to leading EUKL. To add further confusion Virgin had been a member of the original LCR Consortium and had assumed they would be playing a major role helping run EUKL, using their experience of running the UK's West Coast and Cross Country franchises. They parachuted several senior people into EUKL for a time and even tried to rebrand the trains in Virgin livery, even though the majority of them were owned by the French and Belgians who had no time for Virgin. Eurostar had therefore had a very chequered and disrupted first few years of life.

It would barely be an exaggeration, therefore, to describe Eurostar's management culture and decision making structure as anarchic and highly dysfunctional when I arrived. Imposing some structure and discipline on the organisation and working up a coherent strategy to develop the business clearly took some time as a result. I was enormously helped in this task by my deputy and COO of EGL, Jacques Damas. Jacques was a senior and hugely experienced SNCF manager, who knew more about high speed TGV operations than almost anyone else and who exuded quiet competence and trust. As we progressively welded EUKL and EGL into a single team Jacques truly became COO of the entire Eurostar operation and a deputy that I was able to totally rely on. He also of course had in-depth knowledge of SNCF and most of its key managers, so was able to successfully oversee everything on the French side by sheer force of personality, despite having no formal authority there either.

Nick Mercer, the Commercial Director, who I recruited in early 2003, also played a key role bringing together responsibility for sales, marketing and communications into a single team, and quickly developing a coherent strategy to grow the business. Nick brought in or brought on a number of highly talented young managers, many of whom themselves played key roles in Eurostar's subsequent transformation. He also set up small sales and marketing teams in both Paris and Brussels to develop the French and Belgian originating markets, supporting the larger team in London. Nick had an impressive background in travel and consumer marketing, which made him ideally placed to bring coherence and stability to Eurostar's whole marketing effort. Quietly spoken, he was strategically brilliant and empowered his team to achieve some outstanding results in a complex market situation.

I well recall an old colleague from both British Rail and National Express days who succeeded me as the National Express Shareholder Director on the board of ICCRL, Richard Goldson, astutely observing several years into my time at Eurostar that much of my previous career had prepared me uniquely for the challenge at Eurostar. The experiences of working in BR's Matrix of sub-sector management, when negotiation and persuasion were the main tools to get things done, growing diplomatic skills and herding cats as Chair of the Association of Train Operating Companies and being part of the turnaround team at

InterCity, were all invaluable. I had to draw on them all in meeting the challenges at Eurostar.

It is also important to say that there were several aspects of Eurostar that made the job of leading the turnaround rather easier than being a Profit Centre Director within the BR Organising for Quality structure or a Train Company MD post privatisation: I had much more freedom to do what was necessary and right for the business. In the UK Eurostar was technically an open access operation and the ICCRL Management Agreement was essentially a set of financial commitments with none of the contractually committed outputs such as minimum service levels that the Passenger Franchise Agreements included. I could operate at arms-length from the Department for Transport, with LCR, not me, answerable to them, and ICRRL also then technically answerable to LCR for EUKL's performance, putting me at an even longer arms-length.

Nor was Eurostar regulated in the same way that UK passenger Train Companies were. In particular there was no fares regulation, either in the UK or in France or Belgium, so we were free to design our own fares structure and set their level as we judged appropriate. It has always struck me as highly ironic that regulated fares in the UK increase routinely every year, usually by inflation or more, whilst we only changed our unregulated fares three times in my eight and a half years as CEO, with one of these changes actually a reduction not an increase! The key benefit for us was that we could set our fares dependent on what the market could bear and to optimise our passenger numbers.

Surprisingly Eurostar's tri-nation ownership could also have advantages. On several occasions I was able to resist and nip in the bud an unhelpful "request" from one country by claiming that the other two nations would not like it or agree to it. Other than at the Eurostar Board, there was no forum where all three national parties came together, so provided we kept the Board on side we could often hold the line with any unreasonable request from one Government. The tri-national operation was also very useful when it came to mitigating the impact of industrial action in one country. This was a fairly regular event in France in particular, and we were usually able to minimise the impact of rail strikes there by rostering more British and Belgium train crews and using Eurostar Driver Managers, and likewise for rarer strike action by British or Belgian staff.

Finally, it was important that we had generally very supportive shareholders in SNCF, SNCB and LCR. They generally had a much more strategic and long-term perspective than more conventional shareholders and recognised that turning Eurostar round would take some years.

SNCF in particular were hugely supportive. They understood the challenges and opportunities of high speed rail services, took the long view rather than always pressing for short term results and were always helpful in seconding the small number of highly able managers such as Jacques Damas that strengthened Eurostar's management team. Much of this was down to the leadership of Eurostar's Chairman, Guillaume Pepy, who in due course became SNCF's President. LCR, led by Rob Holden, were also very supportive. They too were able to take the long view as they were contracted and, importantly, financed over a number of years to build the Channel Tunnel Rail Link. They were not subject to the often short-termist shareholder pressures that a listed company would have. Both SNCF and LCR were in effect patient investors who understood our business and could see the benefits of taking the long view.

The secondment of an albeit small number of managers from SNCF made a valuable contribution to changing Eurostar's management culture and making it much more international in outlook. We quite quickly got a reputation amongst the SNCF management cadre as being a good place to spend some time as part of career progression and so were able to attract some very talented managers. SNCF, like many French organisations, had a very hierarchical culture and younger managers in particular found it hugely refreshing to spend time with Eurostar and the much more open culture we developed. There were several occasions when a younger SNCF manager expressed amazement and delight that they were actually able to chat with me as CEO!

Exploiting the benefits of the Channel Tunnel Rail Link

Strategically the biggest opportunity to turnaround Eurostar's performance was always going to be the opening of services on the new Channel Tunnel Rail Link (CTRL). This was being constructed in two phases, Phase 1 from the tunnel to a new connection with the classic railway at Fawkham Junction in north Kent, and Phase 2 from there under the Thames and East London to Eurostar's new home at St Pancras International. This would allow two bites of the cherry, with each Phase giving a saving in journey time to Paris and Brussels of twenty minutes, as well as the chance to significantly improve punctuality since our trains would no longer have to share track with slower commuter and freight services. So an early priority was to smoothly launch services on each phase with as much fanfare as possible to start to rebuild the service's reputation with customers.

Phase 1 was due to open in September 2003, so much of my first year was spent working closely with Jacques and Nick and their teams preparing for the launch both operationally and commercially. Eurostar had developed a somewhat defeatist attitude to projects by this time, partly a result I suppose of its failure to realise its initial promise and also the lack of project management disciplines. It was increasingly accepted as "normal" that projects were late, over budget or failing to deliver the promised outcomes. Making a success of the launch of Phase 1 was therefore essential to changing this negative mind set, and completing the transformation of Eurostar's management culture.

I remember giving a briefing to staff soon after we successfully launched services on Phase 1 and amongst other things saying that I felt we had exorcised the ghosts of Eurostar's past. I was only a little surprised that everyone in the room understood exactly what I was trying to say. Probably the most prominent "ghost" had been the failure of the very first Eurostar train, which had broken down on launch day at Waterloo International station.

The move onto Phase 1 was very much simpler than it would be for Phase 2 and it was more easily encompassed within peoples' day jobs, so there was no need to set up a separate project management structure. We were simply moving on to a new section of railway, identical to the high speed lines in France and Belgium that crews were already well used to. We decided to go for the highest profile launch we could with a huge marquee set up adjacent to the new line near to Leeds Castle in Kent and two days of media and customer presentations and receptions. The original plan was to have the Prime Minister, Tony Blair, lead the launch in Kent but security concerns intervened to prevent this. We were lucky that at the very last minute he came to Waterloo International and, off the cuff, gave a very positive and up-beat speech to mark the event. Our whole objective was to get as much media coverage as possible, both in the UK and abroad, as a way of relaunching Eurostar services and trying to put the past behind us. In this we were encouragingly successful with much positive coverage. We were so successful in fact that we inadvertently upset LCR who were rather put out that all the coverage was of Eurostar with little mention of their successful completion of the first major new piece of railway in Britain for many decades.

This lack of balance would need to be corrected when Phase 2 was launched.

Sales and passenger numbers had already started to slowly grow again in the spring of 2003, but the switch of services onto Phase 1 of the CTRL in September gave a big further boost and numbers grew by 15% in the following twelve months. We were moving in the right direction at last. The buzz created by the opening of the new line was further helped by the setting of a new UK speed record with a train running at 208mph (334.7 kilometres per hour) on a test run on July 30th 2003.

The opening of Phase 1 ironically also precipitated the collapse of Project Jupiter to create a single, unified joint venture between the partner railways. The opening events had created the opportunity for our Chairman, Guillaume Pepy, to meet with the Permanent Secretary of the Department for Transport (DfT) and it became clear that the DfT had a very different view of the progress of the project. It emerged that in my inexperience of dealing with Government I had been dealing with the Department at far too junior a level. I had been given the impression that there were only four or so final issues to be resolved, such as the procedure for appointing the Chairman of the new company. Shortly after Guillaume's and my meeting with the Permanent Secretary I received a letter from a Director level civil servant who I had barely met up until that point, which listed 38 issues of principle yet to be resolved in their view! I was afraid that this would trigger a crisis in relations between the various Eurostar partners, in particular that National Express would withdraw their cooperation within ICRRL, since a key part of their contract with the DfT for management of EUKL was based on Project Jupiter proceeding. Without it they were faced with significant financial losses up to the capped maximum in their contract. This would have made the already complex task of managing EUKL and EGL much harder still.

In the event I need not have worried and at the subsequent meetings of the ICRRL and Eurostar Boards all the parties took a very responsible line. It was agreed to cancel Project Jupiter and continue to manage Eurostar within the existing cumbersome structure. We called this informal arrangement "Jupiter without Jupiter" and I set out a number of key principles in a memorandum to the Boards. I therefore continued to lead the business with this less than ideal structure for the next six and a half years! The upside was that I could now focus entirely on driving the business forward and not have to spend time on Project Jupiter as well.

Improving Eurostar passengers' travel experience

As already noted the key to transforming Eurostar's performance was the need to substantially grow revenue and passenger numbers. This is a story of its own which is told in Chapter 7. But improving the service experienced by passengers was equally important since Eurostar's punctuality and general reputation had started to slip, with passenger numbers falling. Our punctuality was actually on a par with the airlines we competed with, who bizarrely reported their punctuality on departure not arrival, but of course passengers expected a railway to be much more punctual. After all, a railway has its own dedicated "way" so why shouldn't it always arrive on time?

Of course, we didn't actually have our own "way" as prior to CTRL's opening we shared track in the UK with a number of intensive commuter services, and in the tunnel with Eurotunnel's own much more frequent car and lorry shuttles. And on the continent we shared the high speed line to Paris with several other high speed services which together ran considerably more trains than Eurostar. Any hold up to our trains on the classic commuter lines between Waterloo and the tunnel caused Eurostar trains to lose significant amounts of time, because on the southern region's third rail direct current system our trains were able to draw much less power and so accelerated only very slowly after any stop. Fixing this was always going to wait for the opening of the new high speed line, particularly its second phase when Eurostar would be running on purpose-built high speed lines throughout.

But Eurostar's trains were also being regularly held up before entering the tunnel. Eurotunnel's processes for loading and despatching their car and lorry shuttles, which were the most frequent users of the tunnel, required them to time the loading in close synchrony with other trains about to enter the tunnel. Whenever one of our trains was late on its tunnel approach it risked being held until the next shuttle had been despatched, which of course meant it followed the slower shuttle throughout its transit through the tunnel and meaning further delay. Working with Eurotunnel Jacques Damas arranged a pre-advice system, linking the high speed lines signalling system into Eurotunnel's control room. When one of our trains was running out of course Eurotunnel could adjust the loading of their shuttles and our train could enter the tunnel ahead of the shuttle and enjoy a clear run through. When this was implemented on the UK side after the opening of Phase 1 of CTRL as well as on the French side there was a marked improvement in punctuality.

What was equally important to our passengers, however, was how smooth and quick the check-in at departure stations was. Passengers needed to allow enough time for this in planning their journey, and any delays or significant queues can cause irritation and anxiety undermining their overall travel experience. Eurostar is different to all other train operations in having both security screening and passport controls before passenger boarding, as well as a ticket check of course. The security screening is similar to airport systems, and because all journeys were international the whole check-in process was very similar to airports.

Passport control is undertaken by both the UK Border Force and Police Aux Frontiers in France, and is because the UK has never been a member of the Schengen free movement area. The security screening is actually intended primarily to protect the channel tunnel from bombs - it is hard to see how or why you would hijack a train - but the processes are mandated by the relevant national authorities and largely copied from airports. Periodic changes in airline security requirements were usually applied to Eurostar too, with little regard to their relevance to Eurostar or their impact on its operations. The very confined areas available for check-in at central city stations as compared to the much more spacious departure buildings at airports has always been a problem for Eurostar, rarely recognised by the authorities.

To improve matters, we invested in additional new, higher capacity baggage screening machines, increased their staffing levels and worked on improving relations with the border authorities so that their staffing levels were adjusted to better match our booked passenger throughputs. It was often a case of two steps forward and one step backwards, however, as the authorities periodically changed their requirements to match some new policy or perceived threat which almost always slowed the check-in process until we were able to make adjustments to compensate. Airport security processes had also of course got more onerous and time consuming over the same period, but it was always our aim to provide a better experience than flying not just a comparable one.

Likewise, the on-train experience was important too. My predecessor at EGL had already hired a celebrated French designer, Philippe Starck, to design new train interiors, as well as new uniforms and business lounges, in preparation for a full train refurbishment and a design "makeover" for Eurostar as a whole. Starck proved to be a very particular designer, who seemed to largely work on his own and who received feedback and comments very badly. He took it very badly for instance when we refused to approve new light-cream coloured carpets for first class coaches, since they would have been impossible to keep clean. He chose to withdraw from the project rather than compromising on his very individualistic designs. He had however overseen a stylish redesign of the business lounges and chosen a silvery grey colour scheme for train interiors as a colour that would never go out of fashion. After some difficulty finalising his designs we carried out a train interior refurbishment which certainly improved passenger perceptions and experience. An interesting detail is that as part of the refurbishment we actually removed a small number of seats to provide more luggage space, since in practice busy trains run out of luggage space before running out of seats.

The final ingredient in the passenger experience was on-train service, particularly the catering service. Here much of the credit for the improvements made must go to Eurostar's contractor, Momentum Services Ltd, who were a joint venture between an Italian catering group, Cremonini, and Compass Group plc. Momentum not only provided the on-board food and drink but also the on-board staff other than our Train Managers. Their Chairman came to see me soon after I arrived at Eurostar to introduce his company and develop a relationship. I had been very surprised to learn that their on-train staff, who had the closest contact with our passengers, were not directly employed by us. I told him that no airline would outsource the provision of such a key group of customer-facing staff and I didn't see that Eurostar should either. But accepting that we had a contract I said he had the three years left in the contract to prove me wrong.

And so he did! Momentum continued to improve their service, and for many passengers they were "Eurostar", as they wore our uniforms and shared our service values. It was a very straightforward negotiation to renew their contract. This had a very innovative structure with a small annual management fee potentially supplemented by bonuses linked to two service indicators, one tied to the level of complaints and one driven by regular customer satisfaction surveys. There was also a financial incentive based on an annually agreed budget, with Momentum keeping 100% of any betterments in the budget year and 50% of these savings in the following year. Thereafter all savings accrued to Eurostar. It became a true partnership, with Momentum's fortunes closely tied to Eurostar's and supported by owners who ensured the management they appointed were truly collaborative.

Tackling Eurostar's cost base

It may come as a surprise to many that the large majority of Eurostar's financial turnaround until it finally became a properly structured Joint Venture company was achieved by growing revenues rather than driving down costs. At the time we had no real control over costs in France and Belgium and the largest item of cost, some 40% of the total, came from the Rail Useage Contract with Eurotunnel. This contract runs until 2086 and was originally negotiated between Eurotunnel and the British and French Governments. It was designed to give Eurotunnel a virtually guaranteed level of income to help them raise the necessary capital to build the tunnel.

The Eurotunnel Contract had three main components, a fixed fee, a contribution to Eurotunnel's avoidable operating costs and a per-passenger charge. The area of contention was operating costs, as Eurotunnel were supposed under the contract to detail their costs each year so Eurostar's appropriate share could be negotiated. But they never detailed their costs in a form that allowed scrutiny and merely stated what Eurostar's overall share was. It was always our suspicion that the large majority of these costs were driven by the much larger number of shuttle trains operated, but it was impossible to prove this. At one point

Eurostar had taken this issue to court, but the contract unfortunately was written under French law and the case got bogged down for several years in their very different dispute system and no result was achieved. After much haggling I did eventually manage to negotiate a modest discount, spread over ten years from 2006, with the costs then set for those ten years to avoid further rancorous discussions.

So in practice the Eurotunnel Useage Contract represented a largely fixed cost, with annual indexation for inflation. It was a classic case of a monopoly supplier, but without an economic regulator to ensure fair play. Eurotunnel also knew that if Eurostar failed, the contract was guaranteed by the British and French Governments as the original signatories, so they had no incentive to help Eurostar by softening its terms. Equally the two Governments knew they carried the ultimate liability, so were keen to see Eurostar continuing to pick up the full tab. A contractual catch 22 and substantial millstone!

Our commercial relationship with Eurotunnel was always therefore a tense one, not helped by the culture of their senior management. I never ever heard them use the word "customer" in relation to Eurostar. Instead they clearly viewed us as captive and, to them, a valuable financial asset. If anything, they were critical of us in public, for instance over the lack of a service to Amsterdam despite this being blocked for many years by Dutch Railways and their Government owners. The Useage Contract was also ambiguously worded in a number of areas, so further tensions arose for instance over insurance compensation for the sustained disruption to our services after a lorry fire in the tunnel in 2006.

The second largest category of cost was for track access in England, France and Belgium. In France and Belgium these costs were fixed by a regulatory process and we paid per train run, making them a truly variable cost. After the switch onto CTRL we also paid largely on a per train run basis in the UK too, with the level of charge fixed by a Government facilitated contract. Consequently, the only way to save costs in this area was to run fewer trains, which of course made it essential to maximise revenue earned for each train we ran.

The scope for cost reductions was therefore severely limited in practice, and largely confined to EUKL's direct costs within the UK. Even here the scope was quite limited as the company had not been around long enough to accumulate too many layers of management or excessive staffing, had a fixed train fleet and a relatively stable timetable. We ran a modest voluntary redundancy programme at the start of 2003 when sales were still falling, which also helped those people who were uncomfortable collaborating closely with our French and Belgian partners leave the business. We ensured that a number of residual costs still being incurred by the cancelled project to run Eurostar trains north of London were managed out. And we managed to lease out several of the seven redundant train sets procured specifically to operate north of London, firstly to Great North Eastern Railways who needed more capacity for their Leeds to London service and later on to SNCF for their Lille to Paris service. However, the scope for re-use of these trainsets was strictly limited because of their one-off size - a fixed formation of fourteen coaches - and high maintenance requirements. They were eventually scrapped.

The story of Eurostar's financial turnaround was therefore overwhelmingly one of growing its revenue and passenger numbers to cover its high cost base. This meant working to hold the cost base constant, only running additional trains very sparingly where there was demonstrable demand from passengers. This was very much in line with SNCF's philosophy for its TGV operations, essentially to only run trains where there was passenger demand and was very different to the UK practice that I was more used to, with

Intercity type services operating regular interval and frequent services throughout the day. As a result, Eurostar ran hardly any more daily trains when I stood down in 2010 than it had when I arrived in 2002, ensuring that costs hardly went up as passenger volumes increased. Chapter 7 picks up the story of how we grew Eurostar's revenue.

CHAPTER 7 Eurostar's financial turnaround and growing revenue

The strategic choices available to a normal business were pretty much fixed for Eurostar. It's a high speed passenger rail company, operating on fixed routes with a single fleet, when I joined, of relatively new trains and with no choice as to who owns and operates the tracks it runs over. Its markets, potential customers, main suppliers and costs are therefore largely determined by this. So the obvious strategy to turnaround its financial performance was based overwhelmingly on growing our shares of the London to Paris and Brussels travel markets whilst holding down costs. We also saw three other ways of growing revenues and passenger volumes: growing the size of the market by promoting new reasons to travel, increasing our share of passengers' spend and developing new markets. Initially we saw the latter as opening up new destinations such Amsterdam and Charles de Gaulle Airport, but this proved too difficult with Eurostar's disparate ownership structure. It morphed successfully into extending our share of travel beyond our core destinations via partnerships with other railway operators.

Focusing on market share as the key measure of success had the advantage, too, of side-stepping the regular media and public criticism of Eurostar's performance, that it had fallen way short of the original, wildly optimistic traffic forecasts used to justify the construction of the Channel Tunnel. So long as we could demonstrate a high and growing share of the actual market, as opposed to the theoretical market postulated in the original forecasts, we could legitimately claim to be successful. It was also fortunate that we operated in a well-defined market, with clearly identified airline competitors and a wealth of publicly available data on the market, allowing us to regularly track progress with implementing our strategy. For the first few years we became obsessed with our monthly market share results. And our initial analysis of market shares by route, journey purpose and country of sale showed clear opportunities for us to do much better, particularly in business travel, on the Brussels route and for international sales. It was an unusual luxury for a passenger rail company to be operating in such a clearly defined market, and it was exciting and motivating to play and start winning the competitive game.

Winning the business travel market

One of the many surprises I had in joining Eurostar was the stark contrast between its success in attracting leisure passengers and the lack of success in the business travel market. Eurostar's estimated share of the leisure market to Paris was 83% compared to just 50% for business travellers. This was a major problem since business travel generally supports much higher fares, but was also a big opportunity if we could fix it. It was something of an enigma, as door-to-door journey times and punctuality, even without CTRL, were as good or better than flying, and our fares were set to match airlines. It became clear that we had both an image problem - many business people did not see Eurostar as a serious travel option - and a customer service problem, as we did not match airlines' service. On reflection the image problem was not surprising as Eurostar's most successful advertising had been the series of adverts featuring Kylie Minogue, which oozed glamour and relaxation and promoted Paris brilliantly as a leisure destination, but were probably actively off-putting to business travellers. The subliminal message from the adverts was that Eurostar was an attractive and glamorous leisure travel option, but not a serious proposition for business people.

Our research told us that business people felt the need to be seen to be "serious" in their travel choices and that flying was seen as the more natural and appropriate mode for international business travel. It presented the right image for a "serious" business person. There appeared to be almost a club type atmosphere for business flyers, by flying you were in the "club" and clearly a serious business person. Most airline passengers to Paris and Brussels were business travellers, so you were safely in the group, and were often able to use airport first class lounges which had a real "clubby" atmosphere. One of our occasional travellers, who was President of the French Chamber of Commerce in Great Britain and a senior banker, explained to me that his days were divided into hour long periods, with each meeting lasting approximately an hour. He spent roundly an hour in the airport business lounge after priority check-in, where he would usually see and chat with a number of his clients, the flight took an hour roundly, and then the taxi or chauffeur car into central Paris from Charles de Gaulle airport allowed for an hour or so of phone calls or studying papers. Flying therefore dovetailed nicely with the pattern of his working day, highlighting the challenge we had in repositioning the perception of Eurostar as a truly serious way for business people to travel. Privately he became a useful benchmark for me on our progress, as over time a higher and higher proportion of his journeys switched to Eurostar.

Nicolas Petrovic took the lead with the customer service team in streamlining our own check-in process and upgrading our first class lounges at stations to better match or beat flying and foster a "club" type atmosphere in the lounges and on-board, so that passengers could feel comfortable and mix with other serious business travellers. Nicolas had joined us from SNCF as Customer Service Director in early 2003 and had quickly made an impact. He was an outstanding manager and strategically very incisive and in due course became my deputy as COO and succeeded me as CEO in 2010. Working closely with Nick Mercer on what customers wanted he introduced a 10 minute check-in deadline for first class passengers - the normal closing of check-in was 30 minutes before train departure. He also introduced a separate first-class check-in line at Waterloo and subsequently at St Pancras, to reduce or eliminate any need for first class passengers to queue at check-in.

The marketing team also commissioned an entertaining and innovative cartoon-based advertising programme called "Mr Jet Set" which gently poked fun at flying through a stereotypical American executive - Mr Jet Set. He always flew and arrived later and a little flustered at his meetings compared to colleagues who had used the train, but proud of the great effort he had made in travelling. The business sales team backed its launch with a morning of "guerrilla marketing" at Heathrow, handing out leaflets to business travellers and waving banners until asked to leave by Heathrow management.

All this was fairly obvious stuff, but re-jigging the on-train experience for business travellers proved to be much more surprising and interesting. At that time Eurostar had three classes of on-board accommodation, standard, first and premium first. The latter was priced above first class and had a separate coach on each train with a dedicated steward and a separate, more extensive menu for a four-course meal service. It was very lightly used, costly to provide and a waste of valuable seats. We initially thought to replace it with a class of travel between first and standard, aimed at budget conscious business travellers and commissioned a number of focus groups to help shape the new product. But the feedback from these groups was fascinating and hugely insightful.

When asked "what single thing could Eurostar do to make travelling with it more attractive?", the overwhelming majority of business travellers said that they wanted to travel with other business people. They didn't want to be sat near leisure travellers, courting couples going for a romantic break, loudly chatting groups of friends, or families with noisy young children. This was very similar to our previous research which showed that business travellers wanted to be seen as serious, and so travelling with other business people ensured they conformed to this image.

What was just as surprising was that when we then held a number of focus groups with leisure travellers they too wanted to travel alongside their own. They didn't want to be sat near business people on their mobile phones or laptops, or engaged in intense discussions, but wanted to be able to relax and be as animated as they chose. Obvious, when one thinks about it, but not what most train companies or indeed airlines normally provide. It further convinced me of the powerful insights that well designed focus groups and market research can bring.

This insight led us to offer two types of first class, Business Premier and Leisure Select, with separate coaches for each but exactly the same physical accommodation. Because Eurostar train sets have 6 first class coaches we were able to do this easily, with the number of Business Premier coaches varying according to demand but with at least one coach always available. The on-board service offer was also tailored to the two different markets, giving business travellers a wider choice between snacks and a better full meal service than provided to Leisure Select. Differentiation between the two services was reinforced by very different fare conditions, suited to the different needs of travellers, with Business Premier tickets being fully exchangeable and refundable for instance. This simple but relatively revolutionary innovation allowed us to offer services much more closely tailored to what the different markets really wanted. Within two years our first-class ticket volumes increased by roundly 40% as a result, split relatively evenly between business and leisure travellers, enabling an improvement in average leisure fare yields by offering a better premium service, and substantially boosting our business travel market share.

When the post 2007 recession hit, the offer was slightly amended and renamed because of a high level of initial down-trading of first-class business travellers to standard, as many companies banned first class travel as an economy measure. By 2010 when I stood down as CEO our business market share on the Paris route had reached 90%.

What we did at Eurostar was in sharp contrast to the approach that has increasingly been adopted on many domestic franchise services. Rather than finding ways of making better use of first-class accommodation for both leisure and business passengers and so meeting a wider range of passenger needs, the number of first class carriages has been cut on many routes at the behest of the Department for Transport because of poor loadings. Driven by their investment appraisal models the Department has long had an obsession with maximising the number of seats in each carriage, with first class carriages obviously looking less efficient. This approach treats passengers as a single homogeneous group and fails to recognise that different groups of passengers have different needs, so missing the opportunity to better cater for these different groups and attract more people to travel by train. It is the difference between a truly customer led approach and a theoretical approach developed in isolation from a proper understanding of what passengers really want.

The Brussels Accelerator Plan

Eurostar's performance on the Brussels route was even more surprising. It's overall share of the air-rail market was just 44% compared to an overall share of 62% on the Paris route. This was despite the journey time to Brussels being half an hour less than that to Paris, which should normally imply a higher market share! On enquiring why this was, I was given a variety of reasons, such as Brussels Midi station being too inconvenient for the city centre and lack of car parking at the station, many of which were purely anecdotal and not very convincing. I therefore commissioned a couple of ex-British Airways executives who ran a small consultancy to look into our performance and come up with a plan to improve it. Their conclusions were fairly stark, namely that we had the wrong timetable pattern, the wrong pricing and, less surprising, that Eurostar had focused its marketing spend on the Paris route and largely ignored Brussels.

In the business travel market Eurostar had a low share of day trips, so the consultants recommended clustering departures from London in the morning business peak and from Brussels in the evening peak, so day trip travellers had a more convenient choice of trains. It meant three-hour gaps in the timetable in the middle of the day, but this proved not to matter. Eurostar was also seen as more expensive than air, partly because many corporate customers had a policy of flying in economy but using first class for rail, so were comparing our first class prices with short notice airline economy fares. It was clear that in the Belgian market there was an expectation that corporate customers should benefit from significant volume discounts. Finally, because of the lack of advertising there was a low level of awareness of Eurostar's actual journey times on the route, with many potential customers believing the journey time was much slower than it actually was.

The result of all this was a Brussels Accelerator Plan, based on the consultants' recommendations and further refined by Nick Mercer after his arrival. The timetable was changed to cluster departures on the morning and evening peaks, and as volumes grew the weekday frequency was increased from eight to nine and finally ten trains a day. Fares were redesigned and a number reduced, significant volume discounts for corporate customers implemented and a higher share of Eurostar's marketing spend was allocated to the Brussels route. Most importantly Nick set up a small dedicated sales and marketing team in Brussels to champion the route and ensure we built up a proper understanding of the market and passengers' needs. Crucially this team were all employees of EGL not of SNCB, so their success depended entirely on growing our share of the market and they were insulated from the internal political factions that often influenced SNCB's decisions and priorities. One of the more gratifying events of my time as CEO was delivering the case of champagne that I had promised to the team when they succeeded in achieving an 80% market share.

The power of revenue management

The third and probably the most important innovation that helped transform Eurostar's financial performance was the introduction of active revenue management. It was greatly helped by the introduction of single leg pricing, already mentioned, and by the fact that Eurostar journeys were reservation only because of Channel Tunnel safety regulations, so a passenger was always given reservations when they purchased their tickets.

What is revenue management? In essence it is the real time variation of prices according to demand, with the low cost airlines the first to truly do this. The key principle is that the quieter the train, and the longer one books in advance, the more cheap fares are available and the busier the train the higher the prices for the remaining available seats for a last minute booking. This sounds like a recipe for higher prices generally but in practice it meant cheap fares were much more widely available, and could be accurately targeted train by train. There is of course an important difference between trains and low-cost airlines in that trains are much bigger, in Eurostar's case five times the seating capacity of a jet airliner. There is rarely enough demand at any particular time to fill a train with high price tickets, so there is almost always some space left to offer to budget travellers and on some trains a great deal of space.

Eurostar's prices varied in £10 increments up from the £59 return lead-in fare, with both outward and return legs on low price seats, up to the full fare of £285 in standard accommodation with both legs booked late-on on busy trains. The pricing system was simple to understand and fully transparent for passengers, with no need to work out what type of fare would suit one's journey, or how to adjust one's journey plans to get the best fare. Eurostar's website showed availability of the cheapest fares train-by-train and day-by-day making it easy to get the best price for one's journey.

This is in contrast to traditional railway fares which are based overwhelmingly on return fares, with cheaper returns offered with various restrictions such as departure only after 09.30 am for day returns or weekend returns requiring a weekend night away. The restrictions are often quite cumbersome and travel may or may not actually be on less busy trains. Similarly, saver return fares are usually restricted for the outward journey to avoid peaks such as rush hours and sometimes on the return leg too. The restrictions are often confusing for passengers and are a clumsy way of trying to segment demand to avoid overcrowding on peak trains but still offering attractive fares to more price sensitive leisure travellers. They often result in overcrowding on trains immediately before or after a barred period, but less than full trains during the true peak period. The big advantage for Eurostar was being able to really open up the availability of cheap fares, whilst not eroding fares yields at times of peak demand.

Overwhelmingly the biggest increase in usage of different fare levels was in the cheapest, lead-in, fare. And because passengers could then be pointed toward those trains with seats available at particular price levels, it enabled progressively higher train load factors to be achieved. A good example of this was the very first train of the day from London to Paris, leaving London around 05.30 in the morning which saw average load factors increase from around 30% to over 65%. In effect every train could be filled much closer to capacity.

Managing such a revenue management system clearly requires a very sophisticated computer system and Eurostar bought its off the shelf from a company that normally supplied airlines. Some 95% of price variations are automatically managed by the system, with algorithms calibrated from time to time by a small revenue management team. The resulting change in demand for Eurostar at different price levels is best illustrated by a skyline chart - a little like the view of a city centre skyline.

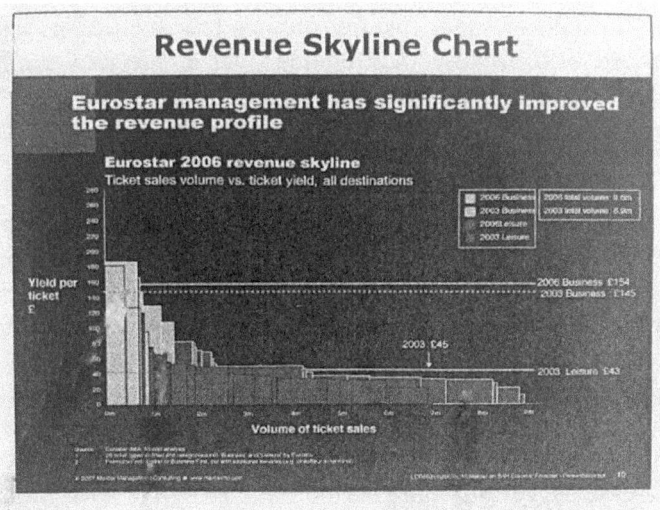

The skyline chart shows numbers of passengers on the horizontal axis and price paid on the vertical axis, with the area of each box representing revenue earned at that price level. The white edged boxes are for 2006, whilst the black edged boxes are for 2003. Total passenger volume increased by 25% in these three years, with the large part of this growth coming from leisure passengers, shown in the darker shaded boxes, travelling at the lowest fares. The size of the highest price boxes also increased, particularly for what might be called the shoulder peak boxes, next to the highest price box, as Eurostar was able to price up on the very busiest trains, mainly affecting business passengers.

A transport economist would recognise the skyline chart instantly as closely matching the price versus demand curve for Eurostar's market. The economic theory is that each individual passenger has a particular price they are prepared to pay for their journey, which will depend on a whole range of factors unique to that passenger. The aggregate of all the passengers in the market leads to the price demand curve for that market. Charging each passenger what they are prepared to pay produces the economically optimum result for the carrier, and ensures only a few passengers are "priced off" because they couldn't get a fare they could afford for the journey they wanted.

Overall between 2003, when single leg pricing was introduced, and 2010 when revenue management was fully mature, average year-round, train load factors increased from 51% to 69%, a 35% improvement in the numbers of passengers on each train. The average fare paid increased from £55.80 to £75.50 over the same period, also a 35% increase. During this seven-year period there was only one price increase (!), in December 2009, averaging 7% across all fares. As a result, revenue earned per train increased by an astonishing 83 %! (71% excluding the 7% fares increase). Over the same period the UK Retail Price Index only increased by 22% and UK domestic rail fares were increased six times. The 83% increase in passenger revenue on each train run obviously had a huge beneficial effect on Eurostar's financial performance.

The £3.5 million investment in Eurostar's revenue management IT system probably paid back in just 2 or 3 months! It remains a mystery and a frustration to me that revenue management and single leg pricing has not been adopted, even on a partial basis, on any longer distance UK train route other than very recently on LNER, despite it having been standard practice on both low cost and scheduled airlines for many years and also increasingly in other markets such as hotels. It is a system that is both simpler and much more understandable for passengers and improves the economics of the rail service. What is not to like?

Expanding Eurostar's markets

As well as steadily winning passengers from the airlines it obviously made sense to work to attract new passengers, for instance by promoting Paris as a destination for weekend city breaks in competition with other destinations such as Milan or Barcelona, or extending our reach beyond London, Paris and Brussels. Negotiating attractive through fares to Paris and Brussels with franchised train operators from towns and cities to the north and west of London was an important part of this. We used the move to St Pancras to launch a wide range of such fares and ran a large number of roadshow briefings around Britain to promote these ahead of the actual move. I was particularly gratified that the fastest growth in use of these new through fares was from my then home city of Derby, although I am sure this was mainly down to Midland Main Line bringing passengers directly into Eurostar's new terminus at St Pancras International, rather than any salesmanship of mine!

We also agreed a simple inclusive "any Belgian Station" add-on for all passengers travelling to Brussels, and paid a 5 Euro fee to SNCB for each passenger regardless of whether they chose to travel on beyond Brussels. Passengers could then travel on seamlessly to any other station and city in Belgium. This was also an elegant way of slightly increasing SNCB's share of the route's revenue, the low level of which had always been a source of dissatisfaction for SNCB. Likewise, we agreed a range of through fares to destinations beyond Paris, although these discussions were often more difficult because of the longer distances travelled to most French destinations and therefore higher share of revenues going to SNCF as the onwards carrier.

To attract more leisure trips to Eurostar we worked hard to develop relationships with a wide range of leisure travel operators such as Rail Europe, Great Rail Journeys, LastMinute.Com and Expedia. Because we had an attractive and increasingly high-profile brand we did not need to offer exclusivity to any of these partners but sought to cast the net as wide as possible reflecting our hunger for volume. We also offered our own short break packages for hotels and travel, in direct competition with some of these leisure travel operators, allowing us to increase our share of passenger spend.

The final push was to attract a much higher share of international travellers, that is non-UK, French or Belgian residents who were visiting Northern Europe either for business or leisure. These people made up some 20% of the total air-rail market between London and Paris and Brussels. But most were flying as that is how they had arrived in Europe and often the easiest thing was to arrange their intra-European travel through their inbound airline. It was also the case of course that such travellers had a much lower awareness of Eurostar, so were much less likely to even consider it as an option. One solution to this was to offer London-Paris fares to airlines that did not fly the route, for them to sell on to their passengers as if it were an airline journey. Our sales team negotiated such deals with a wide range of airlines.

But it was also important to work to raise awareness of Eurostar and what it offered in these international markets. Direct advertising in individual overseas markets was simply not realistic, given the tiny proportion of, say, New

Yorkers ever likely to travel to both London and Paris in a year, so producing an incredibly low cut-through to actual potential customers. Our solution was to use events and stunts to achieve media coverage, which because it was not paid for potentially offered a much more cost-effective route to raise awareness. The best example of this was the special train we ran from London through to Cannes in the South of France in 2005 carrying the cast of the newly released "Da Vinci Code" film from their UK to their French launch events. Paul Charles, our Communications Director, persuaded Sony Films to abandon the traditional film premier TV interviews in key cities and instead do these on a special train. Eurostar benefited from TV coverage of all the interviews throughout the train's journey. More spectacularly the train arrived in central Cannes alongside a Red Carpet allowing the cast to walk to the film's worldwide premiere in Cannes' Palais de Congress. It was estimated the resultant media coverage right around the world was worth £60million of free advertising to us, a wonderful payback for the few hundred thousand the train and associated promotions cost us.

The remarkable thing was that whilst the Da Vinci Code book is set jointly in London and Paris, Eurostar as the physical link between the two did not actually feature in the film at all. Our then Communications Director, Paul Charles, did an incredible job in inserting Eurostar into all the buzz around the film's launch despite this. As an aside Eurostar entered the Guinness Book of Records for running the longest non-stop international high speed train service over 1,421 kms (883 miles). Similarly, extensive international media coverage was produced by the various record speed and journey time runs in the build-up to our move to St Pancras and by the move itself.

A final way to broaden our markets was to extend our distribution as widely as possible: that is where potential passengers could buy tickets, either physically, by phone or on-line. As well as selling on the airline-oriented Global Distribution Systems this meant over time more and more passengers booking through the Eurostar website, which went through progressive upgrades to improve its functionality. By 2010 it accounted for over 50% of sales volume. Probably the most important of these upgrades was the train-by-train display of the availability of our lead-in fares so budget conscious travellers could easily plan their journeys and avoid having to hunt around to find the best fares. Alongside the market wide switch away from sales through travel agents it meant of course that our cost of sales came down substantially over time, from around 10% when I first joined Eurostar to 5% by 2010, saving us many millions of pounds.

It is interesting to reflect on how we were able to achieve such a major turnaround in Eurostar's marketplace performance. It certainly helped that technically we were an open access operator, not subject to fares regulation by the Department for Transport and therefore free to choose our own fares structure and price levels. We were free, too, to innovate and change virtually all aspects of our service without the straightjacket of a detailed franchise specification and all of the obligations and constraints that went with it. We were of a manageable size, allowing us to be fairly nimble in how we worked, and we served a well-defined market. And most importantly we were able to build an outstanding marketing team, using our high-profile brand to attract really good people. Virgin Trains were able to build a similarly strong marketing team, and the new Edinburgh to London open access operator, Lumo, appears to have done so too. There are some important lessons here for how the major domestic rail routes are managed and resourced in future, and how open access operators like Lumo might be used as "innovation hubs" to spread best practice more widely.

Finally, we were successful in establishing Eurostar as a respected brand, widely recognised both nationally and internationally. Getting the basics of service and reliability right were clearly important for this. But having a strong marketing team, including a succession of three widely experienced and professional Communications Directors, was equally important. It meant that there was wide awareness of our service, and for many people an aspiration to travel with us when the opportunity arose. And each PR event and advertising programme could build on what went before, multiplying its impact. In 2010 when I stood down as CEO Eurostar was ranked 52nd out of 500 so-called international Superbrands, with most of those above us on the list being much bigger multi-national companies.

CHAPTER 8 Going green and meaning it

Early in 2007 Stuart Rose, then CEO of Marks and Spencer's, did some something which few business CEOs had done before. With the launch of Plan A he made a series of public commitments to reduce all aspects of Marks and Spencer's impact on the environment, particularly the greenhouse gas emissions for which it was responsible. He justified this not because it would improve profitability but as being the right thing to do. It would clearly require M&S to invest extra time and money to achieve, and the "payback" was justified as an act of faith that in the long run it would help reduce costs and strengthen M&S's customer appeal. He named it Plan A on the basis that given the growing crisis of climate change there could be no Plan B.

I was inspired by Plan A and immediately thought that we at Eurostar should set out to do something similar, and wouldn't it be good if we were the first travel company to do it.

Interestingly, we had already done research on what our carbon footprint was, in response to persistent questions from some of our corporate customers. They had been asking what their carbon footprint was when they travelled by Eurostar, so they could report it in their Corporate Responsibility Reports, hoping that it would be rather lower than flying. I'm afraid our initial answer was that they shouldn't worry about it, it was very low and much lower than flying to Paris or Brussels. Unsurprisingly this did not satisfy them, they needed a number, which had prompted our research using a leading environmental consultancy.

The research was very striking and very encouraging, namely that travelling on Eurostar to Paris produced just one tenth of the greenhouse gas emissions that flying would, and just one seventh for a journey to Brussels. This was based on actual numbers of passengers using Eurostar and flying, the actual mix of aircraft types on each route, the known carbon footprint of each of our electricity suppliers in the UK, France and Belgium, our actual electricity consumption and specifically calculated emissions for London to Paris and Brussels flights. Incidentally because it used figures for specific journeys and passenger numbers it remains a more accurate estimate than a lot of transport emission analyses, which tend to use averages for baskets of journeys and vehicle and aircraft types.

The research had already prompted us to think about how we could use it to promote Eurostar as a greener way of travelling, so Stuart Rose's Plan A gave us a new impetus and sense of urgency. The consumer research we then did to design our Tread Lightly programme proved to be even more striking, and surprising. We first of all asked people how they reacted to the statement that a Eurostar journey was ten times less climate damaging than taking a plane to Paris. The response was "That's interesting and good, but shouldn't you be working to reduce it still further rather than just resting on your laurels. Surely everyone should be looking to reduce their impacts?" Furthermore, they said, "Greenhouse gas emissions are invisible and a bit of an abstract thing, we can't see them, but we can see all the newspapers, magazines and food waste and packaging that gets thrown away on your trains. What are you doing about recycling them? And by the way what about all the water you use to wash your trains, etc etc?"

The launch of "Tread Lightly"

It quickly became clear that to promote our low carbon credentials we needed to do a great deal more than simply boast about them, but ensure we had a convincing programme to reduce our emissions, as well as all of our other environmental impacts. This led us to launch our "Tread Lightly" initiative, which we described as a climate change plan to make high speed rail greener still. There were three main planks to the plan: A commitment to cut Eurostar's greenhouse gas emissions per traveller journey by 25% by 2012; A ten-point plan to reduce the environmental impact of all aspects of Eurostar's operations; and a commitment from 14th November 2007 to become the world's first train operator to make all journeys carbon neutral by offsetting the emissions we could not yet eliminate.

The ten-point plan was itself a very broad ranging and ambitious programme touching all aspects of Eurostar's operations. It was based on the three principles of reducing useage wherever possible, sourcing supplies responsibly and recycling what is not reusable. In effect we sought to follow the simple mantra of "Reduce, Reuse and only then Recycle". The plan committed us to take forward the following initiatives:

*Separating, sorting and recycling all on-board waste, including food waste

*Replacing train air-conditioning refrigerants with less environmentally damaging chemicals

*Helping travellers reduce their CO_2 emissions when accessing Eurostar services, by providing journey planner information and easy ticket sales for public transport options

*Sorting and recycling waste from stations, offices and Eurostar's Temple Mills train maintenance depot, with the goal of zero waste to landfill by 2012, and 80% recycled by 2009

*Ensuring lighting, heating and mechanical plant at stations, depots and offices are as energy efficient as

possible; developing a "switch off" culture and procuring electricity from greener suppliers

*Re-using water from train washing at Temple Mills train maintenance depot and investing in rain water collection

*Reducing paper usage by switching to e-tickets, undertaking direct marketing by e-mail and web-based methods; where paper is unavoidable sourcing from sustainable forests or recycled paper, and then recycling it.

*Ensuring on-board disposable items (eg cutlery, plates etc) are either biodegradable or fully recyclable.

*Refurbishing or de-branding and recycling used staff uniforms

*Sourcing on-train food from local sources in the UK, France or Belgium to reduce food miles, and from Fairtrade suppliers overseas

Rarely has such a comprehensive set of commitments formed part of a corporate environmental policy. So began an exciting and fascinating journey.

Given the relatively high profile of Eurostar as a brand, the launch of Tread Lightly predictably attracted a fair amount of media attention. Only half-anticipated was the close media interest in my personal lifestyle as CEO, probing as to whether this matched and supported our aspirations as a greener business, looking for the flaw or downsides in what was otherwise an unusually "good news" story. This included questions such as what sort of car did I drive, did I know my personal carbon footprint, where was my last holiday, and how did I travel there? It was a further reminder of how demanding today's media can be, always looking for a negative angle and looking to personalise issues. Fortunately, I managed to "pass" the scrutiny, and deny the media any negative angles. The best evidence for this was the headline of a Guardian newspaper leader article about the story which read "Going green and meaning it".

A more tangible outcome of the launch publicity was an approach from Friends of the Earth, wanting us to become a corporate partner. At that time they were lobbying hard for Parliament to pass the Climate Change Act, which would set the Government legal targets to reduce greenhouse gas emissions. They wanted to bring some corporate support and respectability to their campaign, but were understandably very concerned only to partner with businesses which broadly mirrored their values and which would not risk damaging them by association. A further potential barrier of course, was that many CEOs would have been reluctant and nervous about associating with an environmental activist group, whose members often lived in a very different world to them and which was often seen as anti-business. This was not an issue for me as I had been chairman of an environmental pressure group at University, which had a loose association with Friends of the Earth, and I was frankly flattered by the approach and enthusiastic about the opportunity to help support the environmental movement.

Eurostar therefore became one of only two corporate partners of Friends of the Earth, the other being the Co-Operative Bank, which at that time had yet to be tainted by subsequent governance shortcomings. We organised a joint event to promote Friends of the Earth's campaign on climate change at our Waterloo terminus and encouraged our passengers to sign their petition calling on Parliament to pass the Climate Change Act, which in due course it did. Whilst the partnership did not extend much beyond this - in practice our two organisations really did operate in very different worlds - it did encourage us not to be shy about what we were doing and to speak out about the importance of taking action on climate change and environmental damage.

Putting words into action

Implementing the Tread Lightly Programme within the Eurostar operation also proved very interesting and, in some areas, surprising. We appointed a young senior manager, Dr Louisa Bell, to be Head of Environment and Energy to lead implementation, who brought real drive and focus to the task. She had had no previous involvement in sustainability, although she did have a PhD in Physics, and had started her career in general management with British Airways before joining Eurostar. She therefore brought rigour and objectivity to the role, and was completely unfazed by the science, which greatly helped; my subsequent experience is that too often those who follow a career in sustainability from the start approach the issues from a particular viewpoint, can be somewhat siloed in their thinking and are insufficiently objective about what they are trying to do.

It is fair to say we had general buy-in across the senior leadership team and there was no resistance across the organisation, perhaps not surprising as I, as CEO, was clearly strongly committed to it. But it had been our hope that a good number of individuals would pick up the baton and act as local champions of the programme and lead local initiatives as part of it. With some honourable exceptions this did not take off to the extent we hoped, perhaps a reminder that getting enthusiastic buy-in for a corporate-led initiative is rather harder than you think. Some exceptions included initiatives to "up-cycle" old uniforms into shoulder bags and the like, and to set up several honey bee hives at Eurostar's train maintenance base at Temple Mills in East London. The team at Temple Mills also became very good at sorting and ensuring their more industrial waste was recycled. On reflection I think it is very difficult for an individual in a company, or even a workplace team, to do much on their own unless the whole organisation, and the various "cogs in the machine" are aligned and encouraged from the top. Most of the actions which will materially reduce environmental impacts are only addressable by the organisation corporately, rather than by any individual or group of employees.

When we were researching what the Tread Lightly programme should include we started with the assumption that we would invest in carbon offsetting projects, to balance the greenhouse gas emissions that we had not yet managed to reduce, so we could say we were carbon neutral as a business. In the initial research we had asked customers whether they would interested in an option to make an additional payment when booking to cover the emissions generated by their journey. This was an option that some of our airline competitors were then offering. The estimate was that this would be less than a pound a journey. Once again the answer was striking: "Why should we pay for your emissions, we cannot influence or control them so surely you should pay for this, and in any case it is such a small amount, so what's the problem?". We therefore decided that we should indeed pay for offsetting ourselves, which we did for the first couple of years of the Tread Lightly Programme. This was incidentally against the advice of Friends of the Earth, who disapproved of offsetting in principle, on the reasonable basis that in effect it was paying someone else to solve a problem that one was unable to address oneself. Offloading, or outsourcing the problem might be a more accurate description than offsetting.

Our experience of offsetting was disappointing and a sharp lesson in the realities of the politics and economics of decarbonisation. Despite working with a very enthusiastic and knowledgeable partner company who specialised in sourcing offsetting projects, we struggled to find worthwhile projects. The theory of offsetting is that you pay per tonne of CO_2 saved by the project you are supporting, with the payments making the difference between the project being viable financially and non-viable. You then claim credit for the greenhouse gas reductions, to offset your own continuing emissions. Most projects are in developing countries, where costs are lower but finance is scarcer. We were also keen to support projects that were socially useful; we got particularly excited about projects in sub-Saharan Africa to fund charcoal cooking stoves to replace raw wood cooking fires. These both reduced emissions from cooking, but also greatly reduced the health problems caused by wood smoke inside peoples' homes.

But the problems with offsetting start with how to validate the emissions reductions actually produced. We wanted to be watertight about this, and had decided only to invest in projects endorsed by the so-called Gold Standard, which limited our choices. There is also a chicken and egg problem involved. To be able to validate the actual emissions saved one really needs a project to be up and running; but if it is already up and running, it was surely already viable for the operator otherwise how did they finance it, unless they had some form of contractual commitment from an offsetter ahead of knowing what the actual emissions achieved would be. The result of all this was difficulty in sourcing credible projects. Most of those we did support ended up being more industrial type projects in China - wind farms, small hydroelectric schemes and the like - where we had the distinct impression that the projects would have happened anyway and we were merely providing additional profit to the operators.

In 2010 we therefore decided to cease investing in offsetting projects, but to spend the same amount of money on a wider range of more socially useful decarbonisation activities. One of these was a "Walking Bus" programme in Kent, designed to encourage children to walk to school along a pre-set route, picking children up along the way, with an adult accompanying them for safety and security. Another was sponsorship of a new transport award as part of the annual Ashden Awards for companies and organisations developing innovative and potentially scaleable ways of reducing greenhouse gas emissions. Since one of our objectives was to use our spend to promote wider awareness of the importance of reducing emissions and tackling climate change, this felt like a much more useful way forward. On reflection the whole basis of offsetting is very questionable, and certainly should never be used to support claims of being carbon neutral. Fortunately, we saw the "light" eventually and no longer sought to present Eurostar as a carbon neutral train journey.

It should be a source of concern that there are now many companies who are claiming to be carbon neutral, or "zero carbon", most of whom can only be doing this by offsetting their emissions. The only truly rigorous way of offsetting is by sequestering carbon, that is by removing it from process emissions, for instance from power station chimneys, and locking the carbon dioxide away underground. The technologies to do this still need to be proved at scale, and nobody can sensibly claim to be doing this yet. The alternative is to take carbon dioxide out of the atmosphere, for instance by planting trees. But trees take a number of years to reach maturity and only then absorb modest amounts of CO_2 each year, so an awful lot of trees would be needed to truly offset most organisations' emissions.

Another area of some controversy was in choosing how to report emissions from the electricity we used. This is a rather esoteric but real problem. Electricity is generated by a variety of means - coal, gas and nuclear power stations, wind turbines, solar photovoltaic and hydro-electric - each of which produces widely different emissions. Some of these are emissions-free and because the mix varies continuously according to the demand placed on the grid and the amount of wind and sunshine, this is not straightforward. Different suppliers will also have different carbon footprints depending on their generation mix. There are three possible approaches. One could report emissions on a marginal consumption basis, assuming each kilowatt hour of electricity used is the last to add to total demand and so is produced by the most polluting mode of generation in use at that time (usually this would now be gas-fired generation). This is theoretically logical but very difficult to apply in practice, as the generating mix is continuously changing hour-by-hour and day-by-day. Secondly, one could report emissions on the basis of the average for the national grid over a period of time, usually year-by-year. Or one could report emissions based on the footprint of one's electricity supplier, which by law are reported by each supplier periodically.

We chose the third method, since as a responsible user we felt we should try to source our electricity from a lower carbon supplier, even if this might be more expensive. Interestingly this was also the method required in France. However, in the UK the Government ruled, as part of its then Carbon Reduction Commitment initiative, that the grid average of emissions per kilowatt hour should be used to report emissions from electricity consumed. This felt wrong to us and I became involved, along with a number of other businesses, in lobbying the Department for Energy to change it. Our argument was the Government's approach effectively disempowered consumers and businesses from having any influence on how electricity is generated and from taking any credit if they chose to buy lower carbon, but potentially more expensive, electricity. I think we said that the Government was effectively nationalising the task of decarbonising the UK grid. I also joked that if both the French and British Governments made their approaches legally enforceable I would end up breaking the law and being jailed somewhere, as it would not be credible to report on one basis in one country and a different basis in the other for what is a seamless service between the two. Needless to say, we failed to change the British Government's mind.

Initial results and challenges

When we started the Tread Lightly journey we set a target of reducing our per passenger greenhouse gas emissions by 25% within five years. This was overwhelmingly driven by the electricity we used to run our trains, and to a much smaller extent by the utilities and things we used in our offices and depots. Achieving the target would require us to reduce the electricity used per train run, for instance by better driving techniques, switching off so-called "hotel" power on trains overnight (ie power for heating, lighting and air-conditioning the coaches), as well as being successful in attracting more passengers to each train so reducing the average emissions for each passenger.

In the event we achieved our 25% reduction target by 2009 and raised our target for 2012 to a 35% reduction. This was achieved for the most part by a combination of improved train load factors, spreading each train's emissions over a larger number of passengers, Eurotunnel switching its electricity to low carbon French suppliers and the changing generation mixes of other suppliers.

Recycling of our various waste streams was another area of surprises where our initial ideas were rather naive. We learned that what happens to stuff set aside for recycling is a complex and sometimes murky issue. My initial encounter with this was when I first joined Eurostar. A small group of staff at head office had commendably started a recycling project for office waste, with several different coloured bins for different items. Staying late in the office one evening I saw the cleaners emptying the different bins into a single sack, which was clearly not going for recycling. In their enthusiasm the group who set this up had not liaised with the cleaning company to ensure their contract was suitably amended!

With Tread Lightly we set a goal of zero waste to landfill. We quickly learned that this was an exceptionally difficult thing to achieve, and certainly did not mean everything being recycled. A significant proportion of our waste - and most household waste generally - goes for incineration, producing electricity but also CO_2 emissions in the process. This is still better than landfill, where the organic parts of the waste will slowly decompose, producing methane. Methane is a much more potent greenhouse gas than CO_2. Whilst some waste tips succeed in harvesting it, and then burning this gas to power electricity generation, inevitably a significant amount escapes and adds to the greenhouse effect.

The key to recycling is keeping different wastes separated, not easy given the time pressures of cleaning trains and removing "rubbish" on turnaround at terminal stations. It requires close liaison and partnership working with cleaning contractors and their staff, and with waste disposal contractors who take the waste away, hopefully for recycling. In the case of railways, the station owners and other train operators at the station will also have their own waste streams to deal with, and therefore need to be involved as well. In practice waste separation often takes place subsequently, at so called Materials Reclamation Facilities where large volumes of waste are separated for recycling, partly mechanically and partly manually. It became clear that just as a business needs to understand and manage its supply chain, it also needs to understand and manage its disposal chain. When we reported progress against our Tread Lightly goals in 2012 Eurostar had reduced the proportion of on-board waste going to landfill to just 1.6%; not bad for that era, but not quite what we had set out to do.

Recycling of course should only be a last resort, much more important is to try reduce the amount of stuff used in the first place, so reducing waste, or to reuse things rather than throwing them away. One of our mantras of Tread Lightly was simply: reduce, reuse and recycle. When a substantial proportion of waste is generated by one's customers, stuff brought on board, consumed and then thrown away, it's harder to reduce or reuse. Ensuring that the packaging, paper cups etc that we used for on-board service were properly recyclable or compostable was at least a partial solution. By 2011 we had increased this to nearly 90% of items. For things more directly in our control we were able to make more of an impact. Office paper usage was reduced by 28% by the simple switching of all our printers to double sided printing as the default option. Even more was saved by the elimination of our rather elaborate paper tickets and their wallets.

We struggled more when looking to reduce the food miles generated by the food we served on board. It quickly became clear that this is not a simple calculation, as food grown in Britain or the near continent might have low food miles, compared to food trucked in from Spain or flown in from East Africa. But if grown in heated greenhouses or with large fertiliser or other artificial inputs it could have an even higher carbon footprint overall. It was not until my successor brought in Raymond Blanc as Eurostar's food adviser and ambassador that real progress began to be made in sourcing food sustainably. His impressive but common-sense approach is to focus on serving seasonally grown food from regional suppliers, so reducing food miles and ensuring the food is grown in a sustainable and lower carbon way.

One of my favourite anecdotes on our Tread Lightly experience came from a conversation with the MD of the company that ran some of Eurostar's big customer and media events. We had encouraged all of our contractors and suppliers to also adopt our Tread Lightly principles. At a routine catch-up meeting I was surprised and delighted when Richard Beggs, the MD, told me about his initiative to provide bottled water at hospitality events. Rather than buy in bottled water, which of course has a substantial carbon footprint from the transport costs and single use bottles alone, he had invested in a water filter and small bottling plant. By filtering normal tap water, he was filling his own bottles which were then also washed and reused, saving substantially on the costs of buying water in bottles, which might be recycled but rarely reused. He was also able to label the bottles with his customers' logos, and therefore able to charge a premium. All in all, he was drastically reducing his environmental impact, but in his words: "the best thing about it is that it has improved my gross profit by 58%!". It shows that good business and the environment do not need to be in conflict.

I am very proud of what we initiated with our Tread Lightly programme, which continues to run at Eurostar to this day. It undoubtedly helped further strengthen Eurostar's image with its customers, enabling it to promote itself as the low carbon as well as the quickest way to travel between Britain and France and Belgium. It cost very little to mount and certainly quickly paid for itself in the savings in materials and energy costs alone. And it taught us a lot about the nuanced way customers see one's business. Just being relatively greener, or less environmentally damaging, is not enough or particularly impressive in their eyes. To establish and exploit one's credentials requires active promotion, supported by a credible programme of further improvement. I believe there is an important lesson here and, so far, a missed opportunity for the wider rail industry in Britain, whose credentials as a lower carbon form of travel remain unburnished and too often overlooked.

There is also a lesson for businesses more generally as to what are the necessary conditions for a successful initiative on sustainability and carbon reduction. One necessary condition is to have the sponsorship of the CEO of the organisation and at least a critical mass of the wider leadership team, setting the goals, providing support and encouragement, asking questions and ensuring adequate resources are focused on it. It is helpful to have the tacit if not active support of shareholders and owners. In my case at Eurostar my three shareholders were all represented on the Board and when I briefed them on what we were planning they were supportive, albeit in a passive way. It is also helpful to have concerned customers who might respond to the right initiatives. It was some of our business customers after all who provided the initial "spark" which encouraged us to act.

Employees or even potential employees can also be a spur to an organisation addressing its environmental performance. I recall a surprising conversation with the Senior Partner of one of the larger UK accountancy practices when I was describing our own Tread Lightly initiative. He quickly interjected to say his firm too had just decided to offset their carbon emissions, including those from employee travel to work. I queried why they were doing this, suggesting that it surely couldn't give any commercial advantage from winning new accountancy clients. But he explained that the number one question asked by potential new graduate recruits was "what was his company's policy on the environment" and so he saw it as a recruitment aid, helping secure more of the best talent available!

I learnt a lot more about this subsequently when chairing the French Chamber of Commerce in Great Britain's Climate Change Forum. This brought together some 40 Anglo French businesses, all looking to reduce their own or their customers' carbon footprints, to exchange experiences and learnings, particularly between different sectors. In the run up to the COP21 Climate Change Conference in Paris in 2015 we surveyed the Chamber's overall membership of some 400 companies, to assess the extent of their interest or focus on climate change and what they saw as the key drivers for change. Predictably most companies claimed to be doing things, often around recycling or energy efficiency, but the most striking feature was what they saw as having driven them to take action beyond what was required by law or regulation. Most often it was their customers or employees who had first prompted them, but disappointingly it was very rarely shareholders, boards or investors. I came to the view that often consumers are ahead of businesses in wanting to see real action in addressing climate change, and businesses in turn are often ahead of Governments in doing more than required by legislation or regulation.

No longer being involved in Eurostar's Tread Lightly programme is undoubtedly one of the things I miss most after leaving the business. As CEO of a high profile business it gave me a wonderful platform to promote environmental sustainability on a wider scale and to champion and showcase its importance for our future. Eurostar has undoubtedly more than pulled its weight in the drive to reduce carbon emissions, both in beating its own targets to reduce the emissions for which it is directly responsible, but more importantly by attracting passengers away from carbon intensive flying. One of the things I would have wanted to do if I had stayed on at Eurostar was to find ways to invest in our own carbon-free electricity generation capability. I was always very envious of Swiss Railways, who invested widely in hydro-electric power after the Two World Wars, and have sourced the majority of their power from these zero-carbon sources ever since.

CHAPTER 9 Moving home - to St Pancras International

November 14th 2007 was a momentous day for Eurostar. We were "moving home" from Waterloo International Station where we had been based since the service was launched in 1994, to the newly transformed St Pancras International and on to the new High Speed One line. We had ceased operations from Waterloo only on the late afternoon before, and to our knowledge, no major railway had moved its operations overnight like this before. We were therefore understandably nervous about how the first day's operation would go!

I arrived at St Pancras bright and early anxious to check how the myriad of tasks involved in the move were going, and just to "be there" in case of eventualities. My role was principally to front up to the media - who we knew would be there to report on the move in large numbers. I was greeted early on by the British Transport Police Inspector in charge of policing that day, who reported to me "Mr Brown, I need to tell you that we have demonstrators on the roof of the station". My heart sank, and I immediately began to think through the possible ramifications. Would it stop us starting services because of the safety or security risk? How might it play with the media and potentially steal the story? Did the demonstrators have a particular issue?

The Inspector continued "They are from Greenpeace, Mr Brown", pausing, "They are demonstrating in favour of high speed rail". Another pause whilst this sank in. "Would you like me to leave them up there for a few hours?" I could have hugged the Inspector in relief and for his flexibility and consideration and of course readily agreed. Clearly all our hard work on our Tread Lightly programme had had an impact. This brief exchange proved to be a good omen for the rest of the day. Whilst in many ways the highly successful launch of services that day was a close-run thing, it was the first evidence of how all our planning and preparations would pay off handsomely.

All of that planning and preparation work had started some three and half years earlier, soon after the opening of the first section of The Channel Tunnel Rail Link, as it was then called, in September 2003. Whilst this launch had also been successful in the eyes of passengers and the public, it had been pretty fraught for us behind the scenes. And that move was immeasurably simpler than the move to St Pancras, being essentially a switch of route within Kent, onto a relatively straightforward section of new railway. The very last piece of signalling on the first section of the new line had only been finally commissioned and tested successfully in July of that year, giving us just 8 weeks to train and familiarise enough drivers and train managers on the new piece of railway. This was no simple task with crews based in all three countries of operation, and a limit on the number of trainsets we could spare from normal passenger service for training runs in daylight hours.

Communications between ourselves and Union Railways, the company who designed and procured the new railway, and Bechtel who were retained as overall Project Managers, had been poor throughout, mainly focused on several successive failures to commission the new signalling which should have been ready by May at the very latest. Our confidence that the new signalling would actually work as intended was weakened by these misfires. It was therefore one of the harder decisions I have ever taken to go ahead with the launch in September, knowing there was a real risk we would not have enough crews trained in time, and might have to cancel trains for the first few days. Fortunately, I was brilliantly supported by my Deputy at the time, Jacques Damas, who was our Chief Operating Officer and a highly experienced SNCF TGV operator who had overall charge of training and all other operational preparations across the whole of Eurostar. He got his calculations just right, and ensured their delivery. We managed to train some two thirds of crews overall, only just enough to sustain services for the first few days with no spare margin whatsoever.

This fraught experience made us determined to manage things better for the altogether more complex move to St Pancras and on to the final section of what became known as High Speed One (HS1). In the spring of 2004 we therefore set up a project steering group, chaired by the Chief Executive of London and Continental Railways (LCR), who were the sponsor and funder of the new railway and at that time also sole shareholder in the UK part of Eurostar. The other members were the MD of Union Railways as the designer and procurer of the line, the MD of LCR Property who would be owner and operator of the new stations and myself as CEO of Eurostar. We met every month for over three years, to monitor progress, ensure all parties knew what the others were doing and that problems were addressed as they arose, taking key decisions in good time. Early on I also managed to engage Richard George, initially part time, as Project Director for all of Eurostar's preparations and planning who also attended every meeting. Richard was to prove pivotal to our success in 2007 and deserves most credit for the smooth transfer of operations to St Pancras and HS1.

The regular steering group in effect brought together the builders and operators of the new stations and railway and provided the foundations for eventual success, ensuring there were no surprises, keeping everyone on the same page and addressing the inevitable conflicts in good time. Too often railway infrastructure projects do not involve the eventual operators nearly early enough in the design and specification of what is being built and, even more importantly, how it is to be commissioned and operated.

The resulting fraught service implementations too often result in substantial teething problems, the launch of the new Thameslink service in 2018 being but the most high-profile recent example.

The move of Eurostar's home to St Pancras International was in practice not one but at least five linked moves: to not one but three new stations, Ebbsfleet International and Stratford International being the other two, to a new Train Maintenance Facility at Temple Mills in East London, and onto the new section two of HS1, the large majority of which was in tunnel with all of the additional safety management issues involved. For Eurostar, effective communication and promotion of the move to both existing and potential new passengers was going to be crucial to the commercial success of the move. And we were concerned about the risk of losing key staff, particularly skilled maintenance personnel who needed to move from the existing maintenance facility near Wormwood Scrubs in West London right across London to Temple Mills in Newham, East London. So, for Eurostar there were three major project streams, each of which was managed as a group of projects: Taking our passengers with us; Taking our people with us; and moving operations to the new stations, high speed line and maintenance facility.

It soon became clear that managing and coordinating these projects was going to be a huge task for what was not a large organisation. Richard George brought in CITI Ltd as experts on project management to review our capabilities and tell us how we should organise ourselves. An early recommendation was to set up a Project Management Office (PMO) to oversee and coordinate all the various activities, and for this to identify all of our existing activities which could remotely be described as projects, and then either terminate or suspend all those which were not essential to the move or to business success in the next few years. This was not an easy task, with inevitable resistance to ceasing or suspending pet projects and activities which were not "business as usual ", and with hindsight we should probably have "cleared the decks" more thoroughly. But the process was very helpful in concentrating our minds on the task ahead, and ensuring we were focused on making the move to St Pancras a success.

CITI also ran a very successful training programme for us on the essentials of project management, which most managers went through and led to a remarkable take up. Even colleagues in sales and marketing and HR, functions not normally associated with the disciplines of project management, fully adopted the approach and ran their part of the moving home programme using project management principles. At the peak of activity, we estimated that there were over forty individual projects underway, each with its own full time or part time project manager, all coordinated and overseen by the PMO, ably led by Elaine Davies, and Richard George as Project Director.

Taking our passengers with us

The original plans for Eurostar envisaged services operating from both Waterloo International as well as from St Pancras International, with much higher numbers of passengers travelling according to the original forecasts. Waterloo would have continued to serve its established customer base, whilst St Pancras would open up the new markets north of London. By 2004 it was clear that the original traffic forecasts were hopelessly unrealistic, and as we looked at the options for dividing the service between the two London termini it quickly became apparent how impractical this would be. Service frequency from each individual station would be less attractive, it would be very confusing for continental originating passengers as to which station to travel to, and for UK returning passengers if they returned to a different station, trainset and train crew utilisation would be poorer, and the costs of running two international terminal stations excessive. So, early on we took the decision to switch the entire service to St Pancras, and fortunately were able to convince both the Eurostar Board and the Department for Transport, as ultimate sponsors of the new high speed line, that this was the right way forward.

But our new traffic forecasts suggested there would be an initial dip in passenger volumes after the move, with some loss of passengers for whom Waterloo was ideally located and might therefore be reluctant to cross central London to St Pancras, before the new markets in the north could be developed. As Eurostar's financial position at this time was still fragile, to say the least, we could not afford the loss of revenue that this implied. A comprehensive programme of marketing and communications activity was worked up to try to ensure we took as many of our existing Waterloo passengers with us to St Pancras, and to kick start the attraction of new passengers from north of London so that overall passenger volumes continued to grow without interruption.

The move to St Pancras and commencement of services on the new high speed line, HS1, was of course the last piece in the jigsaw in the original concept for Eurostar, and making a success of it would be crucial to Eurostar's long term success and move to financial viability. And as an iconic international brand we knew that the move would be the subject of intense media interest and scrutiny, both nationally and internationally. A comprehensive strategic communications programme was going to be essential to success. This was an integral part of the overall marketing strategy, and brought home to me the crucial importance of good communications, and of having a top-notch Communications Director in the lead, to running a successful railway. As a public service, but also needing to operate commercially, railways are of above average interest to both the media and politicians, and how well one communicates with them is as important as the quality of one's advertising and marketing. The experience at Eurostar helped me understand that communications need to be a core part of the overall marketing mix, reporting to the Marketing or Commercial Director. They should also have a strong dotted line to the CEO, who is expected to be the public face of an organisation and needs the support and advice of a communications professional to do this to best effect. We were also very fortunate at Eurostar in having a first-rate Commercial Director in Nick Mercer, superbly supported by Communications Director, Simon Montague, Head of Marketing, Greg Nugent, and Head of Sales, Emma Harris.

The marketing strategy had a number of core components. The most resource intensive was a programme of sales briefings in towns and cities around the country to explain the move to HS1 and St Pancras and its impact in each different place. These briefings invited local MPs, Council Leaders, local media, Chambers of Commerce and known potential larger customers, and were each led by a Director supported by sales and communications colleagues. What was crucial was to vary the messages according to the audience, as some places, particularly those in the catchments served by Waterloo, saw the move as potentially a negative change because of the perceived extra time and inconvenience involved in travelling to St Pancras rather than Waterloo. The tone here was not to pretend that everything was wonderful, but to seek to explain about the different options for accessing St Pancras or Ebbsfleet International, stress the fact that it would be 20 minutes faster from St Pancras to the continent, and therefore just as quick overall but more reliable because of the dedicated high speed line.

We also stressed the option of Ebbsfleet International for those who might prefer to drive to the station to access Eurostar. Our market research had suggested that being close to junction 2 of the M25 would make Ebbsfleet potentially attractive to drive to for people living close to the M25 as far round as the junction with the A3. Transport for London were also extremely helpful in arranging to put stickers on every one of their thousands of tube maps in their trains showing Kings Cross and St Pancras tube station as serving both national and international trains, and extending the number 59 bus from Waterloo via Euston on to St Pancras. In the event the large majority of passengers from the Waterloo catchment area chose to travel through St Pancras after the move, attracted by its magnificent environment and facilities and better frequency of trains than on offer at Ebbsfleet.

Putting Ebbsfleet "on the map" proved very challenging as it was not marked on any maps and didn't even have a postcode. The name originally referred to a large proposed housing development site, which had been moribund for several years so didn't yet exist as a place. We sponsored the local Gravesend and Northfleet football club and they agreed to change their name to Ebbsfleet United. This got the name broadcast every weekend on sports channels when the football results were read out. The team had Eurostar branded shirts and, with serendipity for us, went on to win the 2008 FA Trophy final at Wembley against Torquay United. In the end we had to pay the Highways Agency to include Ebbsfleet International on motorway signage around the Dartford Crossing area, despite having signage for Heathrow, Gatwick and Stansted airports all round the M25. Their rationale was that they had many people travelling to them, whereas we had none! - hardly surprising as it was a brand-new location. Land Securities, who were the owners of the housing development site, were no more helpful in putting Ebbsfleet on the map and were happy merely to piggy back on our efforts to put their development on the map.

For towns and cities north of London the tone of the sales briefings was more upbeat, explaining the service frequency and travel times from St Pancras to Paris and Brussels, how to access St Pancras from wherever that briefing was happening, and launching the through fares that we had negotiated with most operators, to show how affordable it would be. The programme of briefings commenced a year out from the date of the move, and each session usually achieved a significant amount of interest and media coverage with the localisation of the content always well received.

The sales briefings were accompanied by a programme of periodic consumer polling in the key geographies we wanted to address, to see how well our key messages were getting over: were people aware of the move to St Pancras and the date we were moving? Did they know what the new journey time to Paris and Brussels would be? And so on. The polling allowed us to target advertising on those areas where the key messages were not adequately getting across, and was a key tool in enabling our inevitably limited advertising budget to be spent most effectively. In the event the sales briefings were so successful overall that we did not need to spend all of this budget.

Nick Mercer, our Commercial Director, had set up an informal advisory group of communications experts to provide a sounding board to help shape our marketing and communications strategy, including such luminaries as Lord Gould, who was Tony Blair's principal pollster, Sir Keith Mills, and Matthew Freud. Their comment, when Nick updated them on the sales briefings, advertising strategy and polling programme, was that we were running our communications exactly like an election campaign!

The second core component of the marketing strategy was a series of events and stunts aimed at getting free publicity. Whilst these required some resource to mount, and carried some risk as we could not control how they might be covered in the media, our experience was that they were usually much more effective in getting our messages across than paid-for advertising. And in any case our financial position meant we could only afford a relatively limited amount of advertising. No doubt Eurostar's high profile as a travel brand, and general interest in the new high speed line being built under east London and through Kent, helped ensure these events mostly got a lot of useful publicity. The events included such railway mainstays as speed record runs on the new line and special trains to both Paris and Brussels carrying the media and key customers to set new records for fast journey times. The announcement of the date of opening of the new line was also timed to be exactly one year ahead, and happily coincided with Eurostar's twelfth birthday.

The final component of the communications strategy was a programme to manage the bad news stories. We were very aware that the scale of the changes involved in the move to St Pancras and onto HS1 were not without a number of downsides for certain communities and customer groups. Foremost amongst these was the fact that with the opening of the new station at Ebbsfleet International in north Kent we would need to significantly reduce the number of trains calling at Ashford International. We were also not intending to stop at all at the new station in east London, Stratford International, contrary to local expectations, and finally, that we would be leaving our old London "home", Waterloo International, empty. Our marketing team gave this programme the rather ambiguous moniker of "protective shelling" ie trying to construct a protective shell around the opening and its good news stories. This was not so much to bury bad news stories as to manage their release into the public domain well ahead of the opening of the new line, so they ceased to have so much resonance later on. It also took the form of a comprehensive and carefully researched Q and A brief on how we would handle potential critical or controversial news stories, and meeting critics of our plans face to face to at least explain our reasoning.

We therefore announced and implemented our planned service reductions at Ashford International some two years ahead of the new line opening which inevitably attracted a lot of protests and much political lobbying from both local MPs and Councils, and from the Department for Communities and Local Government. I had a number of difficult meetings with the local MPs, led by the then Leader of the Opposition, Michael Howard, with Kent County and Ashford District Councils, and with the then Minister of State, Yvette Cooper. Going so early with this bad news meant that it was no longer news when we eventually opened, and also it allowed us to make some modest changes to the eventual service pattern at Ashford in the light of passenger reaction to the changes, including the reinstatement of an additional stopping service which took some of the heat out. I recall the meeting with the Minister as being particularly bizarre, as she had obviously not read the brief from the Department for Transport, which was our sponsoring Government Department, and suggested that because Ebbsfleet was obviously going to be very profitable for us, we should cross subsidise more calls at Ashford. This ignored the fact that overall Eurostar was at that time still significantly loss making and received no public subsidies to operate!

Not calling at Stratford was more a matter of playing a straight bat, not hiding the issue (I think we encouraged the news to get out very early) but patiently explaining the basis of our decisions. We were helped in this by some very clear and thorough market analysis which showed there was only a tiny potential local market which was not served well by either St Pancras or Ebbsfleet, both of which were only a few miles distant. This small market would nowhere nearly justify the costs of stopping. Again, I held a number of meetings with the London and Newham Mayors and the local MP, Stephen Timms who was at that time a Treasury Minister. We were helped by the fact that our new Train Maintenance Facility was opening at Temple Mills in the Borough of Newham, bringing many good jobs to the area including a number of apprenticeships, and our agreement to sponsor a local youth orchestra. So we had some good news to balance the bad.

Handling the closure of Waterloo International Station was more frustrating as its ownership was agreed to transfer to the Department for Transport after our departure, so its future use was in their hands. I had naively hoped that we would be able to explain how it would be reused after we left, but despite regular prompts to the Department that this could prove a running sore and become a white elephant, no decision on its future use was ever forthcoming. It was not in fact until nearly ten years later that it was finally brought back into use for South West Train services on the Windsor lines.

Two other potential "bad news" stories never became an issue. One was the cost of building HS1, which in the early days of its planning and construction had been a very contentious issue, and the other was our concern that the noise of our trains running on the new line would attract complaints from the new line's neighbours. What emerged was that the cost of the line had largely been forgotten as its value became real and appreciated, as is often the case with large infrastructure investments. It's also the case that we did not receive a single complaint about the noise of our trains, nor did Kent County Council as the local authority. This was in contrast to our experience on the old route from Waterloo through South London, where we received periodic complaints about train noise; clear testament to the effectiveness of the noise prevention measures on the new line. I think the fact that the new line was built by a private sector consortium, who had a detailed contract and specification to deliver, with financing in place in advance, and that they delivered within this Budget, headed off any subsequent debate or controversy about its costs or scope. We were therefore credibly able to mitigate any potential bad news stories by making "On time, on budget" a core plank of our communications programme, which proved to be simple and very effective.

A final, interesting, nuance in the marketing and communications strategy was the name change of the new line from "The Channel Tunnel Rail Link" (CTRL) to High Speed One. Some eighteen months ahead of the opening, the marketing team had expressed concern about the name CTRL which they saw as clunky, unfriendly and not really describing what the new line offered. I remember expressing scepticism at the time, because the name had been around for a long time, was well established and known and therefore difficult to change. Nevertheless, the Project Steering Group agreed the team should look for and research better alternatives. The result was High Speed One, or HS1, which we all agreed resonated much better, was shorter and described precisely what the new line was about. We needed Department for Transport approval for the name change, however, as they were its sponsors and would be owners of the line when built. We were concerned they would reject the name as setting an uncomfortable precedent, as the clear implication was there would or should be an HS2 or even an HS3 to follow. I for one was surprised and pleased that the name was accepted with little fuss, and the rest is history as they say!

As the date for moving got close we were reasonably confident that our communications strategy had worked, reassured by the results of our polling. But there was still a concern that some passengers would not have heard we were moving and would turn up at Waterloo as before, only to find no Eurostar trains. Given the millions of passengers who used Eurostar each year, many not from the UK at all but from France, Belgium or even further away, this was a real risk. We therefore left behind a small team at Waterloo for the first few days after the move, armed with taxi vouchers, tube maps and the like, to redirect and assist any passengers who might arrive inadvertently. I well remember visiting the team several days after the move to see how they were getting on and being rather taken aback when they begged me to let them join their colleagues at St Pancras as they were so bored! They had assisted just five passengers in the first few days; a Japanese couple and a small French family of three. Our messaging about the move had clearly worked!

Taking our people with us

The initial plans for Eurostar operation from St Pancras assumed we would continue to use our existing Train Maintenance base at the rather exotically named North Pole depot next to Wormwood Scrubs in west London. Trains were assumed to be moved to and from the depot via the North London Line. But the plans had been made a number of years previously, and not been worked up in any detail. In the meantime the passenger service on the line had at least been doubled and it also emerged that the overhead power supply on the line would struggle to cope with the heavier power demands of a Eurostar train each with its two power cars and eighteen coaches. It therefore quickly became clear to us that the plan would not work and we would need to move to a new maintenance base which could be easily accessed from St Pancras. A number of options were looked at, but the best and only truly practical solution was to build a new facility using the old freight yard at Temple Mills in East London. Persuading the Department for Transport that this was the case took the best part of two years, with several sets of consultants retained by the Department trying to prove us wrong or to come up with "better" solutions. We had to fight for every aspect of the new facility, with the Department or their consultants constantly trying to argue for less than adequate facilities.

With hindsight I can understand the Department's reluctance to agree to our solution as it was a substantial variation to the concession contract they had given to London and Continental Railways (LCR), the builders of HS1, so they would need to finance it. The Department had presumably used the original planning work done under British Rail auspices in setting out the detailed specifications in LCR's contract. This had also assumed operations continuing from Waterloo, alongside the new terminus at St Pancras, so good access would have continued to be possible for at least a proportion of trainsets. In the event logic prevailed and whilst arguments about the precise scope of facilities at Temple Mills continued to the wire, Eurostar did manage to get the large majority of what it needed. With over ten years of experience of operations at the old base at North Pole, itself not a very easy depot to operate, the maintenance team also ensured the new facility was more fit for purpose with a number of improvements in its design.

But the decision to move to Temple Mills presented a new challenge: how were we going to encourage the critical mass of the highly skilled and experienced maintenance staff at North Pole to transfer to Temple Mills, on the other side of London? If we lost any significant number of staff because of the move we would struggle to be able to maintain our trains, certainly for the first year or two until new people could be trained up and become fully familiar with Eurostar's complex and sophisticated trains. A review of the home addresses of our people at North Pole showed many of them already had quite long commutes to work, with many living west of London in places like Swindon and even beyond, so the additional travel time of up to an hour to get to Temple Mills would be a big hurdle.

So we realised that taking our people with us was a critical task. This was only reinforced when we were reminded that the large majority of staff based at Waterloo had been with us since Eurostar's launch in 2004, and for whom Waterloo had been their "home" all this time. Whilst St Pancras was only two miles away, it was north of the river Thames and perceived to be in North London, and it was then little known as a railway station. We could not assume everyone would want to transfer.

All of this was happening at the same time as British Airways were preparing to move into their new dedicated Terminal Five at Heathrow and had embarked on their "Fit for Five" initiative to sort out the widely different and often inefficient employment conditions of their Heathrow employees, which dated back to the merger between BOAC and BEA. I therefore suggested we should do something similar, to address some of the costly and less efficient staffing practices we had ourselves inherited from the original Eurostar operation when it was still a part of British Rail. This might have meant we did not need to take everyone with us. I am pleased to say that all of my fellow directors thought this was a thoroughly risky idea, to be attempting a significant staff restructuring alongside everything else we had to do, and I was outvoted. The various restructurings were quietly achieved in the years following the move, and in the event BA's move into Terminal Five proved to be a fairly fraught one, I believe partly because they had a demotivated workforce who were not prepared to go the last mile to make it a success. In contrast the commitment and enthusiasm of all of Eurostar's staff to make our move a success was to play a really important role.

A number of our younger "rising star" managers had gone on a short "Managing for peak performance" course run by a company called K2. All their trainers were professional sports coaches who applied the same principles to managers as they did for the elite athletes they helped coach. Their whole emphasis was on preparing oneself to be at one's peak of performance on the day or time it was needed, an event at the Olympics for instance. They pointed out that the day we moved our operation from Waterloo to St Pancras was an exact parallel. Once the date was fixed, we had no choice but to be ready to perform then. The whole of our senior management team also attended, and we all benefited from being as personally prepared as we could be for the move.

We did three main things to ensure we took as many of our people with us as possible. The easiest was to agree with our staff representatives to compensate people for their additional commuting time to their new places of work, on a tapered basis for the first several years after the move. Whilst initially quite expensive we were confident it would be cheaper than having to invest significantly in recruiting and training replacement staff.

Secondly, we ramped up our internal communications processes to provide regular briefings on the progress of the building and construction works at St Pancras and on HS1, ensuring these "told it like it was", covering risks as well as opportunities. This culminated in a full-day's briefing in the spring and early summer ahead of the move, with relevant project managers updating on their part of the preparations, a detailed Q and A session with a Director, and finally a visit to view the newly renovated St Pancras. The visit was to raise the levels of excitement about the move, as we knew that people would be highly impressed by what they saw. Sharing the risks and downsides involved with the move, as well as all the upsides, also meant that the many staff who had direct customer contact could talk about the move with greater confidence and respond more convincingly to questions and concerns.

Finally, we tried to ensure that as many staff as possible were involved in the planning and preparations for the move. Some 100 staff from North Pole depot (roundly a third of the total workforce there) were directly involved in planning the design and detailed layout of their new facility at Temple Mills, for instance where best to locate tool lockers and spare parts bins in the maintenance shed, and how best to phase the transfer of the large volumes of parts, stores and equipment to the new location. As a result, there was a real sense of ownership across the organisation of the move and of their new workplaces. A measure of the success of this for Temple Mills was that the teams accomplished the overnight servicing and maintenance of train sets on their first night there in the same time as they achieved in the old location. This was in an entirely new and relatively unfamiliar depot, after a hugely complex transfer of parts and equipment that took place over a number of weeks, which could have resulted in any number of key tools or parts being unavailable on the night. It was a remarkable achievement, clear testament to the commitment and determination of all of Eurostar's people to make a success of the move! Needless to say, only a handful of staff chose not to move with us to their new workplaces.

Moving home

As building and station renovation work proceeded one of the key issues for our planning was when would be the least disruptive time to make the move? Traditionally the UK rail industry does most of its engineering work at weekends, as this is when it is considered to be least disruptive for passengers. There are few commuters or business travellers then, albeit lots of leisure passengers. To start with, our assumption was that we would follow this long-held practice. But it held two significant disadvantages for us. Firstly, there is usually much less of a management presence at weekends, so requiring greater changes to work patterns to ensure the whole management team was around at this crucial time. But secondly, and more importantly, for similar reasons we could expect a much thinner presence from the media at a weekend, so blunting our ability to achieve maximum publicity for the new line and stations.

The marketing team analysed our own daily pattern of passenger volumes and quickly concluded that Tuesdays and Wednesdays were usually our two quietest days, and therefore the obvious time to make the move. The next issue was which month and week to choose. Because of the Project Steering Group process already described, we had good visibility of progress with the construction programme, and it increasingly looked as if everything would be ready for the second half of 2007. We wanted to avoid holiday and half term periods, as these tended to be busier for us, and also months when extreme weather was more likely. We also needed to avoid the early autumn when the Rugby World Cup was being held in France with large numbers of extra passengers wanting to travel to games. A final consideration was our obsession with BA's Terminal Five at Heathrow, which had been getting a lot of media attention, and we worried would overshadow the publicity for our move if they completed the terminal and moved before us. In the event of course, we need not have worried as their move early in 2008 was something of a disaster in terms of media coverage, with many teething problems for passengers in the first few days, particularly with baggage handling.

The night of November 13th/14th 2007 was chosen to meet these various criteria, which happily would be Eurostar's thirteenth birthday, allowing us to confront superstition head on and seek to break with any pattern of earlier misfortunes in Eurostar's first few years. Fortunately, because we were moving onto an entirely new railway, with no other operators on it initially, we no longer needed to dovetail changes in our timetable with other rail operators so could choose any date that suited us.

An overnight move was clearly desirable to minimise disruption to our passengers and consequent loss of revenue, and our planning had established that this was broadly possible. The main constraint was the time needed to move portable equipment essential for day to day operation from Waterloo to St Pancras, and see it safely positioned in its new home. Also, it would be necessary to allow extra time for those trainsets finishing their days work at Waterloo on the 13th to be moved round south and east London in time to receive maintenance and servicing at Temple Mills in readiness for start of service on the 14th. The final departures and arrivals at Waterloo were scheduled for late afternoon on the 13th, and the first departures from St Pancras late morning on the 14th, resulting in a slightly extended "night" of some 18 hours. A short but emotional "Farewell to Waterloo" party was arranged immediately after the last departure, principally to allow the station's staff to say "goodbye" before moving on, with Lily Allen singing the Kinks' hit "Waterloo Sunset".

The logistics and scheduling for moving maintenance and servicing from North Pole to Temple Mills was an order of magnitude more complex. When trains are undergoing maintenance they are obviously immobilised, often partly disassembled, and for more detailed examinations out of action for a number of days. It was therefore necessary to have a maintenance plan that spanned a number of months, detailing exactly what was to be done each day, to ensure no necessary work was missed as equipment, parts and tools were progressively switched over to Temple Mills. This latter was itself a huge task as there was no longer an original equipment manufacturer for Eurostar trains, and the whole stock of parts and spares is held directly by Eurostar itself. The physical move of all the kit took a number of weeks. The task was more demanding still as we wanted the trains to look at their best after the move to St Pancras, in their new terminal surroundings of a freshly renovated and partially brand-new station. So a programme of in-depth cleaning of the fleet was also planned in. To relieve the pressure on North Pole some heavy maintenance work was temporarily transferred to SNCF's high speed train depot at Le Landy on the outskirts of Paris. That it all went smoothly is a testament to the quality of the planning and delivery of the maintenance teams.

As the opening date got closer the pace of preparation activity progressively accelerated, particularly when the new line was sufficiently complete to allow testing to take place. Initially this was of each individual component and installation and was undertaken by the various contractors building the line. But as these tests were completed it was then necessary to test whole systems, often using a programme of test trains to check the wide range of systems needed for a modern high speed railway, particularly with so much in tunnel. On top of this there was a programme of crew training and familiarisation on the new line and, of course, the programme of special record runs as part of the wider communications strategy.

It was fortunate indeed that an early decision had been taken to use identical signalling and power supply systems to those on the high speed lines in France and Belgium. As a result, there were none of the signalling and other system compatibility issues that have dogged other major rail projects such as Crossrail. Strikingly there was one minor exceptions to this, which caused some concern at the time. The "throat" at St Pancras - the complex of switches and crossings to allow trains to access the various platforms off the two running lines - used point machines specified by Network Rail, rather than the standard SNCF high speed line machines, as technically this last few metres of infrastructure would be owned by them. It turned out that Network Rail had specified a new, relatively untried, design which they intended to become their standard design for the future. Sorting out the inevitable teething problems with these machines caused some lost sleep for the engineers who were of course unfamiliar with the different design, and was a reminder of the difficulties of integrating systems of different design.

Access to the new St Pancras station was at an increasing premium in the run up to opening. Whilst the main construction work was long since complete there was a huge programme of fit-out works to be undertaken, at the same time as running test and special event trains into the station, and access for staff and other familiarisation visits. And because the opening would mark the culmination of LCR's contract to finance and build HS1, it was planned to hold a large opening ceremony with hundreds of guests, with Her Majesty the Queen herself opening the station. A large viewing platform and staging to accommodate the guests had to be erected, and then dismantled, at the same time as final fit-out works were still underway.

The last, and in the event most important, access requirement was for five days of what was dubbed "Integrated Volume Testing" (IVT): using several thousand volunteers to act as passengers to test out all of the passenger handling systems and processes at the new station, from check-in, through security to train boarding and despatch, and then train arrival and passenger disembarkation. The IVT used the same shift of staff that would be running the station for the first few days, so they would be as familiar as possible with their new environment and equipment. Suffice it to say that the first day of IVT was little short of chaos, with a huge range of problems identified, allowing them to be fixed without inconveniencing real passengers. But by day five everything was running relatively smoothly. I have no doubt that the IVT programme, the brainchild of Richard George as Project Director, played an absolutely crucial role in the successful opening and launch of services a few days later by giving the staff concerned the confidence to run the station on the day. I have several times wondered if BA and BAA at Heathrow's Terminal Five had done anything similar their opening might have gone more smoothly.

The actual launch of services from St Pancras on November 14th 2007 of course went very smoothly for passengers, with punctuality of 94% achieved on day one, and most importantly for Eurostar's future success, a massive amount of superlative national and international media coverage. Behind the scenes things were rather more fraught, however, because very little of the staff accommodation and other "back office" facilities had had their fit-outs completed. Likewise, very few of the wide range of retail outlets in the wider station had been fitted out. That passengers and the media barely noticed was another mark of the effectiveness of our project management, which had clearly prioritised the completion of all passenger facing facilities ahead of other items of fit-out, and had contingency plans in the event any behind the scenes facilities were incomplete. It was also down to the commitment and determination of Eurostar's staff to make the opening a success, helped I believe, by the fact we had successfully "taken them with us" not just physically but emotionally too. Again, a striking contrast to BA's experience several months later at Terminal Five.

Most importantly there was no "dip" in passenger volumes following the move, as had been forecast, and passenger growth didn't just continue but accelerated as people from the new markets opened up north of London started to use the service from day one. Looking back the successful move to St Pancras International was the highlight for many peoples railway careers, and provided something of a textbook case study of how to integrate construction of a major infrastructure project with its opening and operation.

CHAPTER 10 Managing a crisis - Christmas meltdown 2009

One of the challenges of running a railway is how to manage major service disruptions, either when trains can't run for any significant period, or they can only run in severely degraded mode, or if there has been a significant train accident involving passengers. I have probably had my fair share of such situations both at Eurostar and in earlier roles, although thankfully I have never been responsible for a rail service in which a passenger has been killed in a train accident. The necessary response is fairly simple, in theory: restore a normal service as soon as possible, keep passengers as well informed as you can and where possible make alternative arrangements for passengers to travel. But you rarely know how long it will take to restore normal service, which is of course what passengers most want to know. Initial estimates often have to be revised as the scale of work to restore services becomes clearer, creating a big challenge for how to communicate helpfully and believably to affected passengers. And making alternative arrangements for passengers to complete their journeys is easier for some passengers than others. Regular commuters are more used to the occasional disruption, or worse, and usually have their own alternative arrangements and so largely look after themselves. Long distance passengers are usually less regular travellers and need more assistance in finding alternative routes or require overnight hotel accommodation or taxis home if they have missed last connections.

All of these considerations apply in spades to Eurostar. There is nearly 400 miles of railway between London and Paris, much of it through relatively remote countryside and managed by three separate infrastructure administrations:

Network Rail in Britain, Eurotunnel in the middle and SNCF in France. Getting to site for the necessary technicians to assess a problem and then fix it can take time, with the number of parties involved further complicating both internal communications and the task of rearranging the disrupted train services. Communicating with passengers in three different countries (now four with the extension of services to Amsterdam) is also a more substantial task, although easier now with the ability to text updates where mobile numbers are known.

But the greatest challenge is the lack of alternative means of travel and the fact that passengers when stranded are in what is for most a foreign country. The most obvious alternative route is to fly, but a Eurostar train carries the same number of passengers as five short haul aircraft so the ability of the airlines to take extra passengers is strictly limited. With probably a dozen or more trainloads of passengers in each direction looking for alternatives flying is an option for only a tiny minority. Likewise, cross channel ferries now primarily cater for cars and lorries and have very limited capacity for foot passengers, before any consideration of the availability of trains or coaches to move people to and from the channel ports. Eurostar's average of some 30,000 passengers daily would require some 600 road coaches to transport them all, beyond any imaginable spare capacity in the coach market. All of this means that the overwhelming priority for Eurostar is to restore services as soon as possible and as far as possible to help stranded passengers find hotel accommodation.

My first experience of this was very soon after I joined Eurostar in the autumn of 2002 when the section of line between Lille and Calais was intermittently closed over a 48-hour period. Within Eurostar the event became known afterwards as "Salty Monday". A storm in the Channel and high winds from the west had blown salt spray far inland. Some of this contaminated the insulators supporting the overhead power cables causing power to the trains to trip out, salt water being a very good conductor of electricity. The solution was to turn the power off and spray the insulators with fresh water to remove the salt, but, in the event, it took several passes of the spray train to clear the problem. In the meantime, Eurostar was striving to assist stranded passengers with hotels and alternative travel, all under an intense media spotlight.

One of our efforts was to try to fly home several hundred families who were returning from a weekend at Disneyland on our through service from the Disneyland park outside Paris, for which we chartered several planes from Air France. Arranging the extra flights and processing all these families through Charles De Gaulle airport without normal airline tickets was not easy and Air France were not helpful in the process as their staff didn't see why they should help a competitor. Inevitably the media, including a BBC journalist, were reporting the problems from the airport. I was about to do a live TV interview with the BBC at Waterloo International when I overheard the interviewer speaking to her colleague at Charles de Gaulle so as to try to "ambush" me with questions about the Disneyland families, when the interview was supposed to be about the overall situation and the prospects for restarting services. Fortunately, I just had time to phone one of our managers at the airport who was assisting the families, to get an up-to-the minute brief on the situation, so was able to wrong foot the interviewer by answering her questions fully and countering several misconceptions. This was not the only example I have encountered of the sometimes very underhand ways the media, and I'm afraid to say particularly the BBC, seeks to catch out or discomfit interviewees.

Meltdown in the Tunnel

Whilst being relatively used to handling service disruptions nothing compared or prepared me for the events following the breakdown of five of our trains in the Channel Tunnel on the last Friday before Christmas in 2009. It was an experience that few of the passengers affected and no one at Eurostar will ever forget. The ensuing media storm lasted for days and took many weeks to fully subside. But it was also an experience that we learnt a great deal from and from which Eurostar emerged much better prepared for future problems. It was a real lesson in crisis management. The run up to Christmas is probably the worst possible time to have a major incident because of the emotional importance of travelling to be with family or friends for the holiday.

I first heard we had a problem at around 10.00pm on Friday evening, December 18th, with a phone call from Nicolas Petrovic, my deputy and Chief Operating Officer. He told me that a train had broken down soon after entering the Tunnel and that there was heavy snow in northern France between Lille and Calais so more problems were likely. I was actually already asleep in bed as I was exhausted after an intense few weeks supporting negotiations between Eurostar's three partner railways to set up a formal joint venture to own and manage Eurostar and replace the relatively informal and ad-hoc arrangements that had existed up until then. These were complex and sometimes fraught negotiations which all agreed were crucial to the future of the organisation. I was therefore not in a good state physically to cope with the events that followed. It was also too late to get a train back to London from my home in Derby and I was too tired to drive safely so decided to get the first train up to London the following morning.

Early the following morning I got the news that a total of five trains had broken down that night soon after going into the tunnel en-route to London. Several trains had been towed out of the tunnel to Eurotunnel's transfer sidings at Folkestone and their passengers were being de-trained and transferred to rescue trains to take them on to St Pancras. Passengers on two trains had had to be taken off their train inside the tunnel and transferred to Eurotunnel car shuttles to be taken out of the tunnel, one to Folkestone and one back to Calais, and then finally onwards to Ashford and St Pancras. There are well established procedures for dealing with broken down trains in the tunnel and for safely taking passengers off a stranded train where necessary. Passenger safety was never at risk, and there were no injuries to anyone, but it was a thoroughly upsetting and sometimes frightening experience for passengers nevertheless, particularly as the last train to break down was (again!) from Disneyland laden with families returning after a pre-Christmas treat.

In such a situation it is not possible to determine what exactly caused the breakdowns until the trainsets involved can be taken back to a maintenance depot and properly examined. However, it was clear that the heavy snow that evening in northern France was a prime cause, but not clear how the snow had actually got into the trains' power cars and caused them to fail. So as a precaution we agreed we would not restart services while it was still snowing in France and until we had established what was the cause of the breakdowns and fixed the problem.

Snow and ice were a particular problem for Eurostar trains, as snow tended to stick to the cold metal exteriors and build up into lumps of ice when running at high speed. The ambient temperature inside the tunnel is around 25 degrees Centigrade so the snow and ice quickly melts on entry to the tunnel adding to an already high level of humidity. As well as the melted snow there was often a lot of condensation on the metal surfaces in the power cars, which could be very cold after running at high speed before entering the tunnel. I likened the effect to taking a beer bottle out of a fridge into a very warm, humid room. Within minutes it will be covered with condensation. On the night of December 18th there was very heavy snowfall in northern France, a large temperature difference between outside and inside the tunnel and high levels of humidity in the tunnel.

This was not a new problem of course. Over the years Eurostar had experienced a range of problems from snow and from the heavy condensation that power cars experienced when going from below-freezing outside temperatures into the warm, humid tunnel environment. Our engineers had implemented a considerable number of modifications to tackle the problem, which had amongst other things contributed to a more than threefold improvement in train set reliability from one incident every 20,000 kilometres in Eurostar's early days to one every 67,000 kilometres. An "incident" being any technical issue at any point on its journey delaying a train by more than five minutes.

It might seem surprising that Eurostar trains were still experiencing problems from snow and extreme temperatures. But it is important to understand their unique design and technical features. Eurostar trains have only two power cars, whereas the equivalent TGV trains on which they are based have four for the equivalent length of train. The Eurostar power cars therefore have 50% more installed power than a TGV power car, to be able to operate at similar speeds. And this extra power had to be accommodated in a smaller space because of the constraints of UK bridges and tunnels which were built to a tighter structure gauge. As well as this the Eurostar power cars were designed to run on the third rail, direct current system of the Southern Region of Britain's railways as well as the usual 25,000 volt alternating current system, so requiring additional electrical equipment. All this meant that the clearances between all the electrical components inside the power cars were at their absolute design minima, so increasing their vulnerability to electrical flashovers between different components and resultant failure. The extra power of Eurostar's power cars also produced a great deal of heat requiring cooling via powerful fans sucking in external air. Hence their vulnerability to snow being sucked into the power car interiors and then melting.

It is also of course physically impossible to test new train designs in snow conditions, or when making an instantaneous transition from very cold to very warm and humid conditions as happens with Eurotunnel. A test hall able to accommodate a 400metre-long train and reproduce such different environmental conditions simply does not exist. It is only possible to do theoretical design simulations and then rely on in-service experience to learn how a particular train performs and where necessary to then make design modifications.

As well as the various engineering modifications Eurostar had also developed an agreed set of winter preparedness measures which were implemented on each power car every autumn. The first line of enquiry was to check why these had not worked. A couple of test trains were run on the Saturday with technical experts riding inside the power cars to observe their performance and look for signs of snow ingress. Whilst neither train broke down the technicians did observe some snow getting into the power cars through the driver's cab doors and interfering with the electrics so the decision was taken to further suspend services that day and on Sunday, until a solution could be found. It was then found that the door seals had actually been fitted the wrong way round by the original train builders so an emergency programme of refitting the seals correctly was started to ensure they worked as designed. Rather surprisingly this construction defect had not been spotted or caused problems before.

The engineering teams worked flat-out all day Saturday and Sunday examining the failed train sets as they were returned to Eurostar's maintenance depot at Temple Mills in East London, figuring out how they failed and more importantly what mitigations could be put in place, if only temporarily, to prevent a recurrence. By Sunday evening they believed they had come up with a set of mitigations to reduce the risk of snow penetrating the power cars again so further trial trains were run and a very limited service for passengers was run on the Monday, with technicians travelling in each northbound power car to check things were working ok. A nearly full service was then restarted from Tuesday.

But by then we had not been running trains for some two and half days and there were several tens of thousands of passengers who had not been able to make their booked journeys. The challenge was how to accommodate these passengers alongside those already booked to travel on the Tuesday and following days. Because it was the last weekend and week before Christmas most of the passengers affected had been planning to get away for their Christmas and New Year breaks with friends or family. We were therefore faced with the classic dilemma for travel companies in such a situation: do you honour bookings already made for the days after services are restarted, and use any spare capacity to work through the backlog of customers who had been unable to travel, a process which can take quite a few days? Or do you give priority to those passengers who could not travel, but not honouring many bookings made for the days immediately after the restart of services? This is a problem regularly faced by airlines, because of bad weather or other disruption, and they routinely choose the former solution on the basis that this ensures that only those passengers who could not travel during the disruption are inconvenienced so minimising the numbers of passengers affected overall, but greatly increasing the inconvenience for those affected. Rightly or wrongly we chose the latter solution, influenced by the extreme inconvenience and upset that had already been experienced by all the passengers on the broken-down trains and a view that we should not disrupt them any more. Whichever option we chose would have posed huge challenges as we were not able to run more trains than originally planned because several of the broken-down trains were out of service for repairs for a number of days, and bookings in the run up to Christmas are always high so there was little spare capacity to handle the backlog in passengers. The consequence of course was that many more passengers felt the effects of the disruption creating a huge customer care and compensation challenge.

A particular problem was accommodating and managing the resulting queues at St Pancras station. We were trying to give priority to those people directly affected by the service disruption between Saturday and Monday, but didn't know in real time how many had decided not to travel or found other means of travelling, so we were in effect offering a first-come first-served service, which allowed us to fill each train to its capacity. But this meant some long queues particularly on the Tuesday when a full service was restored. This was the first occasion that we had experienced major disruption at our then still newish London terminal so both we and the station's operators, Network Rail, were on a steep learning curve. After a rather chaotic start, which of course produced more passenger dissatisfaction, a much better queue management system evolved, with a lot of help from both Network Rail staff and many of our own office staff volunteering to assist. The lessons learned provided the blueprint for all subsequent situations requiring some degree of passenger queuing for check-in.

Handling the media and Government

Eurostar has always operated very much in the public spotlight, being a high-profile brand and, in transport terms, a relatively glamorous one. It is also highly accessible to the media with its central city stations allowing TV crews to cover issues with ease. We had enjoyed three or four years of very positive media coverage, particularly with the highly successful relocation from Waterloo to St Pancras in 2007, so it was probably inevitable that at some point we would suffer a fall. The UK and French Governments also took a close interest when things went wrong; as ultimate owners of the service they were usually keen to be seen to hold management to account and, perhaps a little cynically, to ensure no blame could be attached to them.

As CEO it was my responsibility to manage Government relations, and I decided I should be lead spokesman in talking to the media and be seen to be taking responsibility for what happened and for fixing it. I called a special meeting of the Eurostar Board on the Sunday morning, to brief them on what had happened and what we were doing about it, but also to ratify two decisions: firstly, to commission an independent review of what went wrong and how we should prevent a repetition and secondly to agree that there would be no management bonuses for the year in view of what had happened. I was particularly keen that it should be our initiative to launch an independent inquiry, not have it imposed on us by Governments, and that we should be seen to be completely open about what happened and not be hiding anything. I had already spoken to Christopher Garnett, the much-respected former CEO of Great North Eastern Railways, and got him to agree to chair the inquiry. I also wanted to be able to handle any media questions about bonuses without any equivocation. In the event the questions for the first few days were much more about why I was not considering my position and resigning, but at least I was prepared!

I went on one of the Breakfast TV Channels on Sunday morning, still with few explanations as to what had happened and without being able to say when services would be resumed. Not a comfortable position! After being asked a question about why communications with passengers stuck on trains in the tunnel were so poor, I made the mistake of starting to explain how these communications worked, as under their operating rules they were all required to be through Eurotunnel. I was quickly interrupted on the lines "Oh, so you are blaming Eurotunnel". I wasn't, but the impression stood and probably soured our already difficult relationship. Eurotunnel staff had worked very hard on the night to help rescue our trains and passengers, in circumstances where their own car and lorry shuttles were also severely disrupted by the snow, but their leadership was subsequently less than helpful with Christopher Garnett's inquiry and actively hostile to Eurostar. Under the tunnel's operating rules, Eurotunnel is responsible for recovering broken down trains in the tunnel, and a significant part of the overall delays to our passengers were because their resources were overwhelmed, as were ours, their own lack of contingency planning and because of communication difficulties with Eurostar staff. Their approach of revealing as little as possible was the exact opposite of Eurostar's.

Things actually came to a head with Eurotunnel on Christmas Day. I was phoned in the morning by our Communications Director to tell me that Eurotunnel had just put out a Stock Exchange announcement accusing Eurostar of breaking tunnel safety rules on the night of the breakdowns. It turned out that the rule "breach" referred to was that we had allowed passengers to take their luggage with them when evacuating their train in the tunnel and transferring to a Eurotunnel shuttle train. This had actually been agreed on the night with the Eurotunnel and First Responder Emergency Services personnel on the spot, so at worst it was an "agreed" breach. The rules were written in the context of an emergency such as a fire, and designed to assist a speedy evacuation, not for the situation where there was no safety threat. The staff on the night took the pragmatic view that requiring passengers to leave their luggage behind, after waiting two or more hours for rescue, would have caused more argument and disruption.

But the potential for a terrible media storm on what was a very quiet media day was huge. Recognising that I, as CEO, would have an uphill task in defending Eurostar I phoned around contacts and industry friends to try to get them to speak out in our defence. I will be eternally grateful that both Chris Green, a former boss of mine and a hugely respected rail industry leader in numerous roles, and Richard Hope, a widely respected rail industry commentator and journalist, agreed to speak for us if we were asked to comment. In the event it fortunately proved to be completely unnecessary as Richard Reid, the infamous Canadian shoe bomber, chose that day to try to blow a plane up. This became the sole media story of the day.

I did also try to speak to Eurotunnel's CEO, Jacques Gounon, to ask him to explain their actions but was told he was attending a Christmas Day party and not available to talk. I was instead passed to their Head of Communications, who was totally unapologetic and unhelpful, and merely stated they had a duty to report the alleged breach to their shareholders. This was despite the stock market being closed for the public holiday, and their shareholders, like Gounon, also being on holiday. It was clearly a brazen attempt to smear Eurostar ahead of the inquiry we had commissioned. An interesting way to treat their major customer!

The media frenzy continued for a number of days, and required me to give numerous live TV interviews at St Pancras each evening up until Christmas Eve. This was always an exhausting and sometimes harrowing task, with up to eight interviews in succession. I was kept going and encouraged afterwards as I walked around the station and talked to staff, who were all immensely supportive and grateful that I was being up front and trying to explain what we were all doing to put things right. As always, I drew strength and energy from their support. It is fair to say that everyone at Eurostar for several days afterwards was in a state of shock over what had happened, the scale of which was beyond anything anyone had previously experienced.

The contrasting attitude of the two Governments was also interesting. The French Government quietly insisted on appointing their own co-Chair to our inquiry, Claude Gressier, a senior civil servant and respected engineer. He worked closely and helpfully alongside Christopher Garnett in taking evidence but did not stand on ceremony as being a Government appointee.

In contrast when I tried to phone the UK Secretary of State for Transport, who was then Lord Andrew Adonis, I was told he too was on holiday and uncontactable, and was passed to the Duty Transport Minister, who happened to be Sadiq Khan at the time. He was barely interested in my reporting of the actual situation, but very angry when I said we had already set up an independent inquiry. He had clearly wanted to announce the setting up of an inquiry as his own and the Government's initiative.

Winning back passenger confidence

Our major priority as a commercial operator, not getting any subsidy from Governments, was to restore our passengers' confidence in our service. The independent inquiry was an important part of this, taking evidence from a wide range of affected passengers and interested parties. A generous package of compensation for affected passengers was equally important, by way of saying we were sorry for what they experienced. We fully refunded all fares, and paid the extra hotel, taxi and other bills that passengers had incurred as a result of the disruption and on top of that gave a £150 "we're sorry" gesture to affected passengers.

The most striking development was the extremely bad commentary about us that started to appear on social media and individual passenger blogs. In 2009 social media as we now know it was still in its relative infancy, so we had a lot to learn. Some of the commentary was pretty dire: abusive and personally threatening about me. I well remember our Commercial Director, Nick Mercer, saying to me that we needed to try to stop it as it could seriously damage our business. My answer was yes, but how? Nick then proposed we contact some of the most vitriolic bloggers and ask them whether they would like to meet in person with one of our Directors to tell us first-hand what they would like us to do to put things right. This is exactly what his team then set in motion, contacting several dozen of the people involved. To our surprise a good number said yes. I personally met the first half dozen or so of those who agreed to meet, with a colleague present to ensure we didn't miss anything.

I will admit I was pretty apprehensive as to how these meetings would go, given some of the very nasty abuse, some about me personally, that I had read in preparation. To my great surprise every one of them was as nice as pie face-to-face. They gave us their feedback, which in most cases we were already fully on board with, and came across as truly grateful to be given the chance to have their say. The last meeting I had was with someone who had not even travelled on any of the stranded trains, but had cancelled his pre-Christmas trip with his wife because he didn't trust us to get them there safely. He was one of the most abusive on-line, but again the conversation was cordial and went very well. So well, that at the end of the discussion I asked him if there was anything else he would like to say to us, immediately regretting this and thinking "now will come the venom". When he answered "yes there is", I metaphorically slid under the meeting table to hide. To my astonishment he said that he thought that we should be telling people more widely what we were doing with these meetings because he thought it was terrific!

This was a striking illustration of how people can have two, often hugely contrasting, even Jekyll and Hyde, personalities one on-line and one in the flesh. With the anonymity of on-line communication people are quite prepared to say things they would never say to someone's face. It is only scant consolation to those who are being trolled or abused on-line, but it is also a reminder that ultimately there is no substitute for face-to-face contact.

The good news for us at Eurostar was that the combination of the high profile independent inquiry and commitment to implement its recommendations, reasonably generous compensation and talking direct to passengers, meant that our customers seemed to forgive us and sales started to grow again year-on-year from the beginning of January. This was in stark contrast to both the media and politicians who continued to refer critically to our pre-Christmas melt down for many months afterwards

Our pre-Christmas debacle receded further into the background four months later when the Eyjafjallojokull Volcano erupted in Iceland causing huge and widespread disruption to flights for a number of days. On this occasion Eurostar was able to play a significant role in helping stranded airline passengers, helping to further redeem our reputation.

The experience also prompted a range of innovations in the way we communicated with passengers. "Never waste a good crisis" is a useful mantra for any organisation and I'm proud of the fact that we learnt a great deal and made a lot of changes as a result of the Christmas 2009 disruption. One of these was the routine capture of mobile phone numbers so we could text updates and any changes to a passenger's booked train ahead of their journey, and also communicate after travel if there had been any problems. This is of course now standard practice across a range of service industries. As well as arranging for volunteer call-outs of staff to reinforce the call centre and assist at stations, we also created a permanent role in our call centre whose full-time job was to monitor social media, so we could pre-emptively answer passenger queries or correct misconceptions in chat rooms and the like. This was supported by a new facility to update our website in real time during periods of disruption, to provide a further channel of communication with passengers. These are all of course standard practice for many travel companies now, but at the time were relatively cutting edge for train companies.

The aftermath

After our services got back to normal and Christopher Garnett's independent inquiry had reported, there of course followed a great deal of activity to implement his recommendations and fully learn the lessons. I recruited a full time Project Director to lead this programme of work, review all of our operational and customer service procedures and institute a programme of regular management rehearsals to simulate different possible disruption scenarios. This included re-equipping our crisis management room in our head office near to St Pancras with video links with Eurotunnel's control room and with Eurostar's Operational Control Centre in Lille. Managers could then talk instantly with key people rather than having to dial up and wait for an already busy person to answer a phone. Communications between the various parties had been significantly hampered by the need to rely on phones during the meltdown crisis, and by the fact that several key managers, not least Eurostar's Chief Operations Officer, Nicolas Petrovic were in Paris at the time and unable to talk face-to-face with colleagues in London for several days. And, of course, it included a range of modifications to Eurostar's train fleet to further strengthen their resilience to snow and extreme cold weather which were completed ahead of schedule by Eurostar's superb engineering team. To my knowledge there have not been any major further problems of this nature since.

In the event, most of the equipment failures that Eurostar's trains experienced on December 18th were found to have affected different components than previous incidents. At one level this was reassuring, that the various modifications that had been done over the years had been relatively successful in preventing further problems. But at another level it was a concern that despite all the good work done to date the trains had still been vulnerable to extreme weather conditions of cold and snow because of their unique operating conditions in the warmth and humidity of Eurotunnel. Most of the extensive programme of modifications was therefore aimed to protect key components from condensation or water from snow melt. One of the more important of these was the enclosure of the electronic control racks in a sealed locker, with a closed air system to cool them thus eliminating risk of interference from condensation or water ingress.

The recommendations of the Independent Inquiry were mainly for Eurostar itself to implement, not surprisingly as it was us who had commissioned it, and Eurotunnel had barely cooperated with it. But there were several recommendations for Eurotunnel, to review its procedures for train and passenger evacuation when there was no immediate safety risk, such as from a fire, improve its communications with trains in the tunnel and review its provision of rescue locomotives. This latter led them to invest in two additional rescue locomotives, to add to the two which it had in 2009 to rescue our five trains and one broken down shuttle.

The crisis also quietly underlined the importance of sorting out Eurostar's extremely cumbersome structure, which fortunately was achieved not long after (see Chapter 11). At the time Eurostar was still operated by each legally separate railway in their own country with each railway owning a number of trainsets and responsible for their maintenance. It transpired that the first train to break down in the tunnel was a Belgian owned trainset. As they only had three operational sets SNCB had subcontracted their maintenance to SNCF. But the contract did not cover winter preparedness as these measures had only been instituted after the contract was signed when Eurostar started operating. For some reason the SNCF maintenance depot at Le Landy had not completed the necessary winter modifications on this set, so it was highly likely to suffer snow ingress and breakdown. It was in turn the cause of the four other sets that broke down being held outside the tunnel in Calais, in what was then a very heavy snow storm. Considerable amounts of snow built up on the power car roofs of these trains, which would of course have quickly melted on entering the very warm tunnel, further adding to any problems of snow melt and condensation interfering with their electrical systems and increasing the chances of them too breaking down. It is interesting that a Paris train entered the tunnel in a "flight" immediately behind the first train to breakdown and was held behind the broken-down train for some time, but in the tunnel not outside in the heavy snow. This train did not break down and in due course made it successfully through to London.

It is not inconceivable that had that first train through been properly prepared for winter weather it might not have broken down, and the other four trains would have been able to enter the tunnel normally, without standing outside accumulating snow on their roofs, and might not have broken down either. I never shared this thought at the time, either publicly or with the partner railways, as it would have been too divisive and set off an unproductive blame game. But it was a reminder of the vital importance of having unified management control and responsibility for all aspects of Eurostar's operations including a single fleet of trains and clear responsibility for their maintenance.

It was also little realised at the time that Eurostar's UK train drivers were actually on strike on the day of the breakdowns and that the first train to break down was driven by one of our Driver Managers. This had a significant subsequent benefit as he was able to help the engineering teams extensively with their investigations and enquiries as to what had gone wrong, drawing on his long and detailed experience of Eurostar's trains. But it also generated some substantial bad feeling between the drivers and their managers as a member of their union had alleged to the media that the breakdown was caused by the Driver Manager's inexperience.

The strike was over the relatively trivial issue of their meal allowances in Paris and Brussels, which had not been increased for a number of years, and had largely been initiated by a new Local Union Representative who wanted to make a name for himself. Because of the bad feeling there was an understandable reluctance from the Operations Team to give the drivers what they were asking for, even after a further two days of strikes early in the new year. Given that everyone's focus at the time was totally on restoring our service and rebuilding passenger confidence no one on the management side was in a hurry to find a settlement, particularly as the local reps were demanding that the drivers involved got paid for the days they had been on strike! Few people in the company had much sympathy for what was seen as the drivers' selfish action. The impasse was broken by a call to me from the ASLEF General Secretary, the drivers' union, asking to meet me. He had the good sense to realise that his union's local representatives at Eurostar had gone out on a limb and that continuing the dispute could badly damage relationships. I agreed a settlement with him, without of course any payment for the days on strike, but over the heads of the Operations Management team, as there was little to be gained by letting the dispute fester. It was a small but telling example of the importance of having a separate channel of communication with the union, and as CEO, standing aside from the main negotiating forum to be available if necessary as a final backstop.

Some reflections with hindsight

Looking back at the disruption before Christmas 2009 we clearly let our passengers down badly, but could we or should we have foreseen what happened and prevented it or at least been better prepared to handle it? With hindsight we could have had better communication systems in place between the various parties that help run Eurostar - Eurotunnel, SNCF and Network Rail in particular. Had we done more regular crisis management exercises this would most likely have been highlighted as necessary as might some of the improved passenger handling processes that were put in place subsequently.

Because of Eurostar's complexity, operating in three different countries and dependence on the Eurotunnel link, we had regularly had to manage varying levels of disruption, for instance following the lorry fire in the tunnel in 2005, which disrupted services for several months, and during strikes in one or the other country. Crisis management was therefore relatively familiar to us and this probably made us somewhat complacent about the need for regular crisis management exercises and rehearsals.

It was also the case that some of the modifications that were implemented, particularly the closed air ventilation system for the electronic control racks, had already been under development before the Christmas meltdown, but the engineers had assumed that sufficient finance was not available and no investment proposal had been put forward. With hindsight a more open dialogue would have highlighted the opportunities and as CEO, I could have asked more questions and encouraged more open discussion of them. But given that Eurostar at the time was still loss making it is by no means certain that an investment case to its three railway partners could have been successfully made.

Overall, however, whilst what happened on December 18th and the following days could have been better handled, I don't believe it could have been reasonably foreseen or prevented. As is so often the case in major accidents and incidents there is seldom a single cause or point of failure, but a chain of events and circumstances that come together to cause it. What certainly didn't help was the complexity and fragility of Eurostar's structure at the time, underlining the importance of tackling this, as indeed was finally done in the next Chapter in Eurostar's story.

CHAPTER 11 Coming of age

By 2009 we had been running Eurostar for five years with "Jupiter without Jupiter". This was after the effective veto by the UK Government in 2004 of the plan to set Eurostar up as a proper international joint venture with a single, integrated management and corporate structure in all three countries. "Jupiter without Jupiter" meant pretending that an integrated structure was actually in place with me and my team taking responsibility for all aspects of Eurostar's service even though we had no formal legal basis for this other than on the UK side. But this virtual arrangement was beginning to creak. There was no ability to make other than very modest capital investments, certainly not in new trains or new routes, and growing uncertainty over the future of SNCB's involvement given their continuing substantial losses with no prospect of breakeven in sight. So, after the success of Eurostar's move to St Pancras and onto High Speed One, and continuing healthy growth in passenger volumes and revenues, the three Eurostar partners set about negotiating Jupiter mark two.

The negotiations between the railways, with three Governments standing behind them and having to approve the final arrangements, in principle in France and Belgium, and in detail in the UK, were inevitably complex and sometimes tortuous. The financial position of each railway was very different, and not in line with their participation in either Eurostar or the number of train sets they owned. For instance, SNCB owned four out of 31 Eurostar train sets, had a 5% stake in Eurostar, but its financial share of Eurostar's results was persistently loss making. The UK wanted to retain its 40% participation, but its share of the profits was way below this. The other partners also wanted some guarantees they would not be saddled with EUKL's pension liabilities. And so on.

Our role as the management team was to provide a long-term business plan and flex this as the negotiations evolved. It was also of course to design and negotiate the contractual terms for operation in France and Belgium, for instance the detailed terms on which French train crew would be seconded to the new company. Much of this was familiar territory for me having gone through a similar process in the setting up of the UK Train Operating Companies for Privatisation, but it was entirely novel if not alien to French and Belgian colleagues. It was particularly important to us to have sufficient capital in the company to be able to withstand the inevitable downturns in demand and a £100 million initial working capital injection was what was finally agreed. The process was inevitably long drawn out and tiring, and not a little stressful for us as so much was riding on a successful outcome, which was by no means certain right until the end.

From early on it had been agreed that on commencement of the new structure I would step down as CEO and become the Non-Executive Chairman of the new company. This was contrary to UK Corporate Governance practice, but very common on the continent. I think it was because I was long known and trusted by all the railway partners and new shareholders that they wanted me. By this time Guillaume Pepy had been promoted to be the President of SNCF, but had stayed on as Chairman of Eurostar in anticipation of the new company being agreed. As he very generously put it to me, he wanted to "keep the Chairman's seat warm" for me.

As Chairman designate I was particularly keen to design an effective Board structure. As the majority shareholder in the new company, SNCF had initially proposed having five shareholder Directors on the new Board, as was common practice on the continent. This would have meant that most of these Directors would be relatively supine, and left less space for more productive members. Likewise, SNCB wanted two shareholder Directors even though their shareholding was just 5%. I wanted to have a reasonable number of independent Directors to ensure Board discussions were objective and balanced and did not become solely based on shareholder perspectives. We eventually agreed to have three independent Directors, and in the interests of balance we appointed one each from the UK, France and Belgium. SNCF accepted having just two shareholder Directors, alongside LCR's two, and SNCB just one. In addition, we agreed three Executive Directors, the CEO, Finance Director and Commercial Director. All of this meant we achieved more of a UK-style Board structure which worked well in practice. The Board was given wide freedom of decision with only a limited number of key issues reserved for Shareholder decision in the final Shareholders Agreement. The agreed shareholdings were SNCF 55%, LCR (effectively the UK Government, who by then owned LCR) 40% and SNCB 5%. The Shareholders Agreement ensured that even though it owned a majority of the shares, SNCF did not control the company. This was to prove very important subsequently.

We appointed Nicolas Petrovic as CEO. He had originally come from SNCF and been with Eurostar since 2003, first as Customer Service Director and then my deputy as COO, and therefore knew the organisation intimately and was well respected in all three countries. Nick Mercer continued as Commercial Director and Nicolas brought in a new Finance Director from Cable and Wireless plc, James Cheesewright. I think there was some concern on the part of the UK shareholders about how the Chairman-CEO relationship would work, given I was moving from an Executive to a non-Executive role. In practice I had for some time been progressively handing over day to day management to Nicolas when still COO, so in the event the transition worked very smoothly.

The new Eurostar International Ltd company went live on August 31st 2010, roundly sixteen years after Eurostar services first started. It certainly felt like a "coming of age" for Eurostar and finally put in place a structure which allowed it to achieve its full potential. It marked the final completion of what I had originally been appointed to achieve, so was the ideal time to step back into a non-Executive role. What was particularly gratifying was how from day one the new management team and organisation beat the financial forecasts in the Business Plan against which the new structures had been negotiated. Whilst we had made progress in the "Jupiter without Jupiter" structure in reducing costs, the new team made rapid progress in achieving all of the efficiencies originally envisaged, and some. Inevitably there had been a significant degree of triplication of costs in some areas in the old structure, and all of this could finally be addressed and costs optimised across the three countries. And having a proper balance sheet at last meant that cash could be actively managed, and a healthy surplus started to be built up.

New trains at last

The most important initiative taken by the new company was unquestionably the decision to acquire some new trains and retire a proportion of Eurostar's original fleet of Intercapital trains. This was despite these trains only being sixteen years old, which was very young in railway terms.

In many ways they were a triumph of design, incorporating two entirely different power supply systems, one 25,000 volts alternating current and one 600 volt direct current, and four different signalling systems. This was all housed within just two rather than the normal four power cars for a TGV train and a very restricted envelope because of the much tighter loading gauge in Kent. But the consequence was that they were very difficult and expensive to maintain, with much longer downtimes to do this than would be usual, and they were not as reliable as we would have wished, as demonstrated in the Christmas meltdown in 2009, described in Chapter 10.

I well remember being asked by one driver at a briefing session for UK Drivers in 2004, quite soon after I joined, "when are we going to get some new trains Mr Brown?". This was when the trains had been in service for just ten years! Even then their limitations were clearly felt by staff. At the time, of course, Eurostar was hugely loss making, and my reply was that the trains were still very young in railway terms, would not need replacing for many years and I would be happy simply to have put Eurostar on a sufficiently sound financial footing to be able to afford to buy new trains. Needless to say, this reply didn't convince and with hindsight betrayed a lack of vision and ambition on my part.

The ambition came from Nicolas Petrovic who initiated and led the project to buy some new trains throughout. I remember reading Nicolas's first paper to the Board proposing to replace some of the train fleet and thinking that it would be remarkable if Eurostar pulled this off. I freely admit to having been sceptical about its chances of success. Much would depend on the price that could be achieved for each new train, what it would cost to maintain and what reliability and availability it might achieve. It would also depend on being able to raise the necessary finance when at that stage Eurostar did not even have a full set of audited accounts to show to potential financiers. It was indeed a remarkable achievement that Nicolas and his team pulled it off and bought 10 new trainsets, enough to retire 13 of the old fleet, and enough to run the whole Paris route service.

Only two train manufacturers expressed an interest in tendering for the new trains, Siemens of Germany and Alstom of France who were the lead manufacturer of Eurostar's existing fleet. I approached my contacts at

Bombardier to urge them to bid, and secure more competition, but they concluded that at that time they did not have a suitable design platform on which to bid. So it was a straight choice between Siemens and Alstom. At the outset some of us assumed that we would end up buying from Alstom, as Siemens was widely perceived as providing higher quality but significantly more expensive trains: "Siemens' Mercedes compared to Alstom's Peugeot". Would we be able to afford Siemens trains? How wrong we were!

Siemens convincingly outbid Alstom, broadly matching them on price but offering significantly better reliability and performance guarantees and more seats per trainset. The latter was a very important benefit as Eurostar pays for track access per train run, so the ability to carry up to 150 more passengers on each train for no extra infrastructure access cost made a big difference to its economics. Alstom did offer to match the seating capacity offered by Siemens but only by significantly cutting back on passenger luggage capacity, which would have been impractical for Eurostar's largely leisure travel market. We were really surprised by the quality of Alstom's offer, so surprised that at one stage I asked to see the UK President of Alstom to seek his reassurance that Alstom were actually serious in wanting to sell us some trains. I told him that everything that Alstom's bid team had offered so far appeared to indicate they weren't serious. Whatever feedback he gave to the Paris based bid team did not in the event make any great difference.

We set up a special sub-committee of the Board to consider the two final tender offers which was able to make a clear recommendation to the Board that we should buy from Siemens. The business case was so clear that as Directors I believe we would have been in breach of our fiduciary duty to have accepted Alstom's offer. But it was then that we entered the world of international politics! Siemens had a strong commercial incentive to win the tender and, as they saw it, break into a market until then dominated by Alstom and French manufacturers. In contrast, Alstom saw this as their territory, and had assumed that Eurostar being majority French owned would "buy French"; after all, few French companies, particularly those which are ultimately state owned, do other than buy French on such high profile procurements. So, when Alstom learned they would not be getting Eurostar's order, the balloon went up.

SNCF as our majority French shareholder come under immediate pressure from the French Government to not support the deal with Siemens. To a large extent the die was already cast as the Board had already formally accepted the business case to go with Siemens, but we still faced a long campaign from Alstom to block the deal. I learned a great deal about the realpolitik of international purchasing and the support given to "national champions" in Europe as the campaign unfolded! Step one for us was to get Board agreement to actually announce publicly the result of the competition, as the SNCF Directors were under pressure to delay any announcement, presumably to give time to Alstom to rebid or reconsider their position. This needed a special Board meeting which coincided with my summer holiday, so I had to chair the meeting over the phone from the cabin of the yacht we were sailing off the coast of Turkey!

Under UK law there is a standstill period after a procurement is announced for aggrieved parties to challenge the procurement. Alstom immediately announced they were seeking a High Court Injunction to block the deal, pending a full High Court hearing into the validity of the procurement process. This triggered the first of what turned out to be three High Court hearings, and resulted in the injunction being declined. This at least cleared us to agree final terms, sign contracts with Siemens and proceed with the procurement. But Alstom's campaign had only just begun.

Our next step had to be to get the Board's formal authority to sign contracts with Siemens. Although we were never formally told this I understand that the two SNCF Directors were threatened with dismissal by the French Government - SNCF's sole shareholder - if they approved the contract with Siemens. This of course threatened an impasse as such an approval required all three shareholders to agree under the Shareholders Agreement. Several special Board meetings were held to try to navigate through this and the eventual, ingenious solution was to agree a written resolution clearing the way for the next Board meeting to approve the contract. The two SNCF Directors resigned immediately before this Board meeting so as not to be implicated in the decision, but were re-appointed after a decent interval.

Alstom meanwhile had gone nuclear in seeking to block our purchase from Siemens. President Sarkozy had close contacts with Alstom, since his time as Finance Minister when he had arranged special financing after they had lost a lot of money on a major shipbuilding contract. Moreover, it turned out that the Bouygues Group were a major shareholder in Alstom and Monsieur Bouygues himself was a close associate and supporter of the President. The Elysee Palace was therefore mobilised to block Siemens. At about this time I did a briefing for the Board of LCR, then still our UK Shareholder, which of course covered the position on the Siemens purchase. One of their non-Executives was a former senior executive at GEC-Alsthom, from which Alstom emerged. He warned me, not very encouragingly, that of course Alstom would have set up a war room to fight our deal, with the implication that we needed to be aware of what we were up against. It made it feel a little like a David versus Goliath fight!

The Elysee instructed the French Vice President of the European Investment Bank to block the Bank's intended loan to Eurostar to help finance the new trains. This was a serious threat as we had lined up the EIB to be the anchor funder, advancing 50% of the total amount we needed to borrow; their absence would deter anyone else from putting up the finance we needed. We believed that the Elysee also leant on the French Rail Safety Regulator and on Eurotunnel to withhold or at least hinder the process of gaining safety approval for Siemens trains, which were of a significantly different design to those of Alstom. And finally, we learnt that President Sarkozy was going to raise the issue with Prime Minister David Cameron at their next summit meeting, presumably assuming that the UK Government would then pressure Eurostar to change its decision. To counter this, I briefed Sir Jon Cunliffe, then a Senior Policy Adviser to the Prime Minister who was extremely helpful and receptive. Likewise, Siemens briefed Angela Merkel's office in Germany.

In the end, none of these moves prevented us raising the finance or getting safety approval for our new trains but for some months they did hold up the procurement and they certainly cast a dark cloud over the whole process. It did feel as if the might of the French State was lined up against us and was a clear sign of how a national champion business such as Alstom could count on Government support.

In parallel with all this Alstom took us again to the High Court in London seeking to have our procurement process declared invalid. This exposed us to a whole new world of legal process, previously having had no experience of how a complex commercial law suit was handled. I had no idea of the range of moves and counter-moves of the parties seeking disclosure of evidence and the like ahead of the Court Hearing itself. We were very fortunate in having Burgess Salmon as our lawyers throughout who proved to be masters in the tactics and strategy of commercial litigation. They were a Bristol based firm of commercial lawyers who had developed a specialist practice in rail industry law after privatisation, hence their engagement to support our new trains' procurement. Not being a London based firm, certainly not a member of the so called "magic circle", I guess they had something to prove and they certainly gave us their all in representing us. They provided excellent advice at each stage and were patient in explaining how the court process worked and the options open to us.

One of Burgess Salmon's moves was to have a copy of Alstom's internal review of their bid disclosed to the Court, albeit redacted. This clearly revealed what we had suspected, that Alstom had put a "B" team onto running their bid, that is the team who normally prepared bids for SNCF's procurements. They had clearly assumed that since the new Eurostar company was majority owned by SNCF that it was also controlled by SNCF and therefore they would be the preferred supplier and a shoo-in to win the contract. The review identified a number of shortcomings in the way their bid was produced and undoubtedly helped influence the judge's decision at the end of the hearing process. In his final written judgement the judge memorably wrote that "to a significant extent Alstom were the authors of their own misfortune". He rejected Alstom's suit.

But having failed to block our contract with Siemens, Alstom still did not give up but proceeded to sue Eurostar for damages for loss of profit and damage to reputation to the tune of 500 million Euros. This was an interesting way to treat a potential customer! Had they succeeded it would of course have completely bankrupted Eurostar. It was another David and Goliath fight given Alstom were many times bigger than Eurostar as a company. I was very surprised they did this, particularly having already lost two rounds in the High Court, and the conclusions from their internal review. We had learnt that Alstom did make a practice of legally challenging other European procurements that they had lost, but this seemed to be an extreme reaction. I had a theory that their CEO had been only selectively briefed on the whole saga by the President of their Transportation Division, who had been trying to cover up his division's failure. I therefore prepared a long letter with the support of our lawyers, Chairman to CEO, setting out the facts as to what had actually happened, although in the event we decided not to send it. It might have spared Alstom the subsequent indignity of losing in court a third time.

The third High Court hearing which we also won was actually initiated by us. Burgess Salmon had identified that there was a case to be made that whilst we had conducted our procurement process in line with the UK's European Procurement Directive, we were not obliged legally to have done this. The argument was that Eurostar was not a utility within the meaning of the Directive, and that therefore the Directive did not apply to Eurostar. Burgess Salmon estimated that we had a least a 50% chance of success with this case, but that even if we failed it would not materially undermine our defence against Alstom's suit. So we accepted their advice and proceeded.

It was agreed that this time I would be a witness at the hearing and I was given a day's intensive training by a QC on court process and how to handle hostile cross examination. Part of the issue was whether Eurostar was in any way controlled or influenced by the UK Government. I was surprised and actually a little disappointed at how poorly Alstom's lawyers had researched their case, and how they had made a number of superficial assumptions as to how we operated, so I was very easily able to refute their QC's various assertions. I had expected a much tougher cross examination. It was nice to be able to beat top lawyers on their own ground, even if one was a little disillusioned at their quality.

We won our case with costs awarded in our favour, albeit these did not cover all of our expenses or the distraction to management. The purchase of our ten new trains from

Siemens could proceed and the blocks to financing and safety approval in due course fell away. It did feel as if Eurostar had indeed finally come of age, and had proved it could hold its own and thrive in the cut and thrust of the real world.

The financing of the new trains' purchase was in itself a remarkable feat as Eurostar International was still then a very new company, with no trading history and not yet even with any audited annual accounts. A straight commercial loan was the eventually chosen route rather than the more conventional option of leasing, this being simpler and more flexible. Securing the EIB as the principal funder, advancing half of the total needed, made it much easier to then assemble a consortium of lenders for the balance. Both the EIB and Credit Agricole, who were the lead bank in the consortium, were very helpful throughout. The lending banks looked principally at Eurostar's track record of actual and forecast revenue growth as the main measure of our financial strength, and of the market that the trains would serve - a nice compliment to the performance of the Commercial team in forecasting and delivering consistent top line growth over the years! The loan was also secured against the new trains, so if Eurostar had then failed financially, the banks would have been able to find a new operator to serve the market using their trains.

Having secured financing the next task was to agree a design for the train interiors. Nicolas Petrovic had already retained Pininfarina, the famous Italian design house best known for designing Ferraris, to prepare designs for the refurbishment of Eurostar's existing fleet. They proved to be an inspired choice as they were expert at considering passenger ergonomics and producing functional but very stylish work. Their concept for the First Class interiors, which catered primarily for business travellers, was to design each seat as if it was a travelling work station, with pockets and space for laptops and mobile phones as the key tools of the modern business person, with table space, too, for meal trays, coffee cups etc and adjustable spot lighting. In Standard Class they had designed a seat that reclined, had foot rests and an under-seat extension which could be pulled out to increase the length of the seat base to cater for taller passengers. This of course made the seats as good or better than many First Class seats in domestic trains. It was an easy decision to ask Siemens to use the same interior designs as Pininfarina had already produced. I have always been surprised that train manufacturers are generally very unimaginative in their choice of seat design, presumably seeing the engineering of the train itself as a more important focus for their skills; witness the relatively uncomfortable seats on the UK's new Thameslink trains, also built by Siemens. It is really important as a train operator to take a proactive role in seat and interior design not just leave it to the manufacturer.

Postscript

It was as the new trains were being built that I stepped down from the Board after my three-year term as Chairman, and severed my ties with Eurostar. Two events after I left gave me particular satisfaction, however, and I believe proved the strength of the integrated Eurostar business and the team that had been built up.

The first was the order for an additional six new Siemens trains. The first order had included a capped liquidated damages clause, to compensate Eurostar for each month that each new train might be late. In the event Siemens hit this cap because of significant problems with their in-cab signalling sub-contractor struggling to get the necessary technical approvals. Eurostar did not want cash to be paid for these damages as it was by then generating significantly more cash than in its business plan, and instead negotiated several extra sets to be supplied at an equivalent value. It also then used some of the cash surpluses it had been building up since the new company went live to finance the remainder. A fantastic deal, and a great reward for its financial performance.

The other event was the UK Government's sale of its 40% share in Eurostar, held through LCR Ltd. Rightly or wrongly it had long been UK Government policy not to hold onto shares in commercial enterprises and for most of my time at Eurostar the expectation was that they would want to sell at some point. The problem was of course that until the integrated company was set up the shares in EUKL were worthless, partly because of continuing losses and partly because EUKL was not in full control of its business. So when Eurostar International started to build up a financial track record the UK's 40% shareholding started to have real value. It was eventually sold in 2015 for £757 million, a far cry from EUKL's loss of £80 million in 2002. I felt some quiet pride in having helped the UK Treasury and taxpayers realise this £757 million in value, by turning a heavy loss into a sustainable profit.

CHAPTER 12 At the Board Table

After stepping back from a full time executive role at Eurostar I started a second, much shorter career as a Non-Executive Director on several different Boards including three directly involved in the rail industry. This gave me a privileged view of how things worked at the "top" of the industry, through a very different lens to what I was used to. It proved to be both a further interesting experience and an eye opener on some of the limitations on the role and influence of Boards particularly those in the Public Sector. My first appointment was to the Board of HS2 Ltd, then the Department for Transport and finally Network Rail. I was also Chairman of one of the larger London Housing Associations, a quite substantial business with 33,000 homes owned and managed and a £3 billion balance sheet.

My involvement with HS2 had in fact started much earlier, in 2008, when I was contacted by the Conservative Shadow Secretary of State for Transport, Theresa Villiers, who asked me whether Eurostar could assist with a review she had commissioned into the business case for a second UK high speed line to follow HS1. I of course said yes and we provided information on high speed rail operation and economics and introduced her team to people at SNCF too. The outcome was a proposal for a new high speed railway from London to Manchester and on to Leeds - a sort of "s" shaped line - presented to and adopted as policy at the Conservative Party Conference that autumn. Geoff Hoon was at that time the Labour Secretary of State for Transport and was reported to have been furious, saying that the policy "should have been Labour property" and "we've been asleep on watch" to let this happen. He was very soon afterwards moved to be Secretary of State for Defence and was succeeded by Lord Andrew Adonis as Secretary of State.

He quickly moved to set up HS2 Ltd as a subsidiary of the Department for Transport to take forward the development of the project and its business case. So the project always enjoyed cross party support and was in fact instigated by the Conservatives.

The first Chairman of HS2 Ltd was Sir David Rowlands, a recently retired Permanent Secretary of the Department for Transport who had not been seen as particularly supportive of railways. He appointed a hitherto unknown senior civil servant as Chief Executive, Alison Monro, who was well regarded within the Department but had no previous experience of major projects. I remember at the time a number of people in the rail industry assuming that the two appointments were an attempt by the Department to quietly kill the project. Against this expectation Alison proved to be a very capable Chief Executive bringing in several very competent planners and engineers to start to define the route and David Rowlands set up and chaired a number of "challenge panels", to critique and contribute to the project development process. I sat on the strategic challenge panel, which critiqued the option selection process. I was therefore already familiar with the project when I joined the Board in 2012 and, as one of the very few people in the UK who had ever run a high speed passenger railway, I suppose I was something of a shoo-in for the role.

Sitting on a Company or statutory Board as a Non-Executive or as Chair is a very different proposition to being an Executive on a Board. You have generally much less influence over what the company or organisation does or how it does it. Even as a Chair one's influence is limited. I well remember my Chairman at National Express, when welcoming me to the main Board as an Executive, explaining to me the key role of the Chair being to sack the Chief Executive if they were not performing adequately and then to find the right person to succeed them. Do those two things well and half the job of Chair would have been done, he said. In reality, of course, the role goes beyond that to ensuring the Board - executives and non-executives together - develops a coherent strategy for the organisation, keeps progress against it under regular review and takes those decisions reserved to the Board in an effective and timely way. The usual model is that the Chairman runs the Board and the Chief Executive runs the business. Ideally there will be a close working relationship between the two, with a high degree of mutual trust and the chair acting as something of a mentor and sounding board for the CEO with an occasional prompt or direction. The CEO is accountable to the Board, but between meetings it is in effect the Chair to whom they are accountable. The role of a Non-Executive Director (NED) is usually described as being a critical friend to the CEO and Executives, generally supportive of the business but critical and challenging when necessary.

Like most things involving real people the reality is seldom so simple. I came to learn for instance that one's ability to influence an organisation and its strategy as a NED is entirely dependent on both the Chair and Chief Executive wanting to "let you in", particularly the CEO being prepared to listen and utilise an NED's knowledge and experience. If the CEO is determined to keep the Board and its members at arms-length and merely to "yes" them as appropriate, then one's scope for impact as a non-executive is limited. And as a NED it is important to come across as supportive and constructive in one's suggestions and criticisms, that is as a friend even if critical.

Public sector Boards only partially conform to this model. For a start the Chair and usually other Board members too are appointed by the Government, or as a minimum their appointment is approved by the Government. In most cases Board members are selected by a public sector appointments panel who have little or no knowledge of the organisation whose Board they are selecting for or, more importantly, what background and experience might be particularly useful. The person specifications against which candidates are chosen are usually very generic, I suspect partly in order to be seen as inclusive and not discriminatory. This is taken to the point where experience in the sector concerned may even be seen as a drawback rather than an advantage. The result is that a lot of Public Sector Boards are made up of apparently worthy individuals who often lack the knowledge to be able to challenge and critique effectively and who can too easily accept what they are told by management. Diversity is an increasingly important criterion for selection and having what looks like a nicely diverse Board can begin to trump its real effectiveness. Add to that the facts that Public Sector Board Member pay is very low compared to the private sector and Board Members' influence is more restricted because of Government oversight and intervention, and the result is that it is very difficult to attract individuals with the right level of experience and knowledge.

When I joined the Board of Network Rail I was only the second person on the Board who had direct experience of running a railway, the first being Chris Gibb who had been COO of Virgin Trains and had had in depth rail sector experience before that. The weakness was made much worse by the fact that no one on NR's top management had had direct experience of running a railway either. Too often the Board did not know what questions to ask or what aspect of performance needed challenging. After a few months we were joined by Rob Brighouse who had been MD of Chiltern Trains and helped build railways in Hong Kong. When we then recruited a new CEO, Andrew Haines, who had been MD of both the Great Western Railway and South West Trains as well as CEO of the Civil Aviation Authority, the quality and relevance of Board discussions improved enormously. A much better balance of experience and backgrounds on the Board resulted.

This is not to say that Boards should be dominated by sector experience. As with a management team, what is important is to have a balance of skills and experience, ideally with several of the best people from the sector concerned as well as a number of people from entirely different backgrounds who can bring different perspectives and help prevent group think. Public sector Boards, however, are too often overwhelmingly comprised of the latter group. They risk becoming rubber stamps, providing window dressing for the organisation but potentially being more a burden than a source of advice and wisdom for management.

The approval process for public sector Board members has become incredibly centralised, requiring Cabinet Office and often No 10 approval, not just the approval of the sponsoring Government Department's minister. My appointment to the Board of HS2 Ltd nearly fell foul of this process. After my interview with the selection panel which consisted of the Board Chair, the then senior civil servant for the HS2 project and a member of the Civil Service Commission, I then heard nothing for ten weeks. When the DfT Director responsible for HS2 eventually phoned me to congratulate me my immediate reaction was that I must be the third or fourth choice candidate for them to have taken so long to get to back to me and I wondered whether I wanted the role on this basis. It was then explained that the excessive delay was caused by the approval sitting on the desk of someone in the Cabinet Office who was on leave and that I was of course the first choice candidate. It is quite normal for the process for Government approval to take a number of weeks, hardly conducive to securing top rate candidates. When I was recruiting senior people I would make a point of calling them on the evening of the interview or at the latest the day after to signal clearly that we wanted them, that the appointment was a priority and that as an organisation we did not hang about. The Government's cumbersome and leisurely approach to making appointments hardly inspires confidence and gives the impression of the appointments being anything but a priority.

Public sector Boards are not of course "sovereign" in the sense that they have final accountability for the performance of the organisation they oversee. As arms-length bodies created by Government, public sector companies or organisations are accountable to a sponsoring Government Department, and therefore to a Secretary of State. In the case of both Network Rail and HS2 Ltd, this was to the Department for Transport. This accountability can be quite blurred, sometimes through the Chair, sometimes through the Chief Executive and more rarely the Board, with both Ministers and Civil Servants involved in exercising it. The problem is magnified by few Politicians and Civil Servants really understanding the respective roles of chairs, chief executives and boards. Very often the role expected of the Chair starts to overlap with management, so putting a substantial additional burden on the chair and making it more of an executive than non-executive role, creating further ambiguity within the organisation. The role becomes closer to a full time one, which of course restricts its attractiveness and limits the range of people prepared to take it on.

HS2 Ltd Board

"Managing upwards" to the sponsoring Department is never an easy task and in the case of HS2 Ltd it was a huge one. Inevitably HS2 was always a very political project and HS2 Ltd was intended as the delivery arm for the Department, with policy and all key decisions the responsibility of Ministers. Very few decisions were ever wholly owned by the company's Board, most being either approved, changed or directly taken by Ministers and Civil Servants. There were several committees within the Department tasked with overseeing various aspects of the project, and all key decisions had to go through the relevant committee after "approval" at the HS2 Ltd Board and before going to ministers. Accountabilities were very blurred to say the least.

There were tensions around budgets and cost estimates from the earliest days. Governments and Civil Servants never like bad news so there was always a tendency to use the low figure from a range and pressure to low-ball estimated costs. Costs were always going to be spread over a considerable number of years, so there was often misunderstanding about the difference between constant prices and emerging prices after inflation, and the provision for potential cost inflation was always set by the Treasury at an unrealistically low level.

Taking forward the planning and delivery of HS2 was a huge undertaking, the scale of which was never properly appreciated. When I joined the Board the main work underway was finalising the exact route to be used between London and Birmingham and managing a huge public consultation exercise on this. A subset of the consultation was production of a detailed environmental impact assessment, the published report on which amounted to a 50,000 A4 page document to fulfil all the necessary legal requirements! This was on Phase 1 alone, with comparable documents following later on for Phases 2a and 2b, and of course it required wide involvement of a large number of environmental experts and ecologists. In responding to the issues raised in the consultation, Ministers added several billions to the estimated costs of the project, through the agreement to additional tunnelling for instance.

The next phase of work was preparing the necessary Parliamentary Bill seeking powers to build the planned line and then supporting its passage through the Parliamentary process. This too was a huge document, with much supporting material, and we were told at the time it was the biggest Bill ever to have been presented to Parliament. After detailed examination by both House of Commons and House of Lords Committees, who heard hundreds of objections, and in responding to them added hundreds of millions more to the estimated costs of the project, the Bill was in due course approved with a ten to one vote in support of it in the House of Commons. We understood this was the largest ever majority approval for any comparable Bill so there was again total cross-party support. The whole process was very professionally managed with a senior Civil Servant seconded to HS2 Ltd to lead the work.

What is not generally understood is that getting parliamentary powers to build HS2 is only the start of an almost continuous stream of more detailed approvals, literally thousands of them, from Local Planning Authorities, Government Agencies such as the Environment Agency and Natural England, for virtually every aspect of the programme: detailed design of bridges and structures, road closures, utilities diversions to name but a few. The administrative work involved undoubtedly added significantly to construction overhead costs.

With Parliamentary powers secured the land acquisition team was greatly expanded to manage the acquisition of several thousand separate parcels of land and properties under Government standard compulsory purchase procedures, another vast undertaking on a scale larger than anything since the motorway building programme. And once land had been acquired work could also start on preparing for construction, for example undertaking building demolitions and conducting archaeological excavations at potential sites of interest. The latter included exhuming a large number of graves in an old graveyard adjacent to Euston station where there were an estimated 40,000 remains to be individually exhumed, catalogued and re-buried elsewhere. It was estimated that at its peak this archaeological programme would absorb the whole of the

UK's archaeological resources. The scale of each packet of work for HS2 was quite simply enormous.

The role of the HS2 Ltd Board in all of this was not that of a normal Board at all, with all key decisions taken by Government and many tasks either following legally required processes or those prescribed by Government policies. The role was therefore more of an advisory one, as well as overseeing the performance of HS2 Ltd as an organisation and ensuring it was adequately resourced and supported. This included trying to ensure that the leadership of the organisation had sufficient flexibility to recruit people with the necessary experience and skills for such a mammoth project. Central to this was the level of remuneration and salary they were able to offer, which was consistently a bone of contention with Government. The latter was and still is obsessed with benchmarking all public sector salaries against the the salary of the Prime Minister. This salary has of course been artificially held down for many years, and did not reflect any of the very substantial "fringe benefits" including a free flat, country house, car and chauffeur etc. But hiring anyone with a salary above this very arbitrary level was a major issue, despite private sector salaries and remuneration packages being substantially more generous and few of the many specialist skills and experience we needed being available in the public sector. It took us nearly two years to get Cabinet Office and Treasury agreement for a limited package of delegations on pay and benefits for management to use. Before that, the organisation had to use an extensive number of individuals employed as short-term contractors which actually cost significantly more than if they had been directly employed. Even then Treasury approval was required for appointments and salaries above a certain level.

As one of the few British people who had actually managed a high speed rail service I saw part of my role to advise on how services on HS2 could be operated and managed once built. I fear I had very little effect on the Department's planning for this, despite convening a small group of UK experts to suggest options and issues that needed to be addressed. The Department opted for a "least change" approach in every case, including operating HS2 services as an extension to the existing West Coast Main Line franchise, with no real consideration of alternatives. I lobbied hard, too to persuade the Department to plan to use active revenue management and single leg pricing on HS2 services, as we had so successfully done on Eurostar and HS1, to maximise their appeal to budget conscious passengers as well as maximising revenue and load factors. Again, to no avail; when I left the Board the plan was still to replicate existing, very outdated, rail fares structures on HS2 services!

Overall, serving on the Board of HS2 Ltd was a very frustrating experience, with so little actual influence over decisions. Particularly frustrating was the restricted ability to promote the case for HS2 publicly. Until building HS2 became official Government policy, essentially when the Act was passed, HS2 Ltd as a Government owned entity was not allowed to promote the case, and ministers too were largely silent. This left it open for the opponents to "make the case", by focusing on the more easily challenged benefits and then exaggerating how small they were. Whilst the original case was always about the need for additional capacity on the rail network, providing relief for the West Coast, Midland and East Coast main lines, and, importantly, additional capacity for freight, the opponents focused on the journey time benefits, whilst drastically downplaying their size so as to belittle the overall case. It was always an uphill struggle after that to set the record straight in the media.

I served under four different chairs during my six and half years on the HS2 Board, and had my original five-year term extended twice to overlap with the handover to the last two chairs (one of whom was only in the role for four months).

It must have been even more frustrating for these chairs and required superlative diplomatic and influencing skills with Government to navigate the complexity of Departmental decision making and conflicting priorities. The most harmonious period was during Sir David Higgins' term as Chair, and when both the Prime Minister, David Cameron, and Chancellor, George Osborne, were strongly supportive of the project and it felt as if all parts of Government were working together.

For much of my time Sir Patrick McLoughlin (now Lord McLoughlin) was Secretary of State for Transport, who enjoyed the confidence of the Prime Minister and knew how to get things done within the Government. He was already the fourth Secretary of State to oversee the project since it was initiated in 2009, and inherited a number of decisions taken by his predecessors. He oversaw the massive task of successfully steering the Phase One Bill through Parliament and was always good to work with, listening to the arguments and prepared to trust his expert advisers. He had a lower profile than many other Secretaries of State but was undoubtedly one of the most effective behind the scenes.

As I write this, it is extremely sad and concerning that the current Prime Minister, Rishi Sunak, has taken a selective axe to the project, and in doing so risks severely curtailing its benefits. Most concerning is his "decision", apparently taken unilaterally within No 10 with no input from the Transport Secretary or anyone else, to halve the size of HS2's London terminus at Euston to just six platforms. If upheld it will halve the number of trains that could ever be run on the line, despite the rest of it being designed for twice the number of trains. Either fewer cities in the North will enjoy HS2 services, or their frequency will be restricted to the point of being unattractive. He also made completion of the Euston terminus being conditional on it being privately financed. This is particularly galling and ironic since as a Board we tried very hard to get the Treasury to agree to a number of different ways of introducing private sector financing to parts of the project, including Euston, all of which were rejected! It also seems perverse as the land for the original eleven platform station has already been acquired and cleared, so the costs saved from the downgrading cannot be large but the reduction in benefits particularly to cities north of Birmingham would be huge.

There are undoubtedly many lessons to be learned from the way the HS2 project has been taken forward and managed. But how to run such vast public sector projects is a huge subject of its own, way beyond the scope of this book. As a minimum it should be hoped that a way is found to proceed with a revamped Euston terminus, with its planned number of platforms. Without this the line will terminate at Old Oak Common, a station in a deep cutting with limited passenger capacity, that is remote from central London. It really would then be the "white elephant" it has often been accused of being. Ideally too, the Department for Transport and the Treasury should review how the benefits of such projects are appraised, particularly to assign real value to the additional freight capacity created as well as to the value of better regional connectivity. And for the longer-term there are clearly big questions as to what governance and delivery structure is likely to be more effective in progressing such mega-projects, and whether there are ways of streamlining the labyrinth of approvals required.

The Department for Transport Board

Compared to HS2, serving on the Board of the Department for Transport was much more pedestrian. As for all Government Department Boards, it was purely advisory and it was very much up to the Secretary of State and Permanent Secretary what use they made of it. To my knowledge I was the only person who had ever directly managed and led transport organisations to have served on the Board, certainly the only person with a rail and public transport background. The majority of Board members were typically retired partners of the big four accountancy firms. Unsurprisingly therefore our role was primarily to advise on how the Department was managed and to critique its performance rather than input to thinking or decisions on transport policy. We were spectators rather than players.

Two aspects of how the Department and wider Government worked particularly struck me. The first was the extent to which the Department was very much a part of the wider Civil Service. Senior Civil Servants moved to and from other departments relatively seamlessly and clearly owed their allegiance as much to the wider service as to the Transport Department. They were all very bright people but generalists first and foremost, meaning that corporate memory of transport policy and its evolution is not a strongpoint nor is knowledge of how the transport industries work. The Department was also subject to wider Civil Service policies and initiatives with surprisingly little influence over these. For instance, the Cabinet Office had signed up an outsourced provider of payroll and other HR services, with Transport being the first department to use it, in effect as a trial. The provider proved to be very poor on delivery, but with the contract being held and managed by the Cabinet Office, the Department had very little control over its performance or ability to hold the supplier to account. I had the impression that the Cabinet Office was one step further still removed from the real world.

The second striking thing was how risk was treated. Risk reporting was something of a cottage industry, with the risk register regularly updated and religiously reported and discussed at each Board meeting, but with rather less attention to potential contingencies or mitigations.

There was even less attention to probing or indeed rehearsing contingency plans, or updating them in the light of experience or new information. A major pandemic was always one of the top risks and subsequent experience with Covid revealed these weaknesses in contingency planning across Government as a whole rather clearly.

The Board only very rarely strayed into any discussion of actual transport issues and these tended to be very superficial. I recall one discussion about how to provide capacity for more container freight trains to and from the Port of Felixstowe, where several expensive options were being considered including double tracking the branch line to the Port. I suggested that one option could be to make it a freight-only branch and withdraw the extremely lightly used passenger service on the branch to free up capacity for container trains. In terms of wider transport policy this would take far more lorry traffic off the roads with minimal cost but it was dismissed as unthinkable. I suspect this was because the Department was now in practice fully responsible for and directing the passenger railway and therefore unwilling to contemplate any worsenment in services on its watch, whereas had the old British Rail proposed this they would have been happy to let BR to proceed.

The most interesting part of the role was when one was asked to undertake a review or provide advice outside of the formal Board process. I led two such reviews, the first into the Department's approach to rail franchising after the collapse of the competition to re-let the West Coast Main Line franchise in 2012, which I describe in Chapter 16, and the second into the resilience of our various transport networks to extreme weather after the winter storms and flooding in 2013/14. Whilst many of the issues around rail network resilience were familiar to me, I learned a huge amount about airport and seaport operations and their resilience, and the challenges that highways authorities face on the road network, all of which was included in our report back to Government. But most of the resulting actions were the responsibility of the various port and network operators not the Department and I am not sure many of the recommendations were ever acted upon. I fear our report quite quickly went on to the shelf to gather dust. Interestingly it was a Cabinet Office Minister, Sir Oliver Letwin, who took far more interest in our review than any Minister from the Transport Department.

One of the recommendations of my Review of Rail Franchising was that the Department set up an advisory board to help guide the implementation of the Review and subsequent evolution in franchising policy. I therefore chaired the resulting Panel for several years, initially reporting periodically to the Secretary of State. This more than anything else gave me an insight into how the civil service operates and its organisational culture, which I describe in Chapter 15. The role of the Panel gradually reduced, with the influence of the wider Department and the Government's approach to procurement and contract management slowly supplanting it, so eventually the Panel was wound up.

The Network Rail Board

My time on the Board of Network Rail was much more interesting but barely more influential. It was very much a tale of two halves. The first half was when Mark Carne was Chief Executive. Mark had spent his whole career before Network Rail in the oil industry and with Shell, mainly involved with big oil and gas projects. He was very supportive, even protective of Network Rail's project side, but never really "got" the intricacies or challenges of operating a railway network. I found myself regularly challenging him on operational issues such as the reporting of Network Rail caused train delays. For instance, Board reports showed a steady reduction in the number of Network Rail incidents or equipment failures causing train delays and management took this as a clear measure of success. But the average minutes delay to trains caused by each incident were rising even more sharply so the resulting train punctuality was actually declining. There was no reporting of how long it was taking to rectify equipment failures or how well Network Rail controllers were working with Train Operators to restore normal services as soon as possible and minimise consequential delays.

The second half was after Mark Carne retired and Sir Peter Hendy (now Lord Hendy) as Network Rail Chairman managed to attract Andrew Haines as the new CEO. Andrew had in depth experience of the rail industry and enjoyed the confidence of Government having successfully run the Civil Aviation Authority for a number of years. One felt one's role as an NED became much more of a truly critical friend and supporter, than one of an outsider, with a common language finally being used. Andrew understood that Network Rail was a very centralised organisation and so an early priority was to devolve much more responsibility to its regions, and to new Route management teams that he created within each region. I readily supported this having previously been something of a lone voice pressing Mark Carne to go much further with his own, much more limited move to devolve responsibility to regions. As a Board we were able not just to support Andrew's initiative but to offer useful advice on how to shape it.

Almost immediately after Andrew Haines' appointment the then Secretary of State, Chris Grayling, set up a strategic review of the whole rail industry led by Keith Williams, a former Managing Director of British Airways. This of course led to a substantial degree of "planning blight" for Network Rail and a constraint on our deliberations as a Board, as we would not know what Network Rail's position within a reformed industry structure would be until the review was published and resulting decisions taken by Government. We also did not know at the time that the Review would not be published for nearly three years. The role of both the Board and management therefore became much more of that of caretakers, with only limited change being sensible pending the outcome of such a major review. It was a classic case of a well-intentioned Government initiative putting a major brake on change and reform because of subsequent political indecision and changes in ministerial leadership.

Nevertheless Andrew Haines, supported by the Board, embarked on a substantial programme to improve Network Rail's efficiency and reform its culture. The former involved tackling long standing inefficiencies in maintenance working practices and the latter to ensure Network Rail put passengers and freight customers first. There was still a tendency inherited from Railtrack to see the Office of Rail Regulation (ORR) as Network Rail's main "customer", as they determined how much revenue the company would receive over each five-year control period. Certainly, in practice the ORR had an all pervading influence over virtually every aspect of Network Rail's activities within what has become a very demanding and resource consuming regulatory regime. Andrew's initiative could not change this but at least it refocused people's minds on passengers and freight customers as being the reason the organisation existed. I am not sure that, even now, either the Government or wider industry appreciate the extent of the ORR's influence on Network Rail's behaviour or priorities for spending or management attention.

A particular area where ORR's influence has become all pervasive is safety, arguably to the point of being detrimental to rail's overall performance. At privatisation, Safety Regulation of the railways rested with the Health and Safety Executive but after the Hatfield accident responsibility passed to the ORR. The idea was that having a single regulator for both economic and safety performance would lead to a better balance between the two. In practice the economic side of the ORR has never moderated or influenced the approach of the safety side so that safety regulation remains unfettered by economic considerations. Safety has become an absolute requirement regardless of cost. This is a huge change from the situation BR faced before privatisation where safety spend and investments were subject to cost benefit appraisal alongside other investments. Safety schemes had a cost per equivalent life saved benchmark to meet, as do all road investment schemes funded by Government even now. This was in recognition that there was not an infinite pot of money to spend and to ensure it was spent on those things which produced the best safety improvements.

We saw a glaring example of this misalignment between safety and economics at the NR Board when we were being asked to make a billion pound plus saving in NR's spend over the last two years of the 2014 to 2019 control period, to contribute to wider Government public expenditure cuts. Management concluded that the main savings would best come from spend on structures and earthworks, as these would have least impact on train service performance. The Board properly asked for a safety impact assessment before endorsing the proposal. It was reported back to the next Board meeting that the cost per equivalent life saved would have been between £800 million and £1.5 billion if the original spend had continued, an incredibly high figure. The Board of course then endorsed the proposed spending cuts as representing a negligible safety risk, but the ORR's safety chief persisted in maintaining this was the wrong thing to do. The irony has been that as the industry's safety performance has steadily improved safety regulation has not stood back, but with fewer and fewer safety problems or accidents to address it has become involved in an ever more detailed and zealous way. This is not of course to argue that safety is not of paramount importance, but that in a sector that is extensively supported by public funds that are not limitless, cost effectiveness must also be a requirement. The concern must be that the unmitigated priority given to safety has quietly added to the industry's cost base and undermined its economics, so reducing its ability to attract passengers and freight off much less safe road transport.

In conclusion all my experience around the Board table is that Boards have much less influence over how an organisation performs than is generally appreciated, certainly by many politicians and the wider public. It is the CEO and management who overwhelmingly determine this and are the key players. The Board's role is to appoint, support and if necessary change the CEO and hold management to account. But to be effective in holding management to account they need to know what questions to ask and to have enough understanding of the organisation and the work it does to spot potential problems. This requires some Board members having real sector experience. Without this, Boards are too dependent on the CEO and management to keep them appropriately and properly informed and are at risk of missing issues. In the rail industry Boards have even less real influence because of the overarching influence of Government and the power and influence of Regulators.

The end of my own time on the Board of Network Rail was a further example of the Government's and politicians' lack of understanding of how Board's need to work. I had originally been appointed to the Board by the Government itself, as their Special Director, when Sir Patrick McLoughlin was Secretary of State. After four and a half years and a new Secretary of State, it was decided to replace me with a senior member of the Government's Shareholder Executive, a very able merchant banker on secondment to the Treasury. But both the Chairman and Board wanted me to stay on and fill a different vacancy, as I was seen to be making a valuable contribution with my in-depth rail sector experience. This reappointment required Government approval, however, and the minister concerned decided that a "fresh face" was required, meaning someone without a rail sector background! It was a classic case of "experts" or relevant experience being neither valued nor wanted.

PART 3

CHAPTER 13 How to organise a railway - the evolution of BR's organisational structure

It is a fact of life in many large organisations that there are regular changes in structure through reorganisation. In the private sector this may be driven by a new CEO or owner who sees a different way of doing things, a drive to cut costs or reduce tiers of management, or respond to shifting requirements in the market, or just to adjust spans of control of top management. Similar forces affect the public sector, with the addition that regular changes in the responsible minister, as well as in Governments too, often create a need to be seen to be making "improvements" or "reforms", simply to be seen to be "doing something". The UK National Health Service is perhaps the prime example, with periodic major changes in the way it's organised in the vain hope that its performance will be improved. There is also the on-going tension between centralised and de-centralised structures, and between geographical, functional or product based structures.

British Rail was of course no exception to this and in my 19 years with it I experienced three very different structures in the way the railway was organised, with major reorganisations to move from one to the next. The principal drivers of these changes were the need to cut costs and, increasingly, to improve the performance of the industry and become more customer orientated. What was different in the case of British Rail was that these reorganisations were all broadly moving in the same direction and each built on what went before rather than reversing it. Rather than seeking to follow the latest organisational fashion the series of changes amounted to a veritable revolution in how the railways were organised, inventing an entirely new structure different to any other railway around the world. There were of course those within the organisation who were cynical about the changes, who would from time to time quote the anonymous (and in fact mythical) Roman General who complained that "when we reorganise we bleed" and argue that the costs and disruption outweighed any benefits. They were a minority however and were proved wrong in practice.

The railway that I joined in 1977 was organised wholly on geographical lines with four main tiers of management, areas, divisions, regions and Board HQ. This was changed to three tiers at the beginning of the 1980s, with abolition of divisions, and mergers of areas to create larger units. This was principally about reducing administration costs with an estimated 10,000 jobs removed, but still geographically based.

The next change was the creation of five business sectors nationally in 1982 to provide commercial leadership for different groups of markets - three passenger sectors, InterCity, London and Southeast and Regional, together with Freight and Parcels. This was quickly followed by the creation of sub-sectors within each region reporting to the sectors nationally. The sectors and sub-sectors were solely focussed on commercial management, with train service delivery still the responsibility of the Regions and Areas. This was the first step in Sir Bob Reid's "railway revolution" well described by George Muir in his book of the same title ([3]). The driver was the need to improve the commercial performance of the railway and have a number of managers

---

[3] "Bob Reid's Railway Revolution: Sir Robert Reid, how he transformed Britain's railways to be the best in Europe", George Muir, Unicorn Publishing, 2021

who were accountable for the financial performance of their sector or sub-sector, with costs properly matched to revenues for the first time. Until then the Chief Executive of British Rail could rightly point out that costs and revenues only came properly together at his level.

The final step before the industry was privatised in the mid 1990s was the creation of Profit Centres within each sector, with train service delivery and infrastructure management the responsibility of these Profit Centres as well as commercial management. This was what came to be called a vertically integrated structure with each Profit Centre responsible for the totality of its business - revenues, costs, service quality and most of the track it ran over - and trading with each other where services ran onto another Profit Centre's route. Each Profit Centre was a business in its own right, ensuring a much stronger focus on the industry's markets and customers and with real accountability for both financial and physical performance. This was a market or product-based structure, and was a world away from the totally geographical and production-led organisation of the 1970s.

Each of these different organisational structures was an evolution from the one that went before, but in aggregate amounted to a true revolution in the way the British railway industry was organised. Each was conceived as a response to the perceived strategic needs of the industry at that time and each step was designed to address the shortcomings of its predecessor and better support the evolving strategic direction the industry needed to move in. As Britain's rail industry faces a new period of strategic change with the intended creation of Great British Railways (GBR), or the "Integrated Rail Body" (IRB) as the draft Parliamentary Bill referred to it, it is interesting to reflect on the strengths and weaknesses of each model for clues as to how GBR might best be organised. The needs and strategic direction of today's rail industry are of course different so none of these organisational models would either be wholly appropriate or practical, but there are nevertheless likely to be some broad principles and approaches that could usefully be adapted and applied.

The backbone of GBR organisationally will be Network Rail (NR), as its biggest component part by far, and of course NR is organised geographically with five regions which are strikingly similar in their geography to British Rail's five regions in the run up to sectorisation some 40 years ago. The experience and pros and cons of this structure are therefore of direct relevance today. BR's five regions had evolved directly from the four large pre-war railway companies - LMS, LNER, GWR and Southern-with the Scottish Region taking over the Scottish parts of LMS and LNER. The regional structure had itself undergone some evolution, with Areas replacing Districts, a large shrinkage in the number and role of Station Masters, and the existence for a while of a sixth region, the freight intensive North Eastern region alongside the Eastern Region and latterly an Anglia Region immediately prior to the setting up of Profit Centres. But the broad thrust of the structure remained constant.

A big advantage of the regional structure was that it was well understood - as it should have been given its long evolution - both internally and externally. Being geographically based it broadly matched Local Authority and Parliamentary Constituencies so appeared accessible to local communities and their representatives. It also made operational sense in an era when the railway was still much more "mixed use" in any one locality, with many passenger stations also handling volumes of parcels and sundries and being responsible for some small freight flows to local sidings, and freight traffic in general being shorter distance than now.

The focus then was much more on running trains with less differentiation between different types of trains and in particular different passenger markets and needs. This was reinforced by the rather uniform and overweening corporate image developed by British Rail which tended to encourage the perception that "a train was a train" regardless of what it carried, or more importantly its value, and that passengers were a homogeneous market. The structure produced a lot of generalists who knew how to run trains but rather fewer people who had a true market focus and understood the often very differing needs of different markets and customers. Some progress was made in the Beeching era with the creation of the Intercity Brand for express passenger services, but there were few managers whose jobs focused solely on Intercity services and these few were relatively lower down in the hierarchy.

Overall the industry was very production orientated, more focused on running trains than on meeting the changing needs of passengers and freight customers. The pre-war Railway Companies had clearly had a more commercial approach, of necessity, because they were listed companies needing to make a profit to survive, but these commercial skills had been very blunted by nationalisation. The hierarchical and somewhat militaristic culture of the industry post nationalisation also did not encourage a more commercial or market orientated approach. Board Directors and Regional General Managers were godlike figures, far removed from regular contact with customers, other than perhaps the very largest freight customers. And the hierarchy did not facilitate upwards communication of any detailed intelligence or trends in customer needs, so at the top there was at best only a very broad and un-granular appreciation of market trends and performance.

The hierarchy was best summed up for me when I first joined by the arrangements for catering at the BR Board Headquarters. There were five grades of catering: a canteen, a Junior Officers Mess, a Senior Officers Mess, a Chief Officers Dining Room and a Board Members Dining Room! There were even three types of toilet: Ladies, Gentlemen and Officers! Each level was very status conscious as I found out when I was appointed as Personal Assistant to one of BR's two joint Managing Directors. I was given the lowest grade of Senior Officer but because my job was not a minuted one the Mess Committee initially declined to accept me as a member. My boss complained, partly I think because he felt his own status was besmirched, but when the Committee changed their mind I'm afraid I then declined to join: a young man's pique perhaps! More importantly these arrangements of course limited the scope for informal communication up or down the hierarchy, although it did facilitate peer to peer dialogue.

But what the old structure most lacked was any responsibility for true bottom line performance below Board level. Regional General Managers did have both cost and revenue budgets, but the revenue budgets were for revenues originating in their region, alongside the costs which fell within their region. But a proportion of revenues were for services which ran on to other regions, and a proportion of costs were for services whose revenues originated elsewhere. There was no proper matching of the total costs of a route or service with the revenues it generated, so that informed decisions could be taken by a responsible manager on service levels, investment needs, pricing etc., or indeed whether the service was worth running at all.

It was to correct this last weakness that BR created its five business sectors in 1982. Each of the five Sector Directors, as they were initially called, had financial bottom line responsibility for the groups of services included in their sector, and every service was allocated to an individual sector. And this was quickly followed by the appointment of sub-sector managers within the regions who in turn had bottom line responsibility for a group of the sector's services, even where these spanned more than one region. For example, I later became the InterCity Manager in Birmingham within the London Midland Region, responsible for two sub-sectors, the West Coast Main Line extending from London Euston through to Glasgow and Inverness in Scotland, and the Midland Main Line extending from London St Pancras onto the Eastern Region in Sheffield and Leeds. I was also later to have responsibility for InterCity's Cross Country sub-sector which embraced a wide range of services from Scotland, the Northeast and Northwest through Birmingham to the Southwest, South Coast and South Wales and running through all five regions. Both Midland Main Line and Cross Country were cinderellas under the old structure with confused commercial approaches and sub-optimal train service patterns, and no one looking at their potential overall. Because there was no management team or leader to provide a focus and foster any pride in the routes it is also fair to say that staff saw the routes at best as of secondary importance and did not really identify with them.

Both the sectors and sub-sectors were relatively slim organisations but soon began to have a substantial impact on the industry's financial performance. Around thirty senior managers were now taking decisions based on their bottom line impact and striving to drive improvements as they got to know their "business" and its opportunities and weaknesses. The sectors and sub-sectors were responsible for specifying what timetable and train services they wanted to run, setting fares, prices and marketing strategy, allocating rolling stock and sponsoring new investment: all key decisions affecting bottom line financial performance. The Regions were still responsible for actually delivering the train service and maintaining all of the railway's physical infrastructure. This organisation left intact the industry's geographically based "production" organisations, but it was now market led.

The bulk of costs were actually managed at Area level, for both operations and engineering departments, and here too costs were increasingly allocated to individual sub-sectors. Area expenditure budgets had to be signed off both by the relevant Regional Chief Officer or Engineer as well as by the sub-sector manager to whom they had been allocated. In effect this was a matrix structure with both solid and dotted reporting lines and an elaborate process of challenge and negotiation to agree budgets between the sub-sectors and areas quickly evolved. In due course every individual post, at stations, train crew depots and signal boxes, was allocated to a sub-sector and if no sub-sector was prepared to underwrite it the post was expected to be removed. And every item of engineering expenditure was underwritten by a sub-sector. In parallel with the changes in organisational structures, the industry's management accounting and information systems also underwent a comparable revolution. The attribution of costs and revenues became more and more refined and detailed, alongside understanding of the cost drivers, giving managers the information they needed to take good decisions and track their impact.

The process inevitably required a good degree of constructive engagement and collaboration and not all managers responded as well as others. But where the engagement was strong a very productive relationship often developed, with "investment" of additional expenditure in things which improved the service for passengers, such as enhanced attention to maintaining coach air conditioning systems, traded off against savings elsewhere, creating a "win-win" outcome for both parties and for customers. By this time British Rail had been managing costs down for many years and managers were adept at making continuous incremental savings. For instance, whenever a post became vacant managers would first look at merging it with another role or removing it altogether before considering filling it. Undoubtedly this long-standing culture helped smooth the process since most managers were already well attuned to reducing costs and the sub-sector challenges often helped them to better prioritise opportunities.

Inevitably there were cases where the spending manager did not play ball with the process. After a couple of years the process was extended to include the review of British Transport Police Divisional budgets. I well remember the first budget review meetings with at least two Divisional Superintendents who turned up to the meetings in full dress uniform, clearly trying to intimidate and send a message that they were not up for challenge! Every query about an item in their budgets was met with the assertion that it was a statutory responsibility and therefore non-negotiable and every suggestion of alternative things they might do prompted a request for new money to pay for them. But overall the process worked pretty well, with most managers engaging constructively and resulted in widespread downwards pressure on costs and improved efficiencies in a way that protected or even helped revenues.

The sectors and sub-sectors were by no means all about reducing costs, although this was an important outcome, but particularly in the case of InterCity and Network Southeast were equally focused on growing passenger numbers and revenues. Chapter 3 has already described a number of the initiatives that InterCity implemented during my time. And in the case of the larger routes the focus went below sub-sector level with Route Managers appointed for individual services. As InterCity sub-sector manager in Birmingham for instance I had four Route Managers reporting direct to me, three for the West Coast Main Line, for services to and from the West Midlands, North West and Scotland and one for the Midland Mainline. They had no staff of their own but operated within a mini matrix, drawing their support from the small terminals, service planning, infrastructure and marketing teams within the Sub-Sector. Later on, we appointed a fifth Route Manager responsible for what by then were our two large Anglo-Scottish sleeper trains: someone who was a night owl by temperament, as most staff of course only worked nights.

The Route Managers role was to live and breathe their route, getting to know the stations and communities served, building relationships with local production managers and staff, so as to be the sub-sector's eyes and ears picking up problems and opportunities. They were responsible for recommending what train service pattern would best serve the route, identifying local investment opportunities and needs, inputting to fares changes and marketing programmes, as well as leading budget negotiations with local managers and engineers. In effect they were local ambassadors for InterCity, senior people with significant executive authority. They became powerful and passionate champions and advocates for their route. For most of my time in Birmingham InterCity was unexpectedly seeing growth in passenger volumes which could barely be accommodated with the minimal level of train service we inherited. The Route Managers were instrumental in identifying low cost ways of increasing train service frequency to accommodate and further encourage growth as described in Chapter 3, as well as in identifying potential solutions to pinch points in capacity, for instance in station car parks. I have no doubt that the granularity of their understanding and stewardship of their routes was a very important contributor to InterCity's success and the power of the sub-sector approach.

Two other initiatives also contributed to the success of the sector and sub-sector structure. The first was BR's Total Quality Management (TQM) programme, seeking to apply the teachings of W. Edwards Deming and others to how BR operated. It was launched by a programme called "Leadership 500", a series of week-long courses which was required attendance for BR's most senior 500 leaders across all departments to teach the key components and techniques of TQM with a strong focus on the importance of ensuring effective teamwork. This was immediately followed by "Leadership 5000" for middle managers covering similar ground. The Leadership 5000 courses were run by each Region, but with strong sub-sector input. I gave an evening talk to a large number of them followed by an extensive Q and A session for instance. The two sets of courses helped develop a common language across the organisation as well as a shared understanding of the importance of teams. The unstated mantra was that sectors, sub-sectors and TQM were a better way of running the railway. The programme was kept fresh and alive by a cadre of TQM Managers in each main organisational unit, with a national Director of TQM, Brian Burdsall, providing strong leadership.

The other initiative helping to ensure the success of sectorisation, and the subsequent creation of sector-based Profit Centres, was the programme of Safety Management launched by BR as part of its response to the Clapham Junction rail crash in 1988 when 35 people were tragically killed. This was a comprehensive programme addressing all aspects of safety management, in turn requiring all senior managers who would have safety responsibilities to attend and pass a safety leadership course. The sharp focus this put on improving the industry's safety management performance made sure that safety was not compromised during reorganisation as it might otherwise have been, and again helped a common language between the production and business sides of the industry. One of the many innovations of the Safety Management programme was the requirement for Safety Validation of all significant organisational changes. The Management Team of any new organisational unit had to produce a detailed document showing how safety responsibilities migrated from old to new, and how the new organisation would discharge its safety responsibilities in detail. The validation was performed by an external panel to ensure rigour and challenge, and the new unit could not go live until passed by the panel.

Whilst this structure of business leadership by sectors and production delivery by regions generated much positive change in the industry's performance it required managers to navigate what was a complex matrix arrangement, with many managers having both solid and dotted line reporting lines. The difference between solid and dotted line often became blurred and working successfully within the matrix required a significant amount of patience and forbearance, as well as what felt like a lot of meetings. It is fair to say there was a growing dislike of the ambiguity it involved and a yearning to return to a more traditional style of solid line reporting within a vertical structure. It was also the case that as the business sectors and sub-sectors grew in knowledge and confidence they became increasingly directive and demanding in their requirements and specifications to the regions and areas. This produced frustration on both sides, with sectors wanting greater control over delivery and the more forward-thinking production managers wanting greater input to business decisions or to actually become part of the business itself.

Out of this situation came a slowly developing consensus of the need for a final, even more radical, organisational evolution into what became known as "Organising for Quality" (OfQ). This involved transforming the sub-sectors into some 25 Profit Centres directly responsible for operation of their own train services and with bottom line responsibility for all aspects of their performance. Profit Centres owned and were responsible for maintaining the majority of the track infrastructure their services ran over, together with most of the stations and depots they used. In short, they were fully fledged train companies, albeit all owned by British Rail. The Profit Centre Directors and their management teams were therefore responsible for both commercial and operational delivery, track and train, in what was a vertically integrated structure.

Debate on the need for further change started in 1989 and intensified in 1990 with detailed planning commencing that year as a critical mass of managers came on board with the direction of travel. It then took nearly two years to plan and implement the large scale of change required. As an example, I was appointed in 1990 as designate Profit Centre Manager for the Midland Cross Country Profit Centre, took up the role full time at the beginning of 1991 with go live of the new organisation not taking place until April 1992.

The OfQ structure was of course short lived as just a few weeks after it went fully live the Conservatives won the May 1992 election with a manifesto to separate track from trains and break up and privatise the industry in a large number of component parts. OfQ was therefore in place and active for only two years and most energy during this time was devoted to the further major reorganisation in preparation for privatisation rather than driving through the benefits of the new structure. It was therefore never truly "road tested", in particular as to how well it would have coped with the inevitable tensions of Profit Centre sharing much track and facilities but with diverging longer-term strategies.

But the large majority of managers who worked within the OfQ structure would say that it was the best organisational structure they ever worked in. For most of us it felt hugely invigorating running a fully integrated railway with responsibility for and control over everything to do with running the service, accountable for all aspects of performance: financial, safety, reliability and customer satisfaction. For the first time there were 25 Profit Centre Directors who all had to directly juggle the often conflicting priorities of safety, service reliability, finance and customer needs and manage the financial consequences within their budgets. There was no hiding place on who was responsible for train delays or cancellations, with no scope for the blame game between Train Companies and Railtrack which was seen to follow privatisation.

We could quickly see the results of our decisions and interventions. It cut out a lot of the meetings required by the previous matrix organisation and made for quicker, sharper decisions. It became possible to optimise spending, for instance on measures to improve train punctuality, across all teams and departments, if necessary moving money from track to train maintenance or vice versa without having to go through several negotiations first. It was also much easier to vary the times that the engineers were given "possession" of the track to undertake maintenance work, because all the variables involved were within our control. It was possible to directly trade off the disruption to passengers and potential loss of revenue because no trains were running against the potential saving in maintenance costs, or faster fixing of a track problem. Communication both upwards and downwards within the organisation was much quicker and more effective, so local problems or opportunities to improve the service were much more readily apparent and therefore acted on.

Perhaps most importantly the structure allowed everyone to more clearly see how their particular team or department fitted in and contributed to the end service for passengers, so fostering a sense of shared endeavour and achievement. It ensured a strong alignment of everyone involved to an identifiable and understandable market and set of customers. This was particularly motivating for those staff whose roles were furthest away from any contact with passengers. In my profit centre for instance, I well remember how enervated the Plant Services Team was with the structure and how they relished their newfound visibility and leadership attention. Their role was to maintain the kit used by other technical departments, making them even further removed from any customer contact and very remote from the running of the trains. But their role was just as important as many more visible jobs, so acknowledging and showing appreciation and support was very motivating for them. The benefits of clearly feeling part of the whole were most important for those staff whose roles were furthest removed from passengers, particularly for everyone involved in maintaining the track and infrastructure on which the trains ran. But the structure also helped foster a better understanding and appreciation for the role and challenges faced by train crew and station staff who had daily contact with passengers.

Having a multi-functional leadership team running each profit centre made for much more visible leadership and in turn helped foster a sense of shared identity with the organisation. Most railway people have an instinctive sense of belonging to a railway family, but this identification in many railway organisational structures is unfocused and relatively amorphous. Even in the short time Profit Centres were in existence one could see staff starting to identify with them and a stronger esprit de corps developing. Taking pride in an organisation that you can get your mind around and is of a more human scale is much easier and more motivating. A clear parallel is the British Army system of Regimental units; soldiers take pride and strongly identify with their parent Regiment, whilst feeling a clear part of the Army as a whole. The 25 or so OfQ Profit Centres, albeit of varying sizes, were of a scale that most people could much more readily comprehend and identify with and, most importantly, see how they fitted in and the impact their job had on the end service to passengers. It was much easier to ensure that all the component parts worked together and pulled in the same direction.

There were of course inherent conflicts and risks in the OfQ structure. Profit Centres did not directly manage everything but often used stations managed and owned by another

Profit Centres, or ran over a section of another's track, so requiring a system of internal contracting to manage this. Making this work required a spirit of collaboration and partnership, which had developed with the previous matrix organisation, but would this have persisted in the longer term as each Sector and Profit Centre developed in potentially different ways? The structure did away with a single national leadership of the railways' key engineering departments - civil, mechanical and signals and telecommunications- instead vesting leadership within each of the national Sector organisations. Would this have weakened technical innovation and standards in the longer term, or would the diversity of approach of the different Sector teams have produced better and faster innovation more matched to the needs of the different markets? It is therefore not possible to reach any clear conclusions on how effective and sustainable the OfQ structure might have been in the longer term, because it was too short lived to be truly tested.

What is very clear however, is that the experience built up in reorganising the railway firstly into Sectors and Sub-Sectors and secondly into Profit Centres made the enormous task of completely restructuring the industry for privatisation much easier. It is even doubtful it could have been possible within the timescale without it. The managers who led this final, dramatic, restructuring had all learnt the importance of collaborative working, become familiar with buying services from other parts of the railway and were well versed in how to lead and implement major change. It is indeed ironic that the energy which enabled the Sector and OfQ organisations to be created also made their subsequent dismantling easier.

What is also striking looking back is how this new cadre of managers was very largely "home grown", with surprisingly few people brought in from outside the industry. The sub-sectors were often led by younger managers and provided a relatively safe, but hands-on learning environment, to get to know their businesses and markets, with the responsibility for production still lying elsewhere. Shared involvement in the Leadership 500 and 5000 initiatives, and the Safety Management Programme, also helped build a set of shared values. The whole process was remarkably successful in developing a new generation of business focussed leaders, many of whom continued to lead parts of the industry for many years after privatisation.

What then are the lessons on how best to organise a railway that I take from this, particularly in the context of today's railway in Britain which potentially faces another restructuring?

There are four key themes which I believe distinguish a better from a poorer organisational structure: market focus, size, bottom line responsibility and a culture of collaboration.

Firstly, component organisations need to be market focused both at a national and at a regional level. The needs of Intercity type, longer distance passenger markets and the cost structure they support are fundamentally different to those of London commuters or rural travel markets. The necessary ticketing and fares structures are different as are the appropriate types of train and the services needed at stations. Operational units should be market focused wherever possible, but also of a size that staff can get their minds around, identify with and have a visible leadership team. Being able to see how your job fits into the wider organisation and its end customers is more fulfilling for staff, and smaller market focused organisations are easier to run. BR's Profit Centres and the passenger and freight Train Operating Companies post privatisation all conform to this. It is also much easier for the company or organisation concerned to develop a relationship with its customers and be understood by them.

Having a cadre of managers who have effective bottom line accountability for financial performance is vital if the railway is to be run cost effectively. This must be for both revenue and all of the costs involved in delivering the service, including infrastructure costs. This is essential to understand the economics of each group of train services and work to improve them. Without the challenge and scrutiny of such managers, decisions on the capacity to be provided, level and mix of fares and what are affordable technical standards are all likely to be sub-optimal. This is the only way to make informed choices between spending on infrastructure or on the trains to improve service reliability and how to optimise the trade-offs involved in engineering track possessions and their impact on passenger revenues.

A fundamental weakness of the industry's structure since privatisation is that no one has a true bottom line, with infrastructure costs which account for roundly 50% of the industry's cost base "passed through" to train companies or direct to the Government, and Network Rail not seeing or taking account of the impact on customer revenues in its decisions and performance. Network Rail's spending decisions are mainly driven by the requirements of the Rail Regulator, rather than by the ability of the train services on a given route to bear the costs. Infrastructure costs are overwhelmingly an administered, fixed cost for train companies and are subject to a completely different regulatory regime to their own costs which are in effect "regulated" via franchise or concession agreements. The result is that half the industry's costs are set without any reference to the economic viability of the traffic carried or challenge by informed managers.

In BR's matrix organisation of sectors, sub-sectors, regions and areas this challenge was provided by the sub-sector managers and their route managers. It ought to be a relatively simple exercise to create a comparable cadre of managers based in Network Rail's Regions as they morph into Great British Railways. Much harder would be the task of evolving NR's management accounting systems to provide the appropriate granularity of costing by route and train service comparable to BR's infrastructure costing systems immediately before privatisation. And taking fullest advantage of all this would also require major reform of the ORR's Infrastructure Access Charging Regime, moving from administered to actual infrastructure costs.

Finally, a necessary ingredient of all railway organisational structures is a culture of collaboration between the players involved, whether they be departments within an organisation, separate divisions or different companies. Whatever the structure there is rarely any choice of who you are dealing with; there is usually only one route any given train service can run over, little choice of maintenance depots to use or stations to call at for a particular market. Normal market rules cannot apply when all of the infrastructure, track, stations and depots are effectively monopoly suppliers, so it becomes essential for all involved to work together and collaborate. BR managers got pretty good at this. This collaborative culture was initially suppressed by privatisation and the attitudes of Railtrack and initially of Network Rail, but it is to the credit of the current generation of railway managers that a new spirit of collaboration and partnership has evolved.

CHAPTER 14 Railways as a System

It is a truism that a railway is a system, and a relatively complex one at that, but it is sobering that many people involved in and around the industry in the UK have at least partly lost sight of this. Many different job roles and items of equipment need to work in tight synchronicity with each other to deliver a reliable railway service, whether to passengers or freight. Each part of the system is dependent on other parts to be able to do its job, requiring a high degree of orchestration and teamwork to make it all work harmoniously together.

The train driver needs to be given the timetable of the service they are to operate, departure and arrival times and station stopping points, and will assume that the timetabler has worked out a clear path with no conflicts with other trains. They need a train set, with up to date maintenance and all systems functioning correctly, and on many passenger trains they need a guard or train manager and other staff to look after the passengers. They need the signaller to set green signals for them to deliver the timetabled path, or to regulate the service when there is any perturbation, and station staff at busier stations to ensure passengers alight and board safely and promptly, and despatch their train punctually. And they need the track they run over, its signalling system and on electrified routes the electric power supply system all to work reliably. A fault or late completion of a task by any of these people risks their train being delayed, and, on a busy network even a very few minutes delay is likely to cause problems for a considerable number of other trains.

The train maintainer in turn needs feedback from the driver and train crew on any issues which require maintenance attention, and they need the train set to be delivered to the maintenance depot at the scheduled time, to be able to process train sets through the depot smoothly, usually overnight, and deliver the set back into service the following morning on time. The signaller also needs feedback from the driver of any out of course events on the track so they can initiate necessary responses and make informed regulation decisions. And so on. The list of interdependencies is extensive, each example dependent on other people undertaking their tasks within a very tight timeframe.

All of this is of course not hugely different to other complex production or operational industries. What is very different to other industries is that many staff either work largely alone (drivers) or in small teams (most signallers, track maintenance teams etc) hence with low levels of supervision compared to a factory say. The railways' "production line" is highly dispersed, extending from end to end of the line over many miles and, uniquely, is continuously exposed to the elements and the impact of extreme weather. Activity is spread out along the line, at each station for instance, as are hundreds of items of plant and equipment such as points, signals, track circuits ([4]) and electric power supplies. Each of these needs to be functioning correctly to ensure a train runs punctually, and where something does fail it is too often at a relatively remote location leading to an initially uncertain delay in identifying and rectifying the problem. Accurate communication procedures and good asset knowledge are therefore essential, as is the need for close coordination of very different technical disciplines: civil engineering for the track itself, and for embankments, bridges and tunnels and associated drainage, electrical engineering for electric train

---

[4] Track circuits detect the presence of a train on a section of track and automatically set signals to danger behind the train to protect it from any collision.

power supplies, signalling and control systems, and a range of disciplines for points.

Add to this the fact that a railway is largely a 24/7 operation. Even when the passenger service has finished for the night, there will be moves of empty trains to and from maintenance depots in the early hours, and of freight trains and track maintenance plant throughout the night. And, as Sir Peter Parker, Chairman of British Rail in the late 1970s, observed, few other industries operate in the full view of their customers with every interruption to production painfully exposed to them. Passengers are often the first people to be aware of any perturbation or disruption.

All of this clearly makes the railways a complex system to operate smoothly, requiring high levels of orchestration and discipline between different functions. Yet for the past thirty years the industry in Britain has operated in two discrete segments: Network Rail, previously Railtrack, owning and managing the track and signalling infrastructure, and larger stations, and train and freight operating companies running the trains. This split between track and train was introduced for largely ideological reasons, to facilitate different companies being able to run trains and enter new markets in competition with incumbent operators. It came from an unusual convergence of UK Government and EU thinking, both of which wanted to shake up what they saw as a rather complacent, inefficient and customer unfriendly rail sector by creating the conditions where there could be competition on the rails.

The two halves of the industry have worked on the necessary coordination and collaboration between them with varying degrees of success and commitment over the years. For a number of years this was made much easier by the fact that the large majority of managers in both Network Rail/Railtrack and train companies had previously worked in the integrated structure that was British Rail, and many had come through its Traffic Management and Engineering Training Schemes and its Operations Function. As a result, they had a good understanding of how to run the railway as a system, and, importantly, understood the needs and issues their opposite numbers faced in the other "half" of the industry. However, as this cadre of managers retired or moved on, understanding of how the railway operates as a system has slowly dissipated, and a growing proportion of managers now have only ever worked in one half of the industry. At the same time the railway has become progressively busier and on many routes is now operating close to capacity making it a more challenging system to operate. The lack of system understanding and coordination has therefore contributed to a growing number of service problems and inefficiencies, as have contractual barriers and misaligned incentives between the different parties.

A final, major, problem is that over time more and more decisions which affect the running of the railway have been taken by ministers and civil servants at the Department for Transport, who of course usually have very limited understanding of how the railway works or of its complexities as a system. Decisions for instance on timetables or investment specifications, as we shall see below, often have knock-on impacts way beyond the immediately perceived factors that were taken into account in the decision. Likewise understanding of how the contractual and other mechanisms that govern Britain's rail system since privatisation impact on actual operations is too often lacking. Chapter 15 describes in more detail some of the inevitable shortcomings of government decision making.

It is arguable that a training and education programme to rebuild system understanding and a more fundamental rethink of the track-train split is now required. To illustrate the scale of the issue, and perhaps point to answers, it is worth describing some of the problems and inefficiencies the industry has experienced, or is still experiencing, which also demonstrate how closely interconnected the different parts of the industry are.

Managing service recovery

One of the most important problems is the way service recovery is managed after an incident that disrupts the train service. Clearly the objective is to restore normal timetabled operation as soon as possible so the minimum number of passengers and freight customers are delayed.

The majority of minutes delay to train services are attributed to incidents within Network Rail's responsibility, such as a track, signalling or power supply problem. When the cause of the initial incident is established and attributed to Network Rail all subsequent delays, including knock-on or reactionary delays to other trains, are charged to them too under the Schedule 8 performance regime ([5]). This regime is designed to give a real cost to delays, by charging for each delay minute, to incentivise those causing them to take measures to reduce or eliminate them. But the speed with which normal service can be restored depends as much, if not more, on the train operator affected, as on the speed with which Network Rail can locate and fix the problem. Do they have any spare train crews or train sets to stand in for crews and trains delayed? Do these crews have the necessary traction and route knowledge to do this? Are they prepared to accept some cancellations if this would allow normal service to be restored more quickly, given that many franchise operators have separate contractual regimes which penalise cancellations?

---

[5] The Schedule 8 Performance Regime is a standard part of each Track Access Agreement. The cost of each delay minute is separately calculated for each Train Company by the Rail Regulator as part of their five yearly Periodic Review process.

Many train operators have over the years sought to tighten up train crew workings to secure efficiencies by more efficient diagramming, increasingly using computerised systems to optimise efficiency, reducing spare crews and limiting the range of train types and routes, particularly diversionary routes, that drivers can operate to reduce training costs. There has arguably been a perverse incentive on train companies to do this if it increases the amount of reactionary delay that Network Rail must pay Schedule 8 compensation for; the train company then enjoys the benefits both of lower crewing costs and higher Schedule 8 receipts from Network Rail.

Unsurprisingly Network Rail has worked hard both to reduce the number of track and other incidents it causes and to reduce the time to fix, and has substantially reduced the number of delay-causing incidents as a result. Things like broken rails, track circuit failures and points failures are substantially less frequent now than they were in BR days. Significant sums have been spent to achieve this. But total delays have still grown on many routes, as increasing delay per incident has outweighed the decline in the number of incidents, making it feel as if Network Rail was trying to push water uphill.

The benefit of managing a railway as a total system was well illustrated when Network Rail and South West Trains briefly entered into an alliance arrangement where they shared the majority of operating and infrastructure costs on the routes into London Waterloo on a fifty-fifty basis. This made it worthwhile for the partners to reintroduce whole-crew working during peak hours at Waterloo: driver and guard staying together for both inwards and outwards workings. This avoided the need to separately wait for a driver and guard to become available during peak hours, to speed up recovery from disruptions. It deliberately increased train crew costs with Network Rail contributing to South West Train's costs, but it was judged to be a more cost-effective way of improving train performance than other purely infrastructure based initiatives. There are many other such examples where there can be a choice between the train operating side of the industry or the infrastructure side taking action and a whole system view is necessary to determine which is optimum. The flip side is that one side making changes to save costs, such as South West Trains withdrawing whole crew working in the early days after privatisation, can export costs to the other side, in this case increasing Network Rail's Schedule 8 compensation costs.

Whole system planning of investments

Looking more widely there are many situations where there can be a choice between doing something to a rail line or to the trains running on it to improve performance, increase line capacity or reduce train journey times to provide a faster service to passengers. Managing the track separately to the trains makes it much harder, if not impossible, to identify and implement the optimum solution. An interesting macro level example of this was the need to reduce journey times on the West Coast Main Line service out of Euston to maintain their attraction for passengers after the M40 motorway opened. I was InterCity Manager in Birmingham at the time, responsible for business management of the West Coast route. InterCity commissioned a detailed study to work out whether it was better to invest in improving line speeds, principally by realigning the large number of bends on the route where speeds were restricted below the ruling line speed, or to procure tilting trains which could go round bends faster without affecting passenger comfort.

The clear conclusion of this study was that it was more cost-effective to invest in track improvements and we briefly started to implement this with realignment works, before the programme was halted ahead of privatisation. One of the benefits was that speed improvements potentially benefitted all trains on the line, not just InterCity Trains, and because line speeds would be more uniform, line capacity would also be increased. It is striking that after privatisation Virgin Trains, who became the franchise operator of the Intercity services on the line, chose to invest in a tilting train fleet to be able to cut end to end journey times and offer a more attractive service to passengers. This strategy was part of Virgin's winning bid to operate the franchise. Virgin had no real interest, or indeed the necessary information, to take account of the impact or potential benefits or disbenefits to other operators on the route or to worry about the impact on line capacity. It was also much simpler for them to look primarily at investing in the trains to improve journey times on the route given they were not the infrastructure operator. The studies they undertook to put their successful bid together presumably involved input from Railtrack, but they would not have been in a position to look at the impact on other train operators either, and were then less interested in the impact on line capacity. Whilst Virgin's West Coast service using tilting Pendolino trains proved to be a substantial success, it is an interesting, if now hypothetical, question as to whether this was the most economic solution for the railway as an overall system.

A more striking example of investment decisions which did not adequately take account of their wider system impacts is the new Thameslink train fleet. Procurement of this fleet was undertaken directly by the Department for Transport (DfT), who unfortunately looked at this through a relatively narrow lens. One key decision was to order a mix of 8 and 12 car train sets, rather than the more conventional 4 car set which could then be combined to form 8 or 12 car trains. The capital cost of these trains per available seat will have been lower, with just two driving cabs to equip for each train rather than the 4 or 6 which would be involved with 4 car sets, and space otherwise taken up by cabs could be used for seating instead. But operating costs are higher because it is no longer possible to run less than 8 car trains, and most will be 12 cars, whereas there are times, for instance on overnight trains or on quieter days, when 4 cars are more than adequate. The significant extra vehicle mileage adds to daily train maintenance, electric power and track wear costs. The investment decision also failed to take account of the impact on infrastructure at maintenance depots and stabling sidings, where significant investment was in the end required to modify maintenance sheds and stabling sidings at a number of locations to accommodate the much longer 12 car trainsets.

This lack of a joined-up system approach extended to the wider contractual management of the whole Thameslink 2000 project, of which the trains were just a part. Financing for the trains was procured by the DfT through a completely separate contract with a special purpose financing consortium, with the trains procured on a build and maintain contract with Siemens Transportation. This contract obliged Siemens to make available a given number of trainsets for service each day, but the specification for this was not calibrated against the timetable which Govia Thameslink Railway (GTR), the franchisee for the Thameslink services, was contracted to operate. On Saturdays for instance Siemens were initially only obliged to provide 50% of the weekday availability. Given the inflexibility of the trainsets this was not nearly enough for GTR to operate the service, but probably would have been had 4 car sets been ordered.

The DfT also had a franchise contract with GTR to manage the entry into service of the new trains and a separate contract with Network Rail to undertake the necessary infrastructure improvement works for Thameslink 2000. These four major contracts were all managed directly by the DfT, but effective programme management of all the various components of successfully launching the new Thameslink service was not put in place until late in the day. It took a special independent review commissioned by the Secretary of State, less than two years before the entry into service, to highlight the need for close orchestration between these four contracts, and for strong programme management of all of the tasks needed to launch the new Thameslink 2000 service successfully. The review was undertaken by Chris Gibb, a hugely experienced railway operator, who was one of my colleagues on the Network Rail Board, so that we were well informed about the issues he identified and remedies he recommended.

One of the recommendations of this review was that implementing the full 24 trains per hour service specified in the original Thameslink investment authority in one step was fraught with risk. A stepped build-up in the frequency of service from 16 trains per hour, coordinated with the commissioning of new automated train control software and digital signalling, was a much more prudent approach. GTR subsequently put a proposal to DfT recommending this and seeking a corresponding variation in their franchise contract, but this took the DfT a number of months to agree because it appeared to be a significant departure from the original investment authority for the Thameslink project. Eventual agreement came four months after the normal cut-off date for GTR to submit its timetable proposals to Network Rail. The result was that the whole timetable production process was very compressed, with more errors inevitably requiring rectification before it could be finalised. It also left GTR with insufficient time to do its own preparation work producing diagrams for trainsets and train crew and resulting train crew rosters, and to validate the availability of drivers with the right route knowledge for the new extended service. The result of course was a seriously flawed launch of the new Thameslink service, with extensive cancellations and associated disruption for several months afterwards.

One of the outcomes of this debacle, and of similar problems with the introduction of new Northern and Transpennine Services at the same time, was the setting up of a Programme Management Office (PMO) led by Network Rail, to ensure that all issues involved in launching substantially new timetables are taken into account and addressed in adequate time. Had such a Programme Management approach been in place from the start of the Thameslink 2000 project, it is likely the problems encountered could have been avoided and key decisions taken in adequate time.

I had direct experience of the benefits of such an approach in my time as CEO of Eurostar when we launched services on the new high speed line in 2003 and 2007, as described in Chapter 9. Because of the relatively fraught launch of services on the first phase of the new line in 2003, we set up a high level steering group bringing together all the key parties involved in building the line and preparing to operate it, more than three years before it opened. And we set up a Programme Management Office to track the myriad of different projects and tasks involved and ensure they were synchronised. It also ensured feedback from ourselves as the operator could influence aspects of the detailed design, for instance of stations, and the phasing of commissioning and completion of different facilities to dovetail with our staff training needs.

With such large projects there are a hundred and one things that may not go according to plan - extreme weather or unforeseen ground conditions affecting on-site construction, technical or component supply problems, necessary design changes etc. - so it was recognised that we should not commit to an opening date until we were sufficiently confident everything would be ready. The date we chose was only decided on one year beforehand. There is a popular expectation, particularly amongst politicians and the media, that big projects must be delivered on time and on budget. But given the fact that their scope is very largely fixed, through the Parliamentary Powers process or planning conditions, there needs to be at least one free variable, between scope, cost and timescale, to allow for the many things that might not go according to the initial plan. We chose the timescale for the opening date as our free variable.

In the event, Eurostar's launch at St Pancras International Station, and what by then had been rebranded as High Speed One, although still stressful, went flawlessly in the public's eye. Had the Department for Transport, as sponsor of the Thameslink project, also set up a similar Steering Group process at an early stage to bring together all the key parties needed to deliver the project successfully, supported by an effective Programme Management Office, the eventual launch of services might have gone much more smoothly. The key is not just coordination between the various parties physically delivering the overall project, but to ensure close involvement of the organisation that will eventually operate the service from the very earliest stages of its conception and planning. This is of course more difficult, but even more important, when the parties are different contractual entities and responsibilities for infrastructure and train operations are split.

Optimising access for track maintenance

But the importance of understanding how the railways operate as a system is not just confined to managing big projects and optimising service recovery. It is also important for a host of other issues. Access to the track to undertake maintenance and renewal work is one such issue, which has always been a source of some tension between the various engineers responsible for the infrastructure and those operating the trains. The engineers generally want more convenient access, ideally during daylight hours for maintenance and routine inspections, and for longer periods for renewals to be able to complete jobs rather than undertake them in stages. But giving access for engineering work clearly prevents or severely restricts the running of trains, so train operators prefer to limit access to overnight hours, when few, if any, trains would be running, and to confine it to pre-planned timings so as to be able to publish timetables well in advance.

There are clearly trade-offs involved as short access times increase the costs of maintenance and renewals work, and the potential loss of passenger and freight revenue from not being able to run trains is not a constant but will vary very substantially by day of the week and time of the year. Ideally a whole system approach would involve estimating the revenue at risk for different patterns of access, as well as how these would affect the costs of a particular renewal or enhancement project, so as to optimise the net result. This requires good revenue and cost information, understanding of what drives each, full transparency of information and, crucially, close communication and team working between the train operators and infrastructure engineers on a route by route basis.

For much of the time since privatisation of the industry in Britain this has rarely taken place or been possible. The passenger franchises are contracted to operate a very specific set of timetables and are therefore reluctant to accept any flexibility around pre-planned access patterns. The franchise letting process has also encouraged bidders to offer to run more trains to provide a more attractive service to passengers, including earlier first trains of the day and later last trains, with the result that access times particularly for maintenance work have become increasingly constrained over the years. At the same time Network Rail, as the infrastructure provider, is disincentivised from seeking different patterns of access for maintenance and other work by Schedule 4 of the track access regime. This requires it to compensate train operators for any changes to access other than those long pre-planned. Schedule 4 payments to train operators can form a significant proportion of enhancement project and renewals costs, encouraging Network Rail to work within relatively rigid patterns of access to limit these payments regardless of whether this is the best result for the industry as a whole.

The result has too often been something of a standoff, with Network Rail reluctant to seek different access because of the Schedule 4 costs and train operators constrained by their franchise agreements from agreeing to changes in timetables to accommodate more cost-effective engineering work. A potential better way of doing things was shown by the London Underground when they introduced all night services on selected lines on Friday and Saturday nights. Overnight maintenance was then confined to five nights a week, Sunday through to Thursday nights, producing a more efficient use of staff with a regular five-day (or in this case, night!) work pattern. Would not a similar pattern on some London commuter lines also be more efficient as well as being more customer friendly? It would require the DfT as franchise authority to agree to an earlier end to services on Sunday through to Thursday evenings, giving more productive access for the engineers, but give much better late-night services for passengers on Friday and Saturday nights, which are busy nights for socialising.

Some work I led as InterCity Business Planning Manager in the mid 1980s and described in Chapter 3, illustrates the sort of dialogue that is necessary to find better solutions. At the time InterCity was looking to reduce end to end journey times for passengers to improve our attractiveness compared to car travel on the then still new and growing motorway network and so grow our passenger revenue. We were also keen to find ways to reduce our infrastructure engineering costs which accounted for roundly half of all our costs, to help achieve our target to make InterCity profitable by 1988. We started our discussions with the civil engineers with a blank sheet of paper, with the engineers saying that the short times they had to undertake track renewal work at weekends were very constraining and inefficient, and us saying that their track renewal costs were very expensive to us and that we also wanted to reduce the time built into timetables to allow for temporary speed restrictions on recently relayed track. There was 20 minutes extra in the timetable between London and Edinburgh to allow for this, as an example of its large impact. Their solution was the introduction of 30-hour possession times on Saturday evenings/Sunday mornings giving sufficient time to complete track renewal work rather than do it in stages over several weekends, followed by a further short possession on Sunday nights to bed in the newly laid ballast. This allowed lines to reopen at full line speed on Monday mornings potentially shaving a full 20 minutes off the journey time London to Edinburgh, with comparable savings on other routes. The "price" was the need to invest in some new kit, Dynamic Track Stabilisers, to consolidate the track ballast on Sunday nights which InterCity was easily able to make the investment case for and happy to sponsor and fund.

Clearly track renewal techniques are now different, with new and better plant and equipment, and each line of route has different characteristics, but this sort of open book and win-win dialogue between those responsible for track infrastructure and for train services could only lead to better solutions. It does need the DfT as franchise authority to relax its approach to timetable specifications, and an approach which seeks the best whole system solutions rather than those which optimise things for one party in isolation. There are signs of this starting to happen with a growing number of "blockades" - closure of a line for a number of days at a time - to allow much more efficient delivery of major enhancement work. The same open-minded approach to agreeing access arrangements for track maintenance and renewal would undoubtedly pay dividends.

Another area where the lack of a joined up whole system approach is evident is in the dovetailing of infrastructure improvements with train service planning. There are a number of examples of new stations being built or promoted, whether by DfT or a local authority, with little or no thought as to their impact on train services. Serving a new station on an existing route will clearly inject additional time into trainset diagrams, to allow for the stopping time at the station, which at the margin could worsen utilisation or impact on connectional times at other stations. More importantly the additional stop will worsen the capacity of the line, other things being equal, particularly if there are other services using the line not stopping at the new station. If the station is on an already busy route the knock-on impacts could be substantial and require working through prior to committing to build the station. A good example is the new station planned at Brent Cross in North London and committed to by DfT a number of years ago, but with no evaluation of its impact on the already very intensive Thameslink service that will service the station, on line capacity, or on the reliability of other services using the line, particularly the busy East Midlands Trains service whose workings are closely intertwined with those of Thameslink. An even more extreme example is the new station at Kenilworth in Warwickshire, where no thought was given to which train operator might serve the station or their capacity to do so when committing to it.

A more surprising example of the lack of system thinking is when infrastructure layout changes or improvements are implemented without making corresponding changes to timetable planning parameters. Several years ago platforms 1-4 at Waterloo Station were extended to accommodate 10 car trains rather than the previous 8 car trains, facilitating a 25% increase in passenger capacity of the services using these platforms; ostensibly a very cost-effective investment in additional capacity. The very constrained layout at Waterloo necessitated moving the points allowing access to platforms 1-4 further to the south west, away from the buffer stops, so that the time taken for the extended 10 car trains to clear or re-occupy each platform was increased. But this increased time was surprisingly not initially built into the timetables, or allowed for in the platforming plan, with a resulting material negative impact on punctuality of the services using these platforms. These were already very intensively used with inbound trains occupying each platform immediately after the departure of an outbound service.

These are all examples of the importance of looking at the railway as a single, integrated system, and some of the pitfalls and shortcomings when this is not done. They are based on my own personal experiences and I am sure many railway professionals, particularly those who have worked under an integrated system, can produce numerous other examples. But do they really matter? Can we not continue as we are, accepting a degree of imperfection in the way track and train are only partially integrated? I believe there are three strategic reasons why a return to more joined up, whole system thinking is essential.

Why whole system thinking is important

First and foremost is the vital importance of reducing the industry's cost base. The industry is heavily subsidised by Government and given the intense pressure on UK public spending the industry needs to do all it can to reduce its call on the public purse. This was an issue pre-Covid but the fall in passenger revenue post-Covid makes it even more important. It is essential the industry fully understands the true costs of each train service, properly matching costs to revenues as British Rail achieved with its sectors and sub-sectors. Only then can informed decisions be taken on what level of service to run and what level of infrastructure cost can be supported by the services run on each section. This is simply not possible with the current split of track from train and largely fixed, administered, charges for track access, giving no useful price signals to either Network Rail or its train company customers. In short, the industry needs to recreate a management accounting framework similar to BR's sector and sub-sector accounts, with a new cadre of bottom line accountable managers to challenge and facilitate better decisions. The loss of BR's management accounting framework for the rail system as a whole after privatisation created a huge and much overlooked gap.

Two examples above of the trade-off between track and train costs - optimising the pattern of maintenance possessions on each route and optimising spend on improving train punctuality between infrastructure and train-based initiatives - are obvious areas where costs overall would be reduced. But a more important opportunity is in introducing bottom line challenge to the many "standards" that now govern much railway activity, and varying them in the light of their financial impact or, as a minimum, actively encouraging derogations. These standards are produced by Network Rail nationally and by the Rail Safety and Standards Board (RSSB). By their nature they are usually "one size fits all" solutions across the whole railway network and are rarely subject to an effective cost-benefit analysis in setting them. But the UK rail network is not a homogeneous thing, having been constructed or renewed at different times to different standards and with different equipment, so applying any one size fits all standard will inevitably add to cost. This is especially the case if the standard has not been subject to any affordability challenge. If nothing else, having bottom line focused managers challenging standards may lead to a different solution, or to varying a standard taking account of particular circumstances.

A second area where a return to more joined up system wide thinking is needed is in maximising the capacity for passengers or freight on an increasingly heavily used network. The recent neutering by the Government of the longer-term capacity benefits that HS2 would have brought to the West Coast, Midland and East Coast main lines, make this even more important. This is particularly important on routes shared by two or more train services. Network Rail's Route Utilisation Studies were a worthy attempt to address the issue, but of course in the absence of a single guiding mind with a long-term perspective on how each route might develop, and authority to achieve this, Network Rail was not able to enforce any of the necessary decisions or take a sufficiently informed view of the likely and desirable level of growth to be accommodated. A system perspective is necessary to try to ensure that when new or different trains are being considered for a route, they are chosen so as to have compatible braking, acceleration and speed characteristics with other trains on the route, otherwise capacity will be wasted by longer headways between the different trains. Likewise, it is important when planning new stations to have an overall system understanding of their impact on existing services and how best to serve them.

An even more telling example of the need for a system perspective is the introduction of digital signalling. This has the potential to revolutionise how the railway is operated, increasing line capacity by tailoring signalling control to each individual train type and its braking capability so reducing headways between trains. Implementing it in a cost-effective way requires closely coordinated planning of the necessary investments in trains and infrastructure, with inevitably some premature replacement investment in one or the other. With multiple train operators and owners on a route, close collaboration is also needed between the various parties. At the same time, it has the potential to streamline many operational management processes, for instance allowing temporary speed restrictions and possessions and power supply isolations to be implemented virtually instantly, and doing away with the need for temporary line-side signage, with useful cost and safety benefits for Network Rail and its operations staff. Realising all the potential benefits requires a true system wide approach, and people with a detailed whole system understanding of railway operations, both track and train, will be essential.

Which points to the third reason for building system thinking and understanding, which is the planning and management of investment schemes. This is partly to avoid the pitfalls encountered by the Thameslink 2000 project described above. But it is also necessary to ensure best value from what will always be a restricted level of investment, reconciling the different priorities of asset renewal, growth and decarbonisation. Plans for electrification should be dovetailed with signalling and train replacement programmes and with emerging plans for hydrogen and battery powered trains, instead of the very piecemeal approach that has applied since privatisation.

Effective system thinking and planning does not necessarily require a single, unified ownership structure for the industry. But it does require sufficient experienced individuals with a good understanding of how the railway works as a system to do the thinking and planning. To ensure cost effectiveness and value for money it also needs a management accounting system that matches costs and revenues service by service and line by line. Finally, it would be easier and less time consuming if there was a single guiding mind, hopefully a capable and leanly resourced Great British Railways. The Department for Transport is the de facto single directing mind at the moment, except of course it is not well resourced with experienced railway professionals and is focused by politicians on short term, largely non-strategic issues. Quite simply it is not, and cannot ever be, an effective or capable "directing mind", as we will see in the next two Chapters.

CHAPTER 15 Public or private?

For all of my time in the rail industry it has been dogged with an almost perpetual tug of war between privatisation and nationalisation. For a number of the later years that it was in the public sector under British Rail there were calls for privatisation, and since it was privatised (even if only partially) this switched to calls for it to be renationalised. Any actual debate tends to be at the ideological level of "public good, private bad", or vice versa, and often the issue led to the industry being used as a political football between Labour and Conservative governments and oppositions. Often, too, it obscured the reality on a particular issue and complicated many relationships. The railway trade unions have always been strongly opposed to privatisation and more recently their rhetoric has sought to demonise the privatised Train Operating Companies and clouded their actual roles and influence compared to that of the Government.

The reality of course is that both the public and private sector operation of the industry have their shortcomings, neither is a "perfect" solution. And because the industry has long been in receipt of public funding it could never be fully privatised, because governments will rightly require the say on how public funds are spent and on what. At the same time the industry has a large supply chain which has long been in the private sector, without controversy. Government and the private sector will therefore always need to find a way to work effectively together and, ideally, they should seek a structure that combines what each does best whilst avoiding as many of the shortcomings as possible. This is of course much more easily said than done and any attempt to work through the issues and options objectively is not only constrained by political dogma but also by a widespread lack of understanding of how the public and private sectors each actually work and how they differ.

My career in the industry has been divided between time in the public sector and time under at least partial private ownership. I have served on both public sector and private sector Boards and also on Boards which sought to bridge the gap between sectors. I was also privileged to serve on the Board of the Department for Transport for a number of years and therefore observed how the civil service works. Operating at the interface of the public and private sectors for much of my career has therefore given me a number of relatively unique insights which I attempt to share in this chapter.

My first encounter with how much the sectors differed was when I joined the board of the Derby City Partnership in the early 1990s. This was a new board set up to try to build bridges between the public, private and voluntary sectors in Derby which until then had largely operated in silos with little dialogue or interchange between them. At the time I was still working for British Rail, and therefore technically in the public sector, but for some reason it was assumed I was from the private sector, perhaps because we were then in the run up to privatisation. I found it interesting and striking how different were the respective approaches and concerns, and regularly found myself re-presenting and re-phrasing what people had said, because it was clear that the other party had misunderstood. I now understand that this was partly because people made assumptions about each other's knowledge and understanding, which were often wrong, and partly because they used a somewhat different vocabulary. The scope for misunderstanding, or simply not understanding, was significant. When I later stepped down from the Board I well remember being thanked by one of the more outspoken members, who was President of the Derbyshire Chamber of Commerce, for being so helpful in translating what people said to ensure others understood! I had inadvertently become something of an interpreter and a bridger of cultural gaps!

Reflections on the public sector

There is certainly a significant difference in the language used by the public and private sectors, with the same words quite often meaning different things. "Investment" in the public sector is usually used to refer to spending on any sort of public good, whereas in the private sector it tends to be more narrowly understood, for instance expenditure on physical assets that have a lasting use and a tangible return or sometimes on things like training. Politicians who announce they will be investing in something often really mean they will be spending more money on something. A "business plan" in the public sector is often really what the private sector would describe as a three year or even one-year expenditure budget and "strategy" is loosely used to describe an organisation's approach to any number of issues. Most public sector entities will have multiple strategies, each addressing a particular subject of concern. Strategy in the private sector tends to be a more holistic thing, embracing how the organisation intends to position itself relative to its markets, competitors and suppliers and how it will shape its business going forward.

There is also language used uniquely in the public sector, which is initially at least a mystery to an outsider. "Socialisation" was a particular example for me, meaning the process of running a document or policy proposal past a number of colleagues partly to gauge and hopefully gain support for it, and partly to ensure that if it is adopted it will not be opposed or criticised by others. Language is of course easily learned and many of the more outward looking individuals from both sectors will often try to adopt the language of the other sector when engaging with it, although not always understanding what the other means by it. And language is easily copied and absorbed by others, leading to blurring of its use and meaning between sectors and organisations.

More importantly the somewhat different use of language also camouflages much more fundamental differences in culture, assumptions and attitudes between public and private sectors. The public sector tends to look inwards and upwards for direction and inspiration, whereas the private sector tends to look outwards to its customers and the market. This is of course the direct result of where the money comes from and how organisational success and personal advancement is achieved. The public sector is a creature of government and is overseen and given direction by ministers and councillors with everyone ultimately accountable to them. Resources flow down from above and in the UK overwhelmingly from HM Treasury. Success is measured by how well a policy area is formulated, too often a subjective and political judgement, and on occasions on how well a particular budget is defended and grown. And too often Minsters see the announcement of £x million funding for a particular initiative as the end of the matter, "problem solved", and quickly move on to the next initiative.

There is a particular difference in attitudes to budgets between the two sectors. In the private sector a budget is something to be beaten, often the more the better because sales are higher than promised or costs lower. In the public sector a budget is seen more as something to be delivered and spent fully, since the result of an underspend is often a cut in next years budget making future life harder. The size of one's budget can also be a mark of status in the public sector. Chatting with an outgoing Permanent Secretary at the Department for Transport, who was moving to the same role in another Department, I asked him why he was moving given he seemed to be enjoying the job with plenty of challenges still to address. His answer was simply "it has a bigger budget".

In contrast, private sector success depends on customers and markets as they provide the organisation's income, and keeping pace with and anticipating changing customer needs and competitive developments is essential to long term success. This encourages much more outward looking cultures, with faster and wider innovation to try to keep up with technological and market changes. Whilst some resources, such as investment, still come from higher up the hierarchy, organisational success will be at least partly dependent on how sales are grown and customers satisfied, or how well specific projects are executed, with relatively objective and hard measures of success predominating.

I have seen similar differences in approach and attitude to customer demand between the two sectors. The public sector tends to see demand as something received, to be met if possible, but is determined exogenously and which cannot and probably should not be stimulated. This was very much the case at British Rail, where business plans focused overwhelmingly on cost reduction and control, with little credibility given to revenue growth. The Plans had of course to be accepted by the Department for Transport, and standing behind them the Treasury, so reflected the public sector instinct. In sharp contrast the private sector sees customer demand as something to be stimulated and grown if at all possible. They work hard to attract new customers to use their service, using new marketing approaches and product innovation wherever possible, as well as to keep existing customers.

I saw similar tendencies in the Social Housing sector in which I served as a Housing Association Chair for nine years. Whilst it is in practice independent of Government, its culture is closer to the public sector than the private. A significant part of its income is either directly or indirectly dependent on Government through Housing Benefit payments or capital grants for building new affordable homes. It is regulated and many of its people come from local authorities or have grown up in the sector. I was regularly struck by how religiously many people in the sector followed each nuance and shift in Government policy on housing. With the high rate of turnover of Housing Ministers, there were many such shifts, and much time was spent speculating on what these might mean and hoping for new initiatives which might help their organisation do more. Too often they seemed to be looking upwards to Government for direction and inspiration rather than looking outwards to customers or developments in the wider housing market.

The accountability of the public sector to ministers and Parliament nationally also has an impact on how decisions are taken and attitudes to risk. Ministers are of course ultimately accountable for all of the decisions and actions of their departments, even though in practice these are so numerous as to be way beyond the capacity of even the most able and energetic minister to be involved in and keep on top of. But any mistake or misplaced act can become politically embarrassing for the minister if it becomes public, so the public sector can be very unforgiving of mistakes. This is of course exacerbated by opposition politicians wanting to score points when mistakes come to light and the media also looking for stories that make good copy.

Civil servants tend therefore to be relatively risk-averse and cautious when involved in decision making, seeking shelter in collective decisions through socialisation, to reduce the risk of making mistakes in the first place, or spreading the blame if things then go wrong. This is partly in order to protect their minister, on whose behalf they may be taking decisions, as well as protecting themselves. One of the things I found hardest to get used to when engaging with the Department for Transport was the collectivisation of decisions and how few individuals were prepared to take any decisions on their own. This struck a strong contrast with private sector organisations where good managers and CEOs readily take decisions and accept accountability for them, albeit after consulting with colleagues and subject experts. A practical consequence is that public sector decision and policy making is often very slow. A further consequence is that the public sector often finds it difficult to acknowledge mistakes, with an instinct to quietly cover them up wherever possible rather than investigate and learn from them.

A more subtle consequence of the accountability of civil servants to Ministers is their overwhelming confinement to central London and Whitehall. Most Ministers are also MPs of course, and have to regularly attend Parliament to vote or attend Cabinet or other committee meetings. They therefore have to be based in central London close to Parliament and Downing Street, which means their senior Civil Servants likewise have to be there too to brief or report to ministers and at the latter's beck and call. And more junior Civil Servants in turn need to be readily accessible to brief and report to their seniors. All this is difficult to break away from as Parliamentary business varies from week to week and the timing of votes is rarely capable of being anticipated much in advance, so ministers are frequently required to be on call in the Westminster area. Add to this the reactive nature of much Government business, reacting to media stories, opposition campaigns or merely "events", as Harold MacMillan would have said, and it becomes understandable that much of the policy making part of the civil service feels it has to stay close to Westminster for most of the time. It would also not be unfair to remember that few politicians and ministers have prior experience of managing or working within a large organisation and are therefore relatively unaware of their impact on the diaries of others. They expect their civil servants to be instantly on hand.

The practical consequence of this is that civil servants spend most of their working lives in their departmental offices and rarely "get out and about" to see how the wider world operates. Meetings with those outside the government overwhelmingly take place at the relevant Government Department, rarely at the other organisation's premises. You go to Whitehall if you want to talk to civil servants or ministers, they rarely come to you. This tends to further reinforce the inwards looking nature of the public sector and certainly blunts their ability to keep up with developments outside. It has not always been like this. There used to be a set of Regional Government Offices, responding jointly to the Departments of Transport, Environment and Business whose role was to act as a liaison point with Local Authorities and regional organisations and businesses. They were at least more in touch with the world outside Whitehall and if used effectively were valuable "listening and learning" posts to keep national Government better informed and helping knock some of the rougher edges off national policies.

It takes a very special civil servant to be able to retain a sharp understanding of how the wider world works and is changing. Too often the result is a rather theoretical, simplistic and sometimes out of date understanding of how a particular industry or sector actually works. As a manager and leader I have always found it essential to regularly get out from my office, at least one day a week and ideally more often, to see what is happening on the ground and to meet customers and staff, as well as suppliers, to keep track of trends in their business and often picking up ideas or problems that need to be addressed. This is not a normal habit of civil servants. And it also tends not to be a habit more generally in hierarchical organisations, like most in the public sector, where managers often feel the need to be available in case their superiors call for them.

All of this contributes to a public sector that has insufficient knowledge and understanding of the private sector, tends to be suspicious of the latter's motives and overly cautious and lacking in confidence when engaging with it. Rather than being informed by direct contact most civil servants' perception and understanding of the private sector comes more from the media, or from hearing about public sector outsourcing or other contracts that have gone wrong. The media is of course much more interested in reporting problems and failures, because they are more news worthy, than the many private sector businesses who quietly, honestly and successfully go about their business without sensation. So inevitably the perceptions about the private sector and business amongst many Civil Servants will be distorted.

I was hugely struck by comments on this made to me by Executives from Virgin Group and other train operators, when I was undertaking my Review of Rail Franchising for the Department for Transport (DfT) after the collapse of the West Coast re-franchising process in 2012. In discussing how rail franchising was managed within the DfT they pleaded that they wanted to deal with "people like themselves", who had the confidence to engage as equals, to be tough negotiators and reach clear agreements with pace or just to say "no" in a timely way. They saw this as counter-intuitive from a public sector perspective, believing the latter would assume they would prefer to deal with more junior and less confident and experienced officials whom they could outmanoeuvre and out negotiate. In practice, of course, they were largely dealing with more junior and commercially inexperienced people, but who were consequently overly cautious and suspicious in engaging with them, afraid to do deals and risk "giving something away", so little useful business was actually done. This was not just intensely frustrating for the franchisees but also a sub-optimal way of managing complex and long-lasting franchise contracts.

Virgin's frustration was also of course partly the result of lack of understanding as how the civil service works. As noted already, decisions tend to be collective and socialised and because public funds are involved there are clear rules and authorities. More importantly commercial skills and contract management skills are not a core competence for civil servants. Certainly, one of the "professional streams" in the civil service is commercial, but this is not seen as a route to more senior roles and most civil servants are generalists with a strong focus on the development of policy. The result is that there are not many senior and experienced commercial people in the civil service, either to fill key roles or for generalists to learn from. The commercial competence and confidence of contract managers letting and managing often complex franchise contracts is therefore generally low. The problem is also amplified by the regular turnover of people in post, particularly the more able civil servants working their way up the hierarchy, who tend to move jobs every two or three years, undermining continuity in the management of longer-term contracts. Similar weaknesses are endemic in much of Government procurement - of which franchise contracts are one, albeit large, example - where the instances of projects or service contracts which run late, deliver poor results or exceed budget are legion.

I was likewise struck by Dame Kate Bingham's experiences working with Government during her relatively short spell running the UK's Vaccine Procurement Programme during the Covid Pandemic. In her book "The Long Shot: the inside story of the race to vaccinate Britain" she relates her experiences as someone who previously had worked exclusively in the private sector. She talks about the lack of pace in decision making in Government Departments, their risk aversion and too often their relatively narrow view of risk. She found many of the people she had to deal with had an innate suspicion of the private sector and of private sector people, and had no conception of the importance of being a good customer to get the best outcomes when letting and managing contracts. All of this felt very similar to my own observations.

The interplay between politics and the media also has a profound impact on how policy is developed and managed in the public sector. Ministers have always had to be sensitive to "public opinion" as articulated by the media, but this has become an ever more consuming issue in recent decades with the emergence of the 24hour news agenda and social media. The need for ministers to be seen to take action in response to an interest group campaign or a critical media story too often leads to Ministerial interventions or instructions that are disruptive and distracting for those lower down the public sector hierarchy who are trying to implement policy. Add to this the desire of Ministers, senior and junior alike, to be seen as active and effective by making regular announcements of new policies or initiatives, and the public sector is rarely a stable place to try to implement longer term programmes.

Two examples of such interventions, ironically from the same minister, illustrate the problem. The first was in response to a complaint from a wildlife protection group complaining about Network Rail felling trees during the bird nesting season. The Minister instructed Network Rail to stop all felling during the nesting season, but Mark Carne, the then CEO of Network Rail, rightly refused, saying that he reserved the right to cut trees down for safety reasons at any time. This led to the minister commissioning a review by a third party "expert" of the entirety of Network Rail's vegetation management policies. The outcome of the review was a new set of unfunded obligations on Network Rail to work to improve the biodiversity of its lineside estate; a worthy but onerous new set of responsibilities on an already very stretched organisation.

The second example was the same Minister wanting to make a name for himself as a champion of low carbon and sustainability. He challenged the industry to come up with a strategy to eliminate diesel traction by 2040. The industry duly set up a working group which came up with a well thought through and researched strategy, but which required Government to buy into it and play its part as the owner and de facto guiding mind of the industry. The sponsoring Minister inevitably soon moved on to a different portfolio and ministry, and the strategy has been effectively on the shelf and ignored ever since. The considerable effort involved in producing the strategy was therefore wasted, and expectations having been raised were dashed. A not untypical example of many Government instigated "initiatives".

Reflections on the private sector

An important feature of any private sector business is that resources mainly come from outside the business, from its customers or from investors. The private sector is therefore much more inclined to look outward to customers and to the wider market for ideas and direction, rather than inwards and upwards as in the public sector. This tends to make it much more innovative and responsive than the public sector. In the long run a business will only survive if it has enough customers to cover its costs, so it needs to keep abreast with their changing needs and expectations, and understand and respond to what is happening in its markets or in related sectors which might invade its own. It will always be looking to win new customers by active sales and marketing and by evolving its product. This is a big contrast with the public sector which tends to view demand for its services as something that is just given, or even excessive in the case of some services such as the NHS, and therefore sees no need to try to stimulate or influence the market. In the extreme, demand for a public service can even be seen as a burden, leading to a poor experience for its "customers".

At the same time, of course, a private sector business must ensure that the price it can sell its products at more than cover the costs of producing them. In the long run break-even is not good enough, as there is no surplus to replace worn out assets or in the event of a rainy day. Unless shareholders and investors get a return, they will not provide the funds for new assets, and a falling share price leaves a company at risk of takeover. So, profit is important and the private sector usually pays close attention to managing its costs, so they remain below the prices it can charge. At its very simplest, running a business is about selling something for more than it cost to produce or obtain. And because the margin between costs and revenues from sales is often quite slim the private sector of necessity tends to be quicker and nimbler in adapting to changing trends and much more tenacious in managing its costs.

The contrast between public and private sectors is not confined to financial issues. There is also often a significant difference in their attitudes to and treatment of their employees. As a manager in the private sector you are generally better able to choose the people who work for you or with you, and you in turn are more likely to make an active choice of the company you work for. There is therefore a better alignment in aspirations between employee and employer, with stronger loyalty to the company. Being a good employer and place to work is important to be able to attract and retain people of the right capability and experience. Often in the public sector you will inherit the team or teams that work with you, and you will move on to a new job before you have had much opportunity to reshape your team. Ironically in my experience from British Rail, public sector managers can sometimes end up as better leaders of people because of the necessity of getting the best out of the people you inherit.

Part of this difference is driven by different approaches to hiring and firing, despite employment law applying equally to both sectors. The private sector tends to be much quicker to act when an employee is not performing so they don't become a drag on the business. This is also out of fairness to other employees who may feel and resent a colleague who is not pulling their weight.

The public sector tends to be more sluggish in addressing such performance issues with strong focus on procedures, often exacerbated by the much higher degree of unionisation in the public sector. Ironically this can sometimes be a lot more uncomfortable for the individual or individuals affected, with weeks and even months of uncertainty and worry about the outcome. In managing wider reorganisations an important principle for me was to appreciate that if people are expecting change it is better to get on with it with pace and openness and not to disappoint them. Delay and prevarication can be very unsettling.

In my experience private sector managers are often better and quicker at judging people. This is partly of necessity when considering doing a deal with someone, when you don't have long to decide whether you can trust the other party to deliver in good faith. The law of the "survival of the fittest" comes into play, as too many wrong judgements probably mean you don't stay in business, those who do make more of the right calls. I am often amazed at how poor many politicians are at judging people's capability and how many poor appointments they make as a result.

It is axiomatic in the private sector that it is necessary to pay the rate for the job to hire the right people, and to pay what it takes to get the best person when that is important. It is also usually understood that having chosen, hopefully, the right person they will almost certainly have other choices available to them and so need to be courted. The best interviews are two way, with employer and potential employee both selling themselves. This is not the case in the public sector where interviews tend to be tightly scripted in case of subsequent appeal and it is rarely recognised that the best people are likely to have other options available to them. Part of the "courting" is also timely communication of a job offer once decided. I well remember a case at HS2 Ltd where after much effort the Chairman had persuaded Government that the organisation needed to recruit a Chief Operating Officer to support an increasingly stretched Chief Executive. An individual had been selected but approval for the actual appointment required a treasury minister's approval (at the time Liz Truss). The individual had other job offers but for whatever reason ministerial approval was much delayed so the individual reluctantly accepted another offer which had a shorter deadline attached to it. When approval did finally come through it was too late. The need to get Treasury and/or Cabinet Office approval for senior level appointments, and for all non-executive roles, routinely adds significant time and uncertainty to all public sector appointments processes.

In parallel with its willingness to pay the rate for the job the private sector is usually more willing to empower and give its managers the freedom to manage and to devolve responsibility. Why otherwise pay a good salary; unnecessary layers of oversight cost money. It also implies looking to encourage a "can-do" culture and to recognise and reward successes and good performance. But the logic of paying the rate for the job is a preparedness to buy in talent from outside the company and a weakness of much of the private sector today is a reluctance to invest in developing a long-term stream of talent. Whether this is through apprenticeships or other programmes, there is the perceived risk that talent developed in-house will get poached by others.

In the public sector jobs are closely graded, with rigid salary bands and little flexibility for managers looking to hire people. This problem has worsened enormously since 2010 and the coalition and subsequent Governments who have focussed intensely on holding down public sector pay to contain public expenditure. The Prime Minister's long constrained salary was used as a benchmark for senior positions and paying more than this required special authority from a Treasury Minister or the Cabinet Office. Quotas were introduced for the number of positions that could be paid more, making life very difficult for arms-length organisations such as Network Rail, HS2 Ltd and the Highways Agency, who found it increasingly difficult to recruit high calibre people or those with particular expertise from the private sector. It also suppressed senior civil service pay so that younger high flyers who reach Director level see little further salary progression and many leave for more lucrative private sector roles, greatly reducing the gene pool of future Directors General and Permanent Secretaries. There is little doubt that the quality and capability of the civil service has been materially weakened over this period as a result and there has been a net drain of talent out of the sector.

Much of the private sector's involvement in the rail industry has been through contracts, whether through franchise contracts, contracts to build trains, pieces of infrastructure or supplying a service. Once a contract is signed, fulfilling it becomes the key driver both legally and financially and private companies are good at focusing single-mindedly on delivering it and avoiding distractions. The existence of the contract provides certainty and stability to both parties to it and to its customers. But how the contract is structured becomes all important in determining the outcome, particularly how flexible it is in coping with inevitable unforeseen changes in circumstance, new risks that emerge or new opportunities which arise. This has become a key interface between the public and private sectors in the rail industry, where over-prescriptive or inflexible contracts have too often gone wrong.

As we've seen the public sector is not well provided with the commercial and procurement capability to design and manage these often complex contracts effectively. To get the best from private sector contractors requires strong procurement and contract management skills. If rail services are to continue to be procured through franchises or concession contracts in future, these skills are much more likely to be built up in an organisation at arms-length from Government, such as GBR, or the Strategic Rail Authority and OPRAF before that. Procurement and contract management would be core skills for such a body rather than one which is little more than a sideline for the Civil Service.

It is also the case of course that the private sector contains many different types of companies, both good and bad, and with different ownership structures. A shortcoming of much public sector procurement in the UK is that it is not good at distinguishing between potentially good and bad contractors, awarding contracts on what is promised rather than on their past track record of delivering. This is partly driven by procurement law introduced when the UK was part of the European Union, and ideally needs to be relaxed to ensure a potential contractor's past record of delivery can be taken into account as well as what it promises for a new contract. I well remember bidding for rail franchise contracts in the State of Victoria, Australia, where the State Government's Franchising Authority did extensive due diligence on our record at National Express before awarding us any contracts, in sharp contrast to how the UK Government awards franchises.

It is also interesting how the types of private companies participating in UK rail franchises has changed over the years. The first round of franchise awards in 1995-7 included seven publicly listed companies: National Express, First Group, Stagecoach, Go-Ahead Group, Arriva, Serco and Prism Rail. There are now only two listed companies still involved in running franchises: First Group and Serco. Arriva was bought firstly by Deutsche Bundesbahn, the German national rail operator and sold recently to an Infrastructure Investment fund. Prism Rail was bought out by National Express who alongside Stagecoach subsequently chose to withdraw from the sector. Go-Ahead was sold to a consortium of Australian and Spanish investors. This significant churn in the companies holding rail franchise contracts, in terms of both their identity and type, suggests that the real expertise in managing rail services resides within the franchise operating companies themselves rather than in the holding companies.

So, in conclusion there is nothing magical about private sector operation of rail services. Letting contracts to run services can bring valuable stability and certainty for the term of the contract, particularly if the services are to benefit from any great scale of investment. It will greatly reduce the risk of inadvertent political changes of direction. Doing this via a competitive bidding process can ensure a check on value for money and introduce greater ambition to how the services are developed. But success will depend on how contractors are selected as well as how the contracts are designed and overseen, if the advantages of private sector involvement are to be properly exploited. The contracts need to be flexible enough to respond to unforeseen changes or new opportunities and give maximum freedom to the contractor to innovate and seek new passengers, so harnessing the private sector's instinct to look outwards to the market and customers for inspiration.

CHAPTER 16   Reflections On Franchising

In October 2012 I received a call from the Permanent Secretary at the Department for Transport, Phillip Rutnam, asking whether I would be prepared to lead a review of passenger rail franchising for the Government. The competition for the next West Coast Mainline franchise between Virgin and First Group had just been suspended because of recently revealed shortcomings in the way the Department had been calculating the performance bonds required. The competition had become increasingly acrimonious, with Virgin alleging shortcomings in the process, which proved to have substance. Two of the Non-Executive Directors on the Board of the Department, Sam Laidlaw and Ed Smith, had already been asked to investigate how the competition had gone wrong. I was being asked to look at how franchising should be reformed going forward.

I assume I was seen as something of a "clean skin", not having been involved as a bidder or franchisee since leaving National Express at the end of 2001, but having been closely involved in franchising up until then. I was intrigued by the challenge and was by this time working only part time at Eurostar so immediately accepted the task. I was asked to report by the end of the year which gave me only around ten weeks to undertake the review. Several friends urged me to push for a longer time horizon, but given the urgency of the issue, I stuck with the deadline. In effect the whole franchising programme had been suspended, after an already long hiatus in letting new franchises. The investments and contracts which flowed from each award were effectively frozen too, meaning that the whole industry was in limbo until a reformed franchising programme could be restarted. I took the view that aiming to deliver a report that was 80% right was better than taking rather longer to get closer to 100%, but prolonging the hiatus.

Leading the review (^{6}) gave me a unique and privileged insight into the whole franchising process, from both the franchisees' and Government's point of view. It was an opportunity to reflect on the strengths and weaknesses of the whole process as well as to try to improve it. With hindsight, it was almost inevitable that the West Coast competition would fail as the Department had seriously under resourced it. It emerged that there had only been a single civil servant wholly devoted to working on the competition, everyone else involved continued to have other responsibilities as well. Senior level responsibility had also been passed from one Director General, responsible for "policy", to another responsible for "delivery" midway through the process, hardly a recipe for effective oversight! I calculated at the time that, had the First Group bid been accepted, it would have been a contract worth £20 billion over its 15-year term, an enormous contract by any standards and deserving a strong and highly professional procurement team to run the bid process and contract award.

It was also the case that the Department had lost much "corporate memory" in running franchise competitions, following the major reorganisation and cuts in the numbers of staff over the previous two years as part of the Coalition Government's austerity cuts. The previous Permanent Secretary, prompted by Philip Hammond who was the Secretary of State for the first months of the Coalition Government, had cut staff numbers by 20% and reduced the numbers of Directors General from five to three, so abolishing the role of a dedicated DG for Rail. In the event it was the second Director General involved, Peter Strachan

---

^{6} " The Brown Review of the Rail Franchising Programme", Cmnd 8526, January 2013

who was responsible for delivery, who was held responsible, paying the price by being required to resign. He was not a career Civil Servant and had only recently joined the Department after a career spent in the UK and Australian rail industries. I had worked with him in both countries. It rather felt like a case of the civil service closing ranks and looking after its own, conveniently finding an "outsider" to attribute blame to. Whatever the facts of the case, I suspect that Peter would have found it difficult to defend himself, lacking a network of colleagues prepared to speak up for him and being still rather unfamiliar with how the civil service really worked.

In practice there was a relatively blank sheet of paper as to how franchising should be organised and structured going forward. At the time I had little doubt that franchising remained the right way to continue. Certainly, there was no hint from Government that they wanted to fundamentally change course, so if I had recommended abandoning the policy I am clear my report would have been shelved very quickly. And at the time all the evidence pointed to the policy having been badly mishandled by the Department rather than being the wrong way to proceed.

Certainly, franchising had its critics at the time but subsequently it has become almost conventional wisdom that it is a bad way to organise a railway and attracts widespread criticism. But its strengths should not be overlooked and ideally these should be retained if some form of concession or franchising continues in future. Foremost amongst these is the enormous incentive it gives to franchisees to attract more passengers and grow passenger revenue to fill their trains better. Once a franchise contract is let, most of its costs become effectively fixed for the rest of its term. Infrastructure costs are largely fixed anyway and train leases, station access contracts and the committed timetable fix most of the remaining costs. Passenger numbers are then the one free variable available to the franchisee to achieve its financial targets, creating an enormous incentive to win new customers and grow revenue, whatever the economic climate. Much has been made of the favourable climate enjoyed by franchises for much of the time since privatisation. Growing road congestion, falling car ownership amongst the under 30s age group and city centre populations and employment growing again after a long period of decline between the 1960s and 1980s, all provided impetus for passenger growth. But exploiting these opportunities to grow passenger numbers would not have been achieved on the scale it has been without this powerful drive. Many of the same trends were also present in other European countries, but the UK saw consistently the fastest growth in rail passenger numbers, outpacing every other country in Europe.

As well as incentivising franchisees to seek more passengers throughout the franchise term, the bidding process also strongly encouraged bidders to be ambitious with their plans for train services. New services, increased frequencies of existing services and new and refurbished train fleets all featured prominently in bids. My review noted that passenger train kilometres increased by 60% between 1994 and 2011 for instance, an unprecedented level of growth compared to previous decades. Passenger numbers also more than doubled during this period. This growth created a virtuous circle, with many more trains being run to cater for passenger growth and in turn attracting new passengers because of improved frequencies and new linkages.

Quite simply, to win a franchise competition you had to be ambitious and offer a better financial outcome for Government, in terms either of higher premium payments or lower subsidy than offered by other bidders, and a more attractive offering to passengers. This was competition for the market - given the lack of competition within rail markets - working well in practice. To put together a winning franchise bid you had to undertake a thorough review of that franchise's markets, service structure and performance and work out how you could do better. Such in-depth reviews of the strategy for each franchise, every seven years or so, undoubtedly benefited Government as the ultimate "freehold" owner of each franchise as well as its passengers, and would be unlikely to be either so searching or frequent in the absence of any competition.

Once a franchise had been let the train service levels and other developments within it then had contractual status for the whole of the franchise term bringing much greater stability and certainty for passengers and local communities than existed before franchising. With franchising now suspended, changes to train service levels are now again a regular feature of the Department's short-term concession contracts. This is a frequently overlooked benefit of franchising, or any comparable competitive bidding and contracting process, and contrasts sharply with the uncertainties that British Rail and its passengers faced with its finances essentially only agreed on an annual basis, and therefore an often-perceived risk of service reductions in subsequent years.

The role of the Treasury in the franchising process is important but usually below the radar. The Treasury effectively determines what each Government Department can spend over a four-year period, following a comprehensive spending review. For the Department for Transport this determines what it can spend on franchise support as well as on capital and operational support to Network Rail. Whilst in theory this allows a firm four-year planning horizon of the Treasury's funding for spending, it is not contractually fixed and new Government priorities or external shocks, such as the 2007 financial crash or Covid, can lead to cuts being required within the four-year period. But franchises and their support or premium payments are contractually fixed, so cannot be changed to meet shorter term Treasury requirements, providing important financial and planning stability to the rail industry.

The Treasury supported the principles of franchising because the competitive bidding process provided a way to test the cost and ensure value for money of each franchise package. The costs to Government reduced over time and it welcomed the opportunity to pass revenue and other risk to the private sector. Treasury sign-off of all new franchise contracts has always been a requirement, not just the approval of the Secretary of State for Transport. Realistically, Treasury buy-in will need to be obtained for whatever structure replaces franchising. As an aside, the Department for Transport's Deputy Director, who very effectively provided the support for my Review, made sure that I kept the Treasury abreast of my thinking and briefed them on my emerging conclusions, in recognition of their crucial but largely hidden importance. It is believed that one of the reasons for the long hiatus in implementing the Williams report on the rail industry's structure is the Treasury's opposition to the idea of letting concession contracts without revenue risk to the contractor, because of the importance they attach to it as a driver of improving the industry's economics.

It is fair to say that, at the time of my Review in 2012, franchising as a system was seen in Government and by many in the industry as broadly successful, in need of some reform but certainly not broken. How then is it that at the time of writing, 2024, it is seen much more widely (but possibly not within the Treasury) as having failed and needing replacement by something different? Two key factors have been the constraints on the way franchises are let, demanded by the Treasury, and the growing political pressures put on the process, particularly the political outcry which has accompanied each franchise "failure". The media and political reaction to each case of failure has tended to further sour public perception of the principle of franchising, and the resulting post-mortems have often led to further complexity and tightening of the conditions of subsequent franchises. But the Treasury has in almost all cases insisted on franchises being let to the highest bidder, which other things being equal, also means to the riskiest bid and therefore increasing the chances of a franchise failing with all the attendant media and political criticism. The outcry that accompanies a franchise failure has then done nothing to enhance the reputation of franchising. Several Secretaries of State for Transport have done much to stoke this outcry, making strident statements about how failed franchise owners should be punished.

Two themes of my Franchise Review were the importance of allocating risks to the party best able to manage them and the need to accept that some franchises will fail, as is the case with any contractual relationship. It has always struck me as ironic that franchise failures and subsequent transfer of responsibility to another operator have always been totally seamless, with no passengers ever turned away, no trains ever cancelled, no one losing their jobs except perhaps for one or two top managers. And the Government usually gained financially because of the franchisee forfeiting their performance bond. The outcry has always been purely political and with Secretaries of State too often succumbing to cheap theatricals to signal their indignation. In reality of course the franchiser, as the organisation designing and letting the contract, should not escape a share of the blame for letting an ill-designed contract or selecting an inappropriate contractor or a too ambitious bid. But Governments always find it difficult to admit any blame and it is more convenient to blame the private franchisee.

The issue of risk transfer, particularly for passenger revenue, has continued to be central to the debate about franchising and with hindsight I regret that my Review did not explore more radical ways of managing this. A core theme of my recommendations was that responsibility for risk should be given to the party best able to manage it. Franchisees should not be expected to carry macroeconomic risk for how well the economy as a whole performs over any long period, as this was a risk they could not manage. The transfer of 100% marginal revenue risk has consistently proved a powerful incentive for franchisees, ensuring they received all the revenue gained from attracting more passengers. But assuming this risk over a seven or even longer period without any mitigation has often proved problematic.

The Hatfield crash and subsequent meltdown of services, the 2007/2008 financial crash and more recently the Covid pandemic, were all macro-level events substantially reducing revenues that were impossible for franchisees to avoid or successfully manage. Designing a more flexible mechanism to allow adjustment to franchise premia/support payments is essential. My review explored various means of doing this including linking the franchise payments to national GDP or central London employment levels so franchisees did not have to carry macroeconomic risk. The Strategic Rail Authority (SRA) successfully managed the first of these events, negotiating appropriate changes to a number of franchises' financial commitments to enable them to continue in operation. It was rather easier for the SRA to quietly do this with little fuss, being an arms-length Government Agency less in the immediate political spotlight. A mechanism that allows a rebasing of a franchise contract's premia/support payments every two to three years, depending on events external to the franchise, would largely solve this problem. But it would require a very different approach to how franchise competitions are structured and evaluated.

More importantly my Review inevitably pulled its punches on the issue of who should manage franchising and how any franchising unit should be structured. I outlined three broad options for this: the Department for Transport continuing to let and manage franchises; setting up an Executive Agency similar to the then Highways Agency to do this; or to set up a standalone organisation similar to the original Office of Passenger Rail Franchising (OPRAF), which very successfully led the first round of franchising. Deciding on which option was most appropriate would have been a complex task beyond the capability of my Review and I recommended that in the medium term the Department should consider where best to place the responsibility for the franchising organisation. With hindsight I now recognise that this almost inevitably meant the Department opting for the status quo, as indeed it did, as the line of least resistance. This was also in line with the centralising instincts of UK Governments over the last few decades, where the Whitehall Civil Service machine or Westminster politicians have seldom willingly ceded control to other bodies.

But subsequent experience, as a continuing observer of the franchising process and also as a Non-Executive Member of the Department for Transport Board for four years, has convinced me that the Department is not the right body to manage franchising, or indeed a number of aspects of railway policy. Britain's railways have always been of political interest, going right back to the days of the pre-war private railway companies, during the nationalised British Rail period and since the privatisation of the 1990s. But having the responsibility for franchising procurement and management wholly within a central Whitehall Department has meant the whole process becoming steadily ever more politicised. Each emerging problem or piece of bad publicity for the industry has too often led to ministers wanting to be seen to be in charge and requiring actions which have led to central Government being involved in more and more of the minutiae of rail decisions. To have civil servants based in Whitehall effectively deciding on railway timetables and stopping patterns of individual trains is clearly absurd, but that has become the reality of England's railways today.

Franchises are complex and commercially sophisticated contracts which do not easily lend themselves to being managed by a central Government Department. They require a highly professional procurement team to let them and commercially savvy and experienced contract managers to oversee them once let. My Review recommended substantially strengthening the capability of the franchising teams, bringing in individuals with senior level experience of procurement, commercial negotiation, finance and programme management from outside the Department and from the rail and other sectors, as well as from other Departments. But in the event the Civil Service has been largely unable to attract sufficient experienced people from outside, partly because of severe restrictions on the salaries it can offer and partly because of the lack of effective career progression for commercial specialists as opposed to civil service generalists. I am not even sure the resulting gap is even recognised within senior levels of the Civil Service, who themselves have little hands-on experience or real understanding of large contract procurements and their subsequent oversight. Most people involved are therefore still generalist career civil servants, typically moving jobs every two or three years so unable to build up in-depth commercial or rail expertise. Locating franchising within a standalone agency would at least make it much easier to offer career paths that built the necessary expertise and corporate memory, and highlight the need to pay appropriate salaries.

Re-reading my Franchising Review of 2012 I was struck by the number of times that we made reference to the importance of approaching franchise management on a partnership basis. This is the way that most successful private sector contractual relationships work, treating the contractor as a trusted delivery partner who will usually know better than their customer how delivery performance could be improved. But such a relationship requires trust and respect on both sides, and for the Franchising Authority it requires having confident and commercially experienced people who understand the passenger railway and who can work with and negotiate successfully with their counterparts. As I observed in Chapter 15, too often franchise managers at the Department are relatively junior, not widely experienced, often somewhat suspicious of the private sector and therefore not confident or effective in negotiating win-win amendments or improvements to franchise contracts. The result is that franchise contracts become rigid documents once signed, lacking the flexibility to adapt to changing circumstances or new opportunities that arise.

It is also the case that national level Government finds it institutionally difficult to work in partnership with others. Instinctively it wants to take the credit for successes and look for others to blame when things go wrong and is paranoid about wanting to be seen to be tough and demanding of its suppliers and contractors. Much of this is driven by our system of adversarial politics with the opposition always looking to find fault with the Government's and individual minister's performance, feeding and feeding off the media, and the Government and ministers needing to react and defend their performance. But this all makes building any sort of partnership relationship with franchisees very difficult.

For all of these reasons, due reflection leads me to the firm conclusion that responsibility for franchising, or whatever may replace it, needs to be removed from the Department for Transport and placed with some sort of arm's length body, similar to the original OPRAF organisation. If Great British Railways, or some similar "single guiding mind" for the industry is set up, then clearly this body needs to be an integral part of it. Whilst this would not take franchising/concessions and passenger rail policy out of the political arena altogether, it would distance Ministers allowing them a degree of deniability on many detailed issues and remove them from the need to react to every issue that arises. It would give much greater flexibility to franchise managers to take more difficult and controversial decisions away from the close media and Opposition scrutiny that Westminster Government involves.

So much for some of the strengths of franchising. Further reflection and experience since 2012 show a number of important shortcomings in both the structure and the way in which franchising has been managed by the Department for Transport. Probably the most serious shortcoming has been the lack of reform and of any real modernisation of the whole ticketing and fares regime. Passenger fares are regulated by the Department for Transport through the franchising regime, not incidentally by the Office of Rail Regulation, and their structure remains almost wholly as inherited from British Rail before the 1990s. It is convenient for politicians to point the blame to the franchised rail companies for the lack of reform, but they have their hands tied by the requirements of their franchise agreements, and it is the Department as de facto regulator that holds the key to reform and has been consistently highly cautious and reluctant to agree changes. Fares structures are a highly technical subject and it is questionable whether the Department has the competence to design their reform, but it is equally unlikely that franchisees would collectively be able to agree on a single structure as each is likely to be affected differently and there will inevitably be winners and losers. The absence of a single "guiding mind", as envisaged by the Williams Review, to lead the reform process using its expertise and in-depth knowledge of the rail industry and its passengers has undoubtedly held back reform.

Likewise, rail ticketing and reservation systems increasingly lag behind other sectors and those of Transport for London. The IT systems needed to underpin modern ticketing would require significant investment in a common platform and would need to be mandated by the Department, as the benefits are spread across the industry but costs imposed individually. The fragmented structure of 17 or so franchises, each with different business profiles, simply does not lend itself to the sort of collective specification and investment in system wide IT platforms that the railway needs. One result has been the growth of third-party internet-based ticket retailers, particularly Trainline, who provide a much used service but inevitably capture a significant financial surplus at the expense of the industry's effective owner, the Government. This is in sharp contrast with other rail networks, such as SNCF in France, who have invested heavily in internet based retail and ticketing systems and who see the likes of Trainline as direct competitors.

In the case of both fares structure and ticketing systems it is the lack of an informed and capable guiding mind to design and champion the necessary changes and manage the investments needed that has prevented reform and modernisation. For all the reasons we've seen already, the Department for Transport does not have the capability or industry knowledge to do this. In no sense is it, or could it ever be, an effective guiding mind. Likewise, the franchise sector cannot do the job, as individual franchise companies each have a different mix of fares and markets and therefore priorities for reform, and are in any case beholden to their owning groups for investment funding.

Workforce reform is another area where the franchising model has not been particularly helpful. The rail unions have long been very resistant to changes in working practices to modernise them or to take advantage of new technology and improve efficiency. This has been particularly true of train crew, signallers and track maintenance staff. The gains from such changes are often quite modest in the short term because of the need to "buy in" the change, only yielding real benefit over a longer period than remaining franchise terms, and can be outweighed by the short-term loss of revenue from strike action. As a result, franchises have usually been reluctant to attempt to tackle sometimes very outdated train crew terms and conditions. It is noteworthy that the Southern Railway, part of the Govia Thameslink Railway (GTR) franchise, is an isolated example of successful reform to the role of their train guards. But GTR were contracted to implement this reform under their franchise agreement and the structure of the franchise meant that revenue risk, unusually, was retained by the DfT, making it much less financially damaging for GTR to persist with reform.

Finally an obvious shortcoming of franchising is that it only addresses half of the industry. The track is subject to a completely different financial regime, with the administered charges of the track access regime providing no indication of the true infrastructure costs of an individual route or group of train services. Using administered rather than actual track costs obscures the overall economics of each route or group of train services, leading to the risk that decisions to increase or decrease a particular train service are taken without full knowledge of their impact on whole industry costs. And Network Rail decisions on route by route spending are taken without any knowledge of the overall economics of each route and their relative value. Overall it is very likely that this financial fault-line between track and train will have led to a number of sub-optimal decisions over the years.

For the future, if there continues to be some form of franchising, management contracts or concessions of passenger services to private operators, then the procurement process needs to be run by experienced, confident and commercially savvy people. Contract oversight needs to be managed as a partnership with the contractor, with greater flexibility to adjust terms when external circumstances change. And contract specifications should be much less detailed than they have become, be focused on outcomes not inputs, and give the contractor much more freedom to innovate and improve.

CHAPTER 17 On teamwork and leadership

For the majority of my life I have been involved in or leading teams. Unquestionably the highlights of my career, the things that I'm most proud of or I look back on with fondest memories, all took place when I was part of a wider team. And when I was planning this chapter it came to me that the two occasions in my career when I was least happy were when I was either not part of any team but working absolutely as an individual or when I was a member of a leadership group which simply didn't work as a team. The former was when I was briefly Personal Assistant to one of the two BR Joint Managing Directors. I had a boss who viewed my position more as a status symbol of his seniority in the organisation than as a potential resource and aide. I had no responsibility and no substantive working relationships with others in the organisation.

The other occasion was when I was Commercial Director of National Express Group (NEG), part of a four-person executive team running NEG alongside the CEO, COO and Finance Director. My colleagues were simply not team players. The Finance Director was a strong character who could be something of a bully, was very ambitious and was more interested in commercial projects than accounting and finance. The COO was something of a control freak who ran four of NEG's then five divisions, including their commercial policies. He was an old friend and colleague of the CEO, and whilst he and I got on well, he had no time for the Finance Director, nor the latter for him. And the CEO was not really interested in putting in the effort to get us working more as a team than as a set of strong-minded individuals, despite my urgings. The result was a leadership team that was not really a team at all. I have never been very good at or interested in playing office politics, so my role was progressively squeezed between my colleagues and in due course I was rightly made redundant.

So, teams are important to me, and I believe central to success in a highly interdependent and complex industry like the railways. This has led me to reflect on what is involved in making an effective team and how they are best led. I've been involved in a wide range of different teams, in differing situations, at school, University and at work and so I've tried to tease out below what I think is involved and what are the key factors determining how effective they are. I do so with considerable trepidation and humility as there are numerous books and studies on the subject by people far better qualified than me. I will merely try to relate my personal experiences and learnings. I certainly feel that I was very lucky, and that serendipity played a big role, with each team and leadership experience helping prepare me for the next one.

The first point is that working in a team should be enjoyable, stimulating and rewarding - and ideally fun. If it is just uphill work and no fun there is probably something wrong with the team. Whether it is the sharing of challenges, experiences and successes, a sense of companionship from being part of a shared endeavour or the stimulation and excitement that comes from a group of people with diverse backgrounds, styles and knowledge sparking off each other, people need to feel it is worthwhile being part of the team. They need to be, or at least become, willing members of the team.

Teams and teamwork are always situational. They come in numerous shapes and sizes. Two people can form a team, either in an on-going relationship - how often do you hear the phrase "they make a good team" describing a married couple - or to undertake a specific task together. Early in my career I was in a two-person team with the manager in charge of training and development at Freightliner. The MD had charged me with leading the company's graduate recruitment scheme, after I had been critical of the way it was being organised. (This incidentally was a shrewd move on the part of the MD, Cyril Bleasdale's part, to test out a young manager to either perform or quieten down). I had no experience or knowledge of training or HR issues, and was acutely aware that recruitment was already this other manager's responsibility and I could be treading on toes. Fortunately, Ken Brown, the manager concerned, was not a graduate himself, and was aware he didn't understand universities or their output. Our knowledge and experience were therefore complementary and we were both natural collaborators, so we formed a good team and were successful in relaunching the company's graduate programme together over the next two years. Key ingredients were mutual respect and tact between us, and an appetite to work with and get to know new colleagues from very different backgrounds and learn from each other.

Teams can either have a single focus, as in project teams to deliver an investment project or address a particular problem, or standing teams as in the management team leading an organisational unit. My first experience of the former was in my very first job in the Corporate Planning team at Freightliner. The team was set up to undertake a comprehensive review of Freightliner's strategy and finances and was disbanded after this was completed. We were all young graduates, including several interns from the USA, keen to learn and to make an impact. It was exciting to feel at the centre of things, we had a lot of fun and it proved to be a wonderfully accelerated way to learn about the company.

Two jobs later I then had my first experience of working in a standing team when I was appointed Deep Sea National Account Sales Manager for Freightliner and inherited a team of four as its leader. Two of the team were much older and more experienced and the other two ambitious, recent graduates like myself, so I had little right to be the leader. Arrogance can often come into play and my experience at school as a Head of House and School Prefect at least gave me the confidence to step up to the challenge of leadership. It would have been possible to manage the team as a set of individuals, letting each of the three Account Managers do their own thing and compete to deliver the best results, but I tried to foster an atmosphere where we shared ideas and problems and took some pride in our collective monthly results. The latter was not hard as Deep Sea was the best performing sector of Freightliner's business in terms of both growth and profitability. I hope I was seen as a supportive and not overly demanding boss, although in those days few organisations engaged in any formal team building or 360degree feedback to find out.

Moving to BR's recently formed InterCity Sector I became part of a much larger and geographically distributed team. In many ways it is possible to develop the same sense of belonging and shared endeavour in a company or business as in a much smaller team. As well as a growing central team we had small teams in four of BR's five Regional Headquarters offices and we shared a sense of excitement being a part of a new business unit with a challenging financial target to achieve and the opportunity to make a real impact on the railway. As Business Planning Manager I became de facto project manager for an initiative to take over direct responsibility for all marketing and sales activity, transferring staff into InterCity and greatly strengthening the regionally based teams. I enjoyed working with the managers of each of the regional teams to design their new organisations, trying to ensure a degree of commonality across each team but also being sensitive to the particular needs and ideas of each regional manager. They were all more experienced and senior to me and I suppose an important motivation for me was to earn their respect and demonstrate I could operate at their level.

Trying to impose a single organisational template with them was never an option, so I learnt a lot about the value of collaboration and persuasion and how to facilitate sharing of ideas.

My first substantial leadership role was when I was appointed InterCity Business Manager in Birmingham, responsible for bottom line performance of two of InterCity's sub-sectors, the West Coast Mainline and Midland Mainline. This was one of the regional InterCity managers positions I had just been collaborating with, so at least I felt familiar with the role. I inherited a team of some thirty people who were very able and experienced but surprisingly rather demotivated. It turned out that my predecessor, who was a much more knowledgeable railway professional than myself, tried to do much too much himself so many of his reports felt disempowered. In nearly every case my direct reports knew much more about their specialisms than I did, and were clearly capable, so it felt natural to let them get on with their jobs without any sense of my looking over their shoulder or trying to do their work. With hindsight it was a perfect lesson in the importance of empowering people and providing light touch and trusting leadership. I found it was really very easy being the leader of this team, giving each manager the space to get on with their respective jobs was the key, so morale and motivation improved remarkably quickly. The team came up with many great initiatives and we achieved much in my three years there.

At the same time, I became a member of BR's London Midland Region management team. This was a large team of functional managers and other business managers like myself, but lacked the same common purpose we enjoyed as managers within a defined business. There were also tensions within the team about the way BR's business-led organisation was developing. There were individuals who didn't agree with the idea of business units but it was nevertheless essential to have a productive working relationship with them. It was again important to earn their respect, if not their active support, and to be fully open and above board on everything. I also learnt the value of developing close relationships and alliances with more like-minded individuals within the team to get things done. Again, what was most rewarding was getting to know and forming friendships with people from very different backgrounds and disciplines.

This was at a time when British Rail was attempting a serious culture change across the organisation with its Total Quality Management programme, described in Chapter 13. Both the "Leadership 500" and "Leadership 5000" courses were core parts of this initiative. Both focussed on developing leadership and team building skills in a total quality management framework with around 50 people attending each course and working extensively in smaller teams as well as attending group talks. The concept of starting with the most senior people, including Executive Board Members, and cascading downwards was very powerful and ensured that what people learnt on the courses was reinforced and often practically applied when they returned to their day jobs. People could see that the organisation was serious when their bosses used the same language of change and improvement and participated in or initiated quality improvement teams looking at specific problems.

The Leadership and TQM programmes generated a huge amount of positive energy across the organisation and I have little doubt they made the subsequent huge changes in organisational structure and privatisation much smoother than they might otherwise have been. It also inculcated in a generation of managers a more collaborative, team-based approach that stood the industry in good stead for a number of years after privatisation. In many ways the impact of the culture change programme was masked and overtaken by privatisation and I'm not sure its potential power has ever been properly recognised. The extent to which the ideas of total quality management had become embedded in the organisational culture is perhaps best symbolised in the naming of BR's radical and final reorganisation into business-led and vertically integrated profit centres "Organising for Quality". Sadly, the ideas and ethos were steadily eroded after privatisation as new owners and organisations, who had not shared the same experience, took over.

In 1991 BR's sub-sector organisation began the process of transformation into firstly business-led profit centres and then into the 50 plus organisations into which BR was split for privatisation. I was appointed to lead the new Midland Cross Country profit centre within InterCity, which brought together two "cinderella" routes, Cross Country and Midland Main Line, and which subsequently morphed into Midland Main Line for privatisation. This of course needed me to build two new management teams, the most challenging being Midland Cross Country as it was an entirely new organisation with no previous focus or identity. This was a once in a lifetime opportunity to select all of my own team, rarely possible other than in a business start-up or project situation. Because some twenty-five other profit centres were being set up at the same time there was inevitably competition for the best people to form the new teams. For the most part I chose people I already knew and had worked with, and who I trusted and rated as good managers. In several cases I had to work quite hard to persuade them to join us. I also sought to attract several of the Area Managers and Engineers from the outgoing Regional structure who had responsibility across the East Midlands, to ensure we started with some local knowledge of the railway we would be running. This was also helpful in reassuring some of the front-line staff who would be transferring into the new organisation under familiar bosses.

The result was an entirely new management team most of whom had not worked together before, had a range of personalities and who came from a wide range of different management backgrounds. One of my appointments was a Quality Manager, Christine Taylor, who had worked with me in Birmingham and who played a key role in running a number of team building events to start to build, not just a high performing team culture, but a shared vision of what we wanted the new organisation to achieve. We quickly learnt that even the strongest team needs a clear and fully shared sense of purpose to perform to its full potential. At times it was hard work, and several team members appeared sceptical about the amount of time we spent on the process but I am clear it was worth the effort. Christine's skills were such that she went to set up her own very successful Quality and Team Building consultancy after leaving the business on privatisation.

An important ingredient in a good team culture is that each member has full trust in each of their colleagues, that they will do their jobs effectively and work collaboratively across departmental boundaries. I learnt that this trust can take longer to develop, and only really comes with actual experience of working together over time. There were fairly regular instances of tension between two departmental managers, where one felt the other was not supporting something they were doing or working in a different direction. Often this was simply based on misunderstanding but it also arose where personalities and management styles were different. Defusing the tensions and sorting out the various bilateral relationships was essential, and I came to recognise that this is a key task for the team leader, to ensure everyone is working together harmoniously. "Knocking heads together" would be an old-fashioned term for the necessary leadership action, and, in most cases, it meant requiring the two managers to sit down together and sort out their differences. Getting involved in mediation or arbitration between them was likely to merely paper over any cracks and be very time consuming. But it also required keeping a quiet eye on each bilateral relationship and intervening early rather than letting things fester, whilst ensuring the team remained focused on the agreed strategy and goals. Altogether, ensuring both the team as a whole and each bilateral relationship between team members are working harmoniously is a key task for a leader and I learned is more time consuming than often recognised.

Some tensions between different functional mangers are inevitable and healthy, for instance between marketing or sales and operations or between finance and spending departments. The trick is to ensure these tensions are constructive and result in good outcomes for the organisation and its customers. As well as collaborative and respectful bilateral relationships, it is helpful if the leadership team have agreed and all buy into a shared strategy and set of goals for the organisation, so that any conflicts are resolved within this framework.

On several occasions the use of behavioural analysis tools could be transformational, either in better understanding each other's preferred team roles using the Belbin model, or in understanding their preferred thinking style using the Myers Briggs model. A classic example came later at Eurostar where the Commercial Director and Chief Operating Officer had very different thinking styles and initially found themselves frequently at odds and misunderstanding the other. When they understood each other's Myers Briggs profile and how it interacted with their own it was like a lightbulb going on and their relationship was transformed. I know that, of the Belbin team roles, I am a very strong monitor evaluator and shaper, and that understanding this helped my colleagues tolerate my sometimes overly sharp contributions to a team discussion.

At the same time, I was also a member of the wider InterCity management team which we called the InterCity

Directors Group (ICDG). This was a group of 16 individuals, three of whom had been Regional General Managers in the old structure and most of whom were strong personalities and widely experienced. Whilst there were clearly shared goals and a passion for the business, the "storming" stage of team building lasted much longer than usual before it evolved into the "performing" stage. Group discussions were often heated and laborious, taking longer to arrive at a collective decision. Several of us formed an informal quality improvement team to analyse our collective behaviours and what was hindering and what was helping our deliberations.

The outcome was a "tent" card which we placed in the centre of the table for all of our meetings and which set out a set of meeting rules to which everyone subscribed. This included good meeting behaviours and behaviours to be avoided, with anyone being able to point to the card and call out a colleague who lapsed into one of the latter behaviours. A good example was "violently agreeing", when in reality there was agreement on a particular issue but one or more members felt so strongly that they essentially made the same point, but in an ever more animated way, because they wanted their voice to be heard and counted. It merely took up precious meeting time unnecessarily. The quality and efficiency of meetings steadily improved thereafter although such a large group was always going to be challenging. The same process produced a set of guidelines for InterCity managers and Directors for how to behave when travelling on trains and how and when to provide support to customer service staff on the train. The two together were a powerful statement of intent of how the leaders of InterCity sought to behave and set an example to other managers and staff.

The shared experience of "storming" then "performing" as a team helped build strong bonds within the team, which were reinforced when the chosen route to privatisation became clear. Everyone in the group was variously dismayed or gutted by the decision to effectively wind up InterCity both as a brand and as a business and each of us needing to follow a different path in the privatised industry. The strong camaraderie and trust that had been built up provided a safe place to share this dismay and support each other in the often difficult times that followed. The core of the Directors Group continued to meet semi-illicitly over dinner every month for many months afterwards sharing intelligence and experiences as privatisation unfolded. Nearly thirty years on those of us still alive and well continue to meet annually for a pub lunch; the "team's spirit" lives on.

When InterCity as an organisation disappeared, I reverted to being a member and leader of a single team, Midland Main Line's management team. In practice this was a subset of the previous Midland Cross Country team so we all knew and trusted one another and shared a strong drive to build our business as one of the top performing Train Operating Companies in the new structure and try to ensure we were privatised early. It was a very stressful period as for two years we were effectively each doing three jobs simultaneously: setting up and running a new company, preparing it for "sale" via franchising, and bidding to win the franchise through a management bid.

We developed a brief "check in" routine at the start of each of our management meetings, to share how each us was feeling as well as any wins or setbacks encountered in the previous week. We also came to understand the idea of "passing the ball" where someone stepped in to support a colleague, usually seamlessly and without being asked. This was often in support of me as the leader, where a colleague stepped up to lead at a meeting or on a particular issue, in effect developing a collective leadership. I am very clear that we could not have succeeded as we did without the strength and support of such a strong team. Unsurprisingly, several colleagues went on to lead their own businesses subsequently.

Moving on to becoming Chief Executive of National Express's Trains Division, I tried to foster a team approach across the five Train Company Managing Directors and our two divisional headquarters Directors. But the five Train Companies had very different markets and economics, with little synergy between them, so there was less common purpose to drive a strong team approach. It underlined the importance of needing a shared purpose and focus for a strong and effective team to emerge. There was a good atmosphere of trust and respect within the team but little to show in terms of impact.

In my next role as Commercial Director and main board member of National Express Group, my team skills became rather rusty, buffeted by the tensions between the Executive and Non-Executive Directors on the Board, the office politics amongst my Executive colleagues and the lack of anything like a team environment at the Group's Head Office. I suspect that the rustiness did not help me in my first months at Eurostar. I inherited not so much a team as a set of individuals reporting to me. As I had combined two roles, Managing Director of Eurostar (UK) Ltd, the UK arm of Eurostar, and Chief Executive of Eurostar Group, these individuals came from two distinct parts of Eurostar with only a loose understanding between them. There was no clear leadership or decision-making forum, indeed it was not clear how decisions were made other than by individual directors.

I probably broke many of the rules of building a strong team in the first few months and tensions fairly quickly arose. As already noted in Chapter 6, five of the EUKL Directors complained about me as being "too close to the French" for instance. The majority of the direct reports I inherited chose to leave as they either did not like my approach or couldn't see how they would fit into the emerging structure. Many of them were talented individuals, who were at Eurostar because it was seen as an exciting place to work and who did not find it difficult to move to other senior jobs elsewhere. Very few were actually made redundant. With hindsight crunching two organisations together was always going to produce some fallout. I relied on the extremely strong relationship I had developed with my deputy, Chief Operating Officer Jacques Damas, to help navigate those first few months. In effect we were a two-person team for a period.

Over time a leadership team started to emerge and more importantly I developed a clear strategy for the business. This was very much my strategy as there was a lack of a coherent team to develop it jointly and I sensed an urgent need to get clarity on what we were trying to do. I ran several workshops for middle managers, supported by Directors, briefing them on the strategy and explaining the rationale behind it. Interestingly, what emerged was a kind of distributed leadership team with a good number of middle managers buying into the strategy, working well with each other and each playing increasingly important roles in delivering it. A number of them played a vital part in the successful move to St Pancras and launch of services on the new high speed line, HS1, four years later. It underlines the importance of having a clear strategy for a business, even if its leadership team is less developed initially. Many of these middle managers involved went on to impressive careers elsewhere.

I was CEO of Eurostar for eight and a half years so inevitably the leadership team changed over time as people left for other opportunities or because of changed personal circumstances. I was therefore an important "constant" in the make up of the team, as were Nick Mercer our Commercial Director and Nicolas Petrovic who initially joined as Customer Services Director before stepping up to

COO. Both were absolutely key to the business and we developed a high degree of trust and confidence in each other. As other people came and went I suppose our relationship and style of working influenced and drew others into the same team approach. We did run several team building away-days to start with but these slowly lapsed over time as we felt less need, despite having new team members.

Given this less than textbook approach to building a leadership team I have reflected since on how it was that we successfully turned Eurostar around and what was my own leadership style, both at Eurostar and before. As CEO it is essential to surround yourself with good people, particularly people who you feel are better than you. If you worry that one of your reports might steal your job you probably shouldn't be the boss. I always felt that my direct reports were much better at their jobs than I ever would be, so it was easy to give them space and let them get on with it. At Eurostar I think we were particularly good as well at giving space and empowering the better middle managers to do some great things. Setting out a clear vision and strategy, a narrative for everyone to rally behind, is crucial.

As a service business, where your front-line staff are central to your success, it is essential to be visible as a leader and to get out and about regularly across the business talking with staff at stations, on trains and those looking after the trains at depots. I came to realise that I drew energy from this, enjoying the sometimes humbling and frustrating conversations with staff. It was always a great antidote after a day of meetings in the office, many of which would have been energy sappers. The majority of these conversations yielded problems and areas of frustration for staff, but finding out about these is the essential prerequisite to trying to address them. It can only be motivating for staff to have the opportunity to give voice to their concerns with the boss, and knowing this was motivating in turn for me. I occasionally had a vision of myself as a human "bee", cross fertilising ideas and experiences from one part of the business to another as a result of these conversations. I think it is important that all leaders work out where they draw energy from, and give regular space in their diaries for this to recharge their batteries, since much of a leader's day is energy draining.

I likewise drew energy from talking with customers about their experiences of travelling with us. I found this was best done away from the train, allowing them to be more reflective in their feedback. Whether I received brickbats or bouquets I rarely found it other than helpful and rewarding, because again most customers would prefer to see you successfully meeting their particular needs than failing. As well as one to one conversations, listening in on well mediated focus group discussions could be hugely insightful as to how customers saw your business and how you could serve them better. Being an ambassador and passionate advocate for your business in all appropriate situations should be part of the job; after all, if you don't do this as CEO why should anyone else?

It should be a truism that a business's customers are its most important asset. Developing a direct relationship with them where you can learn from their feedback and understand how and why they use your service so you can improve it or just extend its appeal to more customers can be very powerful. Face to face conversations, where they can be had, are of course the best way of doing this. It is sobering, and in some ways surprising, that despite this, customers do not feature at all on any financial balance sheet of assets.

Language can be surprisingly important in talking about customers. I normally referred to our customers at Eurostar as passengers and occasionally as travellers (always in the plural, as there were many individual passengers with varying needs) as that was how they saw themselves. I recoil at other business leaders who refer to "The Customer", as if they were homogeneous and all the same, or worse still "the punter" or "punters". None of those descriptions convey a sense of respect for customers or a recognition of their often widely varying needs and expectations.

I also enjoyed and got huge satisfaction from building strong relationships and partnerships with suppliers, contractors and professional advisers. These relationships are of course first and foremost commercial, but in most cases these other parties want to see your business being successful - if nothing else it is good for their business to have a successful customer - and often have valuable insights on how your business could do better. Being open to their feedback and suggestions, indeed actively canvassing them, can ensure your suppliers and advisers become some of your most valuable supporters.

I came to understand that if you are doing your job right being the leader results in you being perpetually frustrated and dissatisfied with the business, because you are always wanting to do things better. You should always be ahead of the rest of the business, never fully satisfied with its performance and restless to do better still. Again, if you are not challenging the organisation to do better how can you expect others to? Stuart Machin, the newish CEO of Marks and Spencer, articulates this very well with his mantra of always being "positively dissatisfied" with M&S's performance to drive further improvement.

The most sobering reflection on being the leader of an organisation is when you realise how easily the organisation can over time come to reflect your own values and weaknesses, as well as your strengths. This is very much the case with smaller organisations, whether a school or a business, but also with larger organisations if the leader is in position for any length of time. It is a scary thought if you have any degree of self-awareness of your shortcomings, and underlines the importance of surrounding yourself with people who you think are better than you to provide balance.

CHAPTER 18 Conclusion

Writing this book has been an opportunity for me to reflect on what I have learned and experienced that might be of interest to railway people and others. I've worked in a wide range of different railway organisations, public and private, small, medium and large, freight and passenger. I've seen the industry both from the bottom up as a manager, and top down whilst serving on several different Boards. I've been closely involved in two revolutionary changes in structure - British Rail's move to profit centres and the subsequent break-up of the industry for privatisation. I've seen first-hand how a number of other countries operate their railways and I have had the opportunity to reflect on how Britain's railways were working during my review of franchising policy for the Department for Transport.

Hopefully this account and its observations will be a small contribution to the rail industry's corporate memory. As importantly, given the widespread dissatisfaction with the current state of Britain's railways and its performance, perhaps some of these reflections will prompt ideas on how things might be improved. So, in this final chapter I will venture, with some trepidation and humility, into a number of thoughts on what might be some of the components in a better railway for Britain. What has worked and what, from my experience, needs to change. No doubt some people will disagree or take issue with some points, but if it helps stimulate thinking, informs enlightened debate and shapes ideas, it will have succeeded. My comments apply primarily to the passenger railway. The freight sector has undoubtedly been one of the successes of privatisation and there is no suggestion that it needs to change other than be allowed the freedom and scope to grow further.

This of course prompts the question as to what "better" should look like. For me it is two things. Firstly, a railway that understands and is able to respond effectively to its customers' expectations, and so has more people, passengers and freight customers, wanting to use it. This is important both because rail is a lower carbon and safer mode of transport than the alternatives, and to ensure its capacity is used as fully and therefore as economically as possible. Secondly, it is a railway that is more cost effective than currently, reducing its call on the public purse and taxpayers, whilst still affordable for customers. Achieving the first will help rebuild passengers' trust in the industry, giving them confidence in the service they will receive and at a fair price. Achieving the latter will help rebuild Government and particularly Treasury confidence in the industry and give it licence to operate with greater freedom. Shifting the balance of funding from the taxpayer to the user has long been a desire of governments, and this is only likely to become a higher priority in future as the pressures on public expenditure grow.

I've always tried hard to get to know my customers, and really drill down and understand how to satisfy their expectations, which are often more complex and subtle than simply providing a punctual service, although this is of course important. This involves talking to actual and potential passengers and getting to know the markets and communities a railway serves; in short developing a face-to-face relationship with them, using their feedback to steer improvements. Being seen to act on this feedback can be a powerful way of building strong customer loyalty. Whilst meeting basic passengers' expectations can get you so far, identifying and satisfying particular and individual needs, sometimes quite minor, will over time help fill an otherwise half empty train. All of this takes time to do, involves being with customers and simply cannot be done remotely or sitting at a desk.

Which points to the first thing that needs to change from the current situation: the Government in Westminster needs to get out from its current detailed involvement in running Britain's railways. As I observed to two successive Permanent Secretaries at the DfT, the Department has become like a soviet era Ministry of Railways. It is far too closely involved in the detail of running the industry, stifling innovation and initiative, taking decisions with imperfect understanding of their impact, and far, far removed, both physically and culturally, from the customers and communities the industry serves.

A Whitehall Government Department, directly accountable to Ministers, is no place to direct and try to run a nationwide industry such as the railway. Ministers come and go too frequently to be able to achieve continuity and consistency of direction and policy. They are easy targets for the Opposition and the media looking to find fault with their performance, using rail issues as ammunition, but prompting often disruptive and unhelpful interventions by ministers. It further reinforces the risk averse culture of the public sector described in Chapter 15, deterring difficult or potentially unpopular decisions. And it is not conducive to longer term planning or thinking, as most political time horizons inevitably go no further than the next election.

At the same time the Civil Service is largely populated by able but generalist civil servants, who also change jobs regularly, in and out of transport as well as of railways, who do not generally have the industry knowledge or commercial experience to direct the railway effectively. Their careers are inevitably largely confined to the "bubble" of Whitehall. The pay, career structure and culture of the civil service has shown itself to be not capable of attracting or retaining sufficient industry "experts" to compensate.

Devolving the direction of the industry to an arm's-length organisation is therefore an essential move, as envisaged by the Williams Review and the creation of Great British Railways, or a similar body. Ministers and the Department for Transport should then focus on setting the broad framework of objectives and financing for the industry, including how rail sits within wider transport policy and objectives. It would also distance Ministers from operational and service decisions, giving them "deniability" when the media or Opposition raise concerns or criticisms.

"Getting out" from its current detailed and all-embracing involvement in running the industry is of course much easier said than done, as Whitehall and Westminster have for long found it hard to let go or devolve in many areas of policy. Instead they have tended over the years to increasingly centralise decision making, certainly within England. It is likely to take a bold and reforming Government to do it, and an industry determined to push for it.

But getting the Government out is only half the battle. The other is to ensure the industry regains the market focus and devolved responsibility it had under British Rail's business sectors and in the earlier days of franchises. Britain's railways are not a homogeneous entity, contrary to a view which unfortunately has been encouraged by centralised control by Whitehall. They vary hugely from route to route and region to region, with different operational challenges and inherited infrastructure and equipment, and different mixes of commuter, leisure and business customers. They need to be managed by teams who fully understand the particular features and issues facing their "patch" and can really get to know their customers and markets and then tailor services to meet their needs.

Moreover, many communities have a proprietorial sense for their local railway. Anglian residents, for instance, look on Greater Anglia Railways as "their" railway, as residents of Merseyside look on Merseyrail, with each having distinct expectations on how the railway should serve them. They want to feel their services are being managed by people who understand and are focused on their needs, are accessible and open to influence about their priorities. Their rail services are important to their communities and economies and it is important therefore that the industry is seen to recognise this and be open to dialogue about how they can work together for mutual benefit. This becomes even more essential as the number of Metro Mayors and their Combined Authorities grows.

So, an essential priority for Great British Railways, or whatever body is created, is to ensure it evolves its organisation toward market focused organisational units. These need to have full accountability for running services for their particular markets and customer groups, and be given wide responsibility and freedom to do this. The good news is that the current suite of Train Operating Companies, which are broadly similar in their geography to British Rail's Profit Centres, provide a good foundation on which to build. They have evolved somewhat over the years in their composition and boundaries, and no doubt will continue to do so in future, but they are generally well focused on individual markets and groups of rail services. They provide an excellent starting point to build on.

What then should be be the scope of responsibility of these organisational units? Ideally they should have full responsibility for all aspects of delivering their services, including management of the infrastructure over which their services run. Only then can their management teams make the best trade-offs between expenditure on track or train operations to improve service reliability, optimise the balance between track maintenance costs and disruption to passenger services, and manage all the other interfaces and trade-offs between track and train. Grouping all the various departments who contribute to the smooth running of train services within a single organisational entity makes it much easier to ensure all are aligned and working together cost-effectively. The experience of British Rail's Organising for Quality structure was also that such integrated units were more satisfying places to work, with traditional silos melted and all teams and departments better able to achieve line-of-sight of their efforts through to the final service to customers.

Restoring unified management of track and train was rightly one of the objectives highlighted by the Williams Review, although it was relatively silent on just how this might be done. The way the industry has been structured since privatisation makes realising this more difficult, with the track access regimes being a particular barrier to change. As we've seen in earlier Chapters, Train Companies are charged an administered price for track access, not the actual costs incurred by Network Rail on the track sections they use, and Network Rail receive an administered revenue, fixed by the Rail Regulator, which bears no relation to the value of passengers or freight carried by their customers. The track access charging regime gives no useful price signals to either Train Companies or Network Rail to allow them to manage across the interface. Clearly any new organisational unit which has unified responsibility for both track and train operations will need to manage its actual infrastructure costs, requiring the track access regime to be suspended or seriously reformed.

Fortunately, Network Rail's organisation has evolved recently with 14 Route Management Teams within their five regions, the boundaries of some of which closely match Train Companies. It should be relatively simple to merge the management teams of matching Train Companies and Routes, to create a unified team responsible for both track and train. These Routes already have full management accounting information on all of their costs, as the Train Companies do for all theirs, enabling the new units to manage the totality of their costs and revenues. As an interim step, without suspending or reforming the track access regime, it would be easy to set up an "alliance" type arrangement similar to the one between South West Trains and Network Rail a few years ago. This failed because of the fundamental incompatibility between the financial objectives of Network Rail and Stagecoach, the then owners of South West Trains. But with both parties in future being part of Great British Railways this should no longer be a problem.

Interestingly such an alliance has just been put in place for the South Eastern Railway. This is, I understand, a trial at this stage and the Route Director concerned only has a "dotted line" accountability to the Train Company MD. At least six other Routes could feasibly follow, covering half of Britain's rail network. It would be a first step to bringing track and train fully together again, and will need evolve to a single, unified management structure as reform of the track access regime proceeds. This will ensure infrastructure and train operations are all aligned to better deliver for their particular markets and groups of customers.

Not all these new organisational units need to have responsibility for their track infrastructure. We successfully transformed Eurostar's financial and service performance without it, but we ran over very reliable, purpose built new infrastructure managed by four different entities and were usually not the biggest user. It had been specifically designed for our services, including how it was maintained, so we had none of the optimisation trade-offs that UK domestic routes face. There are also several nationwide users, Cross Country Trains and the freight companies, who run over large parts of Britain's rail network, often as secondary users. But wherever possible the new units should also be responsible for managing the infrastructure they run over, or at least the key sections of it.

So much for structure, what could be the role and scope for impact of these unified organisational units? Giving their management teams bottom line accountability for both financial and train service performance will undoubtedly lead to greater cost effectiveness, with duplications eliminated and more optimal allocation of resources between track and train. Unified responsibility for train service performance will sharpen accountabilities and remove any temptation to lay blame elsewhere. In both cases having a single, strong management team focused on its "patch" will deliver faster improvement in performance.

Decisions on changes to train services, whether to increase or even curtail them, can also then be taken with full knowledge of all of the costs involved, not just the train operating costs. It is sobering that since privatisation all types of rail service - intercity, commuter, regional and rural - have seen significant expansion, with little regard for their impact on infrastructure costs, despite these accounting for half of the industry's cost base. A more economically rational approach would seek to grow those services which were able to cover all of their costs, and ensure the subsidy required for others was transparent and clearly understood in taking service and spending decisions.

With 17 Train Companies currently, and potentially similar numbers of unified organisational units in future, there would be a number of CEO type leaders all driving bottom line performance, mirroring Sir Robert Reid's unique insight that led to British Rail's Profit Centre organisation. It would also lead to a subtle but potentially significant change in the level of challenge to infrastructure costs. The main challenge currently comes from the Rail Regulator via the five-yearly Periodic Review process, which determines what should be Network Rail's cost base and sets its annual income accordingly. To this would be added challenge by the new organisational management teams, looking to improve their bottom line performance and to find better ways of maintaining and renewing their infrastructure. The rate of innovation and improvement in cost efficiency in GBR's infrastructure activities would undoubtedly benefit.

The potential scope for positive impact of these organisational units should go further. One opportunity is in challenging and seeking derogations in standards. One of the less well appreciated changes in Britain's rail industry since the creation of Network Rail has been a proliferation of standards. Some of these have been produced by Network Rail itself, in seeking to regain control of its infrastructure management after the demise of Railtrack and the bringing in-house of their various infrastructure maintenance contractors. Others have been produced by the Rail Safety and Standards Board, also set up after the demise of Railtrack, half of whose raison d'etre has been the formulation and updating of industry wide standards. Whilst mostly necessary, these standards carry the risk of adding to costs when assets are replaced or improvement investments undertaken, unless they are set at a level of the lowest common denominator. Slavishly following them is too often the easiest option, but there will be many instances where seeking a derogation is a more cost-effective option. This requires strong, bottom line focused managers to challenge and secure appropriate derogations.

The sponsorship of investment projects is another area where unified organisational units could have a substantial impact. Most investments are currently undertaken by Network Rail, inevitably at one step removed from the markets or customers they are intended to benefit. The so-called sponsors of these projects also usually report to the Project Director, rather than the other way round as was the case in British Rail, blunting their ability to challenge costs or delivery approaches. Too often the result has been investment projects which fail to deliver all of the original intended benefits, or cost more than they need. Making investment project sponsorship the responsibility of market focused organisational units and their MDs, with the knowledge and incentive to challenge project teams on scope and cost, seek more effective ways of delivering projects and ensure the projected benefits are actually delivered, would undoubtedly drive more successful and cost-efficient investments. It is their financial bottom lines that are affected and potentially improved by the investments, giving them the incentive to be active and challenging sponsors.

These organisational units then need to be led by a capable management team with leaders experienced in rail, balanced with people from other backgrounds to challenge groupthink and bring wider ideas and experience. Too strong a dominance of rail industry people and the culture risks becoming too inwards looking and lacking new ideas, too few experienced industry people and the organisation is unlikely to become a high performing one. The rail industry has people from a wider range of backgrounds now, but increasingly few have experience of more than one side of the industry - track or train, but rarely both - and many Network Rail managers are even more narrowly experienced within a particular specialism. An option for accelerating knowledge of how the railway works as a unified system could be to require managers to go through a purpose designed education programme, requiring them to successfully "pass out" at the end, on similar lines to British Rail's Strategic Safety Management courses in the run up to Organising for Quality.

A strong marketing and communications capability needs to be part of these broader and balanced teams. This is partly about the ability to drill down and really understand customers' varying needs, adapting the service to better meet them and using PR and marketing communications to promote the service. For longer distance services it is also about using active revenue management, single leg pricing and other fares' innovations effectively. This is a vital component in being able to appeal more widely to budget conscious passengers, as well as increasing train loadings and spreading these more evenly to improve a service's economics. Attracting more passengers is going to play an important role in improving the industry's financial performance, as it did for most of the period of franchise operation. Again, the industry has built significant marketing capability, although there are signs this is slowly dissipating as Train Companies are no longer accountable for their revenue and experienced people leave for more stimulating opportunities elsewhere. So, there is urgency to GBR's task in establishing its organisational structure.

Finally, the organisational units should work to build strong brand identities for their services. The industry has partly lost sight of the value of developing strong and enduring brands which chime with the geography of their services. Virgin Trains, GNER/LNER, Chiltern Railways and others all built strong brand identities which helped their appeal to new customers. Building a strong brand was important to Eurostar's turnaround and it was surprising how quickly Midland Main Line established its brand in a previously under-exploited market. But too often the periodic rebranding and renaming of franchised services creates an impression of change for change's sake, and does nothing to build passenger confidence or awareness. A strong and enduring brand helps foster the loyalty of both passengers and staff and develop a sense of ownership by the communities it serves. Ideally the brand should relate closely to the region or regions it serves. ScotRail is an exemplar of such a brand, which has developed under both public and private ownership. In contrast a single, monolithic and undifferentiated national brand, such as British Rail before the creation of its market sectors, or Great British Railways, would be seen as distant, impersonal and much less user friendly.

If the Department for Transport can successfully extract itself from its detailed direction of the industry, and Great British Railways successfully evolves these market facing organisational units, I believe it then matters much less whether these are run as private or public sector organisations. As I observed in Chapter 15, the real expertise and value added by private sector management of franchised Train Companies lay within each franchisee management team rather than in their holding companies. Private sector operation brought greater willingness to devolve responsibility to each management team and provided wide freedom for them to manage. Competitive bidding for contracts ensured competition "for the market" and encouraged ambition for the development of services. And the subsequent contracts ensured stability over their term and disciplined both sides, franchisee and more importantly Government as franchiser, to see the contract through to delivery and not move the goal posts or change direction midway.

If management of the unified organisational units is to be contracted out to the private sector via a competitive tendering process, then it is essential that Great British Railways build a strong capability to design, let and oversee such contracts. This needs to be commercially savvy and experienced enough to be able to manage the contracts with agility and agree necessary changes on a timely and partnership basis. And the contracts need to be designed to give wide freedom to the management teams to innovate and adapt services to passenger needs, including incentives to grow passenger numbers.

But there is no fundamental reason why Great British Railways should not be able to successfully manage these organisational units "in-house" within the public sector, provided it is able to retain and develop managers of sufficient calibre. This will require Government to give greater freedom to GBR to pay market-based salaries for senior leaders (as ironically it does by default for most other groups of staff!). It also requires Government to ensure that those people it appoints to oversee GBR at Board level have the necessary capability and railway expertise. And GBR itself must have the confidence to devolve responsibility and give management teams wide freedom to manage, as we were at InterCity, at Eurostar which for all of my time was technically in the public sector, and in the early days of franchising. It also requires the fostering of a strong marketing and communications capability, encouraging a private sector culture of actively "stimulating" passenger demand rather than passively "receiving" it. This means looking "outwards" to the market and customers for inspiration and ideas, not inwards and upwards.

Directly Operated Railways (DOR) is a useful role model. This is a Government owned holding company who step in and run Train Companies whose franchise has been terminated by Government. It's sometimes referred to as the Operator of Last Resort. At the time of writing, it's overseeing four formerly franchised companies, some of which have been successfully run for a number of years now. It's a very lean organisation, run by highly experienced railway professionals, giving significant freedom to its management teams to manage. One of my former bosses at British Rail once described his job to me as providing a steel umbrella, to intercept any unhelpful requirements or directives that headquarters, or above, regularly issued and leave me free to run my business without undue interference. His actual language was more colourful! In a quiet way this is one of the roles that DOR performs very effectively. It would be a very useful approach for GBR to copy, managing upwards to Government and the various regulatory bodies, and avoid distracting the managements of its operating units from getting on with their jobs.

Success therefore requires the establishment of a set of market focused organisational units, with full cost, revenue, investment and delivery responsibility. They would be focused on better meeting passenger needs, and continuously improving the economics of their group of services. With such units running its railway on the ground GBR could then be the lean organisation so many people hope for, focusing on broad strategy and policy, and such issues as fares and ticketing reform, investment priorities and steady de-carbonisation. I am sure some people would see what I've described above as overly simplistic, and will point to complexities and barriers that would get in its way and details that I have ignored. It would certainly take time to fully establish, but could be introduced on selected routes quite quickly. But unless one has a vision of what "good" looks like and a broad blueprint to work towards, one risks drift and continuing rearrangement of deckchairs. The prize is a better performing railway, more trusted by its customers and making a much smaller call on public finances. What would be not to like?

ABOUT THE AUTHOR

Richard Brown CBE has 43 years of railway experience, 28 of them at Director and Board level. He was a Director of British Rail's InterCity business before privatisation, then set up and ran one of the first 25 Train Operating Companies, Midland Main Line. Following privatisation he became Chief Executive of National Express Group's Trains Division, overseeing five franchises before moving on to the plc Board as Commercial Director. In 2002 he moved to Eurostar as Chief Executive, where he led its successful transformation before becoming non-Executive Chairman. As a non-Executive he served on the Boards of HS2 Ltd, the Department for Transport and Network Rail. He led two Government policy reviews, into Rail Franchising, following the collapse of the 2012 West Coast franchise competition, and Extreme Weather Resilience of Britain's Transport systems after the 2013/14 winter storms. He was also twice the elected Chairman of the Association of Train Operating Companies, President of the Chartered Institute of Logistics and Transport, Deputy President and briefly President of the French Chamber of Commerce in Great Britain. He was appointed a CBE in 2007, and a Chevalier of the French Legion d'Honneur in 2019.

Milton Keynes UK
Ingram Content Group UK Ltd.
UKHW030813071224
3415UKWH00002B/130